Vocabulary and Notes to Ba Jin's *Jia*: An Aid for Reading the Novel

Cornelius C. Kubler

East Asia Program
Cornell University
Ithaca, New York 14853

The *Cornell East Asia Series* publishes
manuscripts on a wide variety of scholarly
topics pertaining to East Asia. Manuscripts
are published on the basis of camera-ready
copy provided by the volume author or editor.

Inquiries should be addressed to Editorial
Board, Cornell East Asia Series, East Asia
Program, Cornell University, 140 Uris Hall,
Ithaca, New York 14853-7601.

CONTENTS

INTRODUCTION

Background

Vocabulary and Notes to Jiā is a reading and study aid designed for use with the revised version of Bā Jīn's novel Jiā. This novel, which portrays the period of social turmoil in China between the abolishing of the Manchu Dynasty and the establishment of the People's Republic, provides very good material for improving one's ability to read Modern Chinese. It contains much dialogue, is fairly limited in its use of vocabulary—which is repeated with great frequency, and is of considerable intrinsic interest. However, a lack of any reading aids has in the past prevented many students from reading the novel with full comprehension and enjoyment, and has necessitated their wasting much time in the tedious process of dictionary-grubbing.

The present notes to Jiā were written for third and fourth year students of Chinese who desire to read an important and well-known novel in its entirety while at the same time continuing their study of vocabulary and grammar. The purpose of the 4,083 vocabulary glosses, cultural notes, and grammatical explanations in this text is to enable the student to use all his available time for reading and vocabulary study rather than spending a large part of it in preparatory work.

When I first read Jiā in the fourth year Chinese course at Cornell three years ago, there were no vocabulary or grammar notes of any kind available and so, the other students in my class that year all being native speakers (and, more or less, readers) of Chinese, I was in for a long

semester of dictionary work. About halfway through the term, a thought
occurred to me: instead of laboriously copying down definition after definition and taking notes which I would probably never look at again, why
not invest a little more time and prepare a set of materials which might
be useful to other students reading Jiā? After discussing the project
with a good many instructors and fellow students, I decided to do just
that.

During the past three years, I have been at work on and off on vo-
cabularies and notes to the Preface and each of the forty chapters of Jiā.
To my original notes I have added all other words which I, with the advice
of instructors and students, thought might be new to third and fourth
year students. After two years of use in a pilot project in Cornell's
fourth year Modern Chinese classes, the notes were further expanded and
revised, based on the criticisms of both students and teachers. The system
of vocabulary coverage described above has worked out to an average of
about ten words per page of running text—somewhat more in the earlier
chapters, less in the later ones. Needless to say, there will be some words
annotated here which are too easy for any particular student, and other
words not given which the student may not yet know. However, as long as
these notes at least somewhat lessen the burden of reading Jiā, this project will not be considered to have been undertaken in vain.

Organization of These Notes

The vocabulary and notes given in this volume are arranged crosswise
in three columns: characters, romanization, and gloss or explanation.

The characters are given as they occur in the text, with common alternate forms and the traditional forms of simplified characters added for

reference. Unfamiliar simplified characters that are not given in the notes

may be identified in the Simplified Character-Traditional Character Conver-

sion Table (p. 258).

The romanization employed here is the Pīnyīn system, which has been

promulgated as the official romanization of the People's Republic of China.

For users of these notes who are accustomed to other romanizations, a

comparative romanization table has been provided in the back of this volume.

In matters of pronunciation, we follow Xīnhuá Zìdiǎn 新华字典（商务

印书馆,北京,1971) with the single exception of the syllable 髮 'hair',

which is there listed as fà but will here be given in the more common pro-

nunciation fǎ. Two syllables having the third tone will be written in their

basic, unchanged form except that when a changed third tone is followed

by a neutral tone, second tone will be written (e.g., 13-101 打扫 dásao

'sweep').

The glosses and explanations given here are primarily for each word as

it is used in the particular context in Jiā. Although other meanings and

grammatical functions of words are sometimes added, these are for reference

only and are not meant to be complete.

In order to save space, vocabulary items are entered in the notes on

their first occurrence only. If a student has forgotten the pronunciation

and or meaning of a word that was introduced in a previous chapter of the

notes, he may locate its first occurrence by consulting the Index (p. 262).

For further information on the organization of these notes, consult the

table of Abbreviations and Conventions Employed on page xix.

How To Use These Notes

In order to gain maximum benefit from Jiā and these notes, the following reading and study procedure is recommended: the student should first read rapidly through a chapter or part of one, glancing at the notes only when necessary to understand the general progression of the story. Then he should study the notes, paying special attention to the starred vocabulary, which is of high frequency. The latter vocabulary, plus whatever other words the instructor may assign, should be learned thoroughly, both to recognize and pronounce in reading and to reproduce from memory in writing (a sheet of paper can be folded in half to cover up the character and romanization columns, so that the student can test himself.)

After he has studied the notes, the student should read the text a second time, this time reading slowly and carefully in an attempt to understand everything. If there are unfamiliar words in the text not given in the notes, they should be looked up and learned immediately. Passages in the text which are still unclear should be marked and asked about in the next class session. Finally, after a lapse of a day or two, the text should be given a third reading, by which time reference to the notes should no longer be necessary.

Classroom procedure at Cornell, where Fourth Year Chinese meets three hours per week, is as follows: class begins with a five minute vocabulary quiz on the starred vocabulary in the notes. Then students are given an opportunity to ask questions about passages in the day's reading assignment which they did not understand (all classroom discussion is in Chinese, no English being allowed). After students have finished asking questions, the instructor asks a few himself. Students are then called upon to read a few

short passages in the text aloud (students can also assume the roles of
the various characters in the novel—someone being chosen narrator to read
the descriptive passages—and read Jiā as a play). The purpose of this oral
reading is to check the students' pronunciation of new words. Finally, there
is class discussion of whatever in the text the students wish to talk about.
In lieu of mid-term and final examinations, two papers are written in
Chinese on topics related to Jiā (cf. Bibliography on page xvi).

The tempo of the class will, of course, depend on the abilities of
the particular students in it. One year at Cornell, the novel was completed
in one term at the rate of one chapter per meeting (most chapters average
about ten pages in length). Another year, when students had somewhat poorer
backgrounds, about five pages were read per assignment and the book was
spread, supplemented by other readings, over a period of two terms. Another
possibility, in order to complete the novel more quickly, would be to read
some chapters in Chinese and others in English translation. However, since
words from earlier chapters are not repeated in the notes to later ones,
vocabulary from chapters not read in Chinese would have to be found in the
Index. The above, however, are only suggestions; the particular procedure
adopted will naturally vary from class to class.

Bā Jīn and Jiā

Bā Jīn 巴金 (1904-   ) is the pen name of Lǐ Fèigān 李芾甘,
well-known Chinese writer, translator, and editor. The name Bā Jīn derives
from the Chinese transliterations of the names of two eminent anarchist
writers whom Lǐ greatly admired: Mikhail Bakunin and Peter Kropotkin.

Bā Jīn was born in Chéngdū, the capital of Sìchuan province, in a

wealthy and educated landlord family. His unhappy childhood experiences
in the large and very traditional Lǐ family are depicted in the novel Jiā.
At an early age, Bā Jīn became interested in foreign languages and litera-
tures, and in the Russian anarchist and socialist political theories that
were popular at the time. When he was 19, Bā Jīn left Chéngdū for first
Shànghǎi and then Nánjing, where he continued his studies of Western culture.
During this period he wrote and translated a large number of articles for
anarchist periodicals and publishing houses. In 1927 Bā Jīn left China for
France, where he wrote and studied for about two years. It was while in
France that he wrote his first novel, Mièwáng 滅亡 'Destruction', which
established his reputation as a writer of fiction.

After his return to China, Bā Jīn began writing a large number of
novels: Sǐqùde Tàiyáng 死去的太陽 'The Setting Sun' (1930), Jiā 家
'Family' (1931), Chūntiānlǐde Qiūtian 春天裏的秋天 'Autumn in the
Midst of Spring' (1932), Léi 雷 'Thunder' (1933), Diàn 電 'Lightning'
(1934), Chūn 春 'Spring' (1938), Qiū 秋 'Autumn' (1940), Huǒ 火 'Fire'
(1941), Hányè 寒夜 'Winter Nights' (1947), and several others. His novels
and short stories were very popular among young readers in the 1930's and
1940's, who identified with his heroes and saw in his works the reflection
of their own lives. At the same time that Bā Jīn lived such a productive
life as a writer, he also continued his editorial and translation work.

Since the establishment of the People's Republic, Bā Jīn has revised
his collected works, published a few new short stories and essays, and
served on numerous cultural and political committees. Compared to his literary production before 1949, however, his writings since the revolution
have been very scanty. At first Bā Jīn was well accepted by the new leaders

of China because, although he himself had never joined the Communist party, his works were considered to have helped pave the way for the revolution. But after the Hundred Flowers campaign and during the Cultural Revolution, Bā Jīn was severely attacked for his old anarchist beliefs as well as for several essays in which he had expressed criticisms of the government. His house was ransacked, many of his personal possessions were destroyed, and, after various humiliations, he was sent off for reeducation. After the end of the Cultural Revolution, Bā Jīn was allowed to return to his home in Shànghǎi, where he still lives today.

Jiā 家 'Family', which forms the first part of the autobiographical trilogy Jīliú 激流 'Turbulent Stream', was Bā Jīn's third novel and remains to this day his masterpiece. For many years after its publication, Jiā was the favorite book of Chinese students. During the 1950's, two different film versions of the novel were produced in China. Although Chūn and Qiū, the second and third parts of Jīliú which continue the story of Jiā, were also quite popular, neither they nor any of the others works that Bā Jīn wrote achieved the success of Jiā.

The original version of Jiā was written by Bā Jīn in 1930 and published by the Kāimíng Bookstore in Shànghǎi in 1931. The version of Jiā which these notes are designed to accompany is the revised version of 1957, in the horizontally printed and simplified character edition published by the Nánguó Publishing Company (南國出版社), Hong Kong. This edition can be obtained at most Chinese bookstores in the United States. As the differences between the 1931 and 1957 versions of Jiā consist mostly of relatively minor stylistic and political changes, these notes could also be adapted for use with the old version.[1] However, pagination and the

exact nature of the vocabulary entries follow the Nánguó edition.

For more information on Bā Jīn and his works, the following sources

are recommended:

Bā, Jīn 巴金. 1934. Bā Jīn zìzhuàn 巴金自傳 (Bā Jīn's auto-
biography). Shídài Yìnshuāchǎng. Shànghǎi.

_____. 1938. Chūn 春 (Spring). Kāimíng Shūdiàn. Shànghǎi.

_____. 1940. Qiū 秋 (Autumn). Kāimíng Shūdiàn. Shànghǎi.

_____. 1958-1962. Bā Jīn wénjí 巴金文集 (Bā Jīn's collected works).
Rénmín Wénxué Chūbǎnshè. Beǐjing.

Lang, Olga. 1967. Pa Chin and his writings. Harvard University Press.
Cambridge.

Pa, Chin. 1958. The family (translated by Sidney Shapiro). Foreign
Languages Press. Peking. [Both this translation and the one below
are based on the 1931 original edition of Jiā.]

_____. 1972. Family (translated by Sidney Shapiro and Lu Kuang-huan,
introduction by Olga Lang). Anchor Books. Garden City, New York.

———————————————

[1]For a linguistic discussion of some of the stylistic changes Bā Jīn
made in the revised version of Jiā, see my Master's thesis A Study of
Europeanized Grammar in Bā Jīn's Novel Jiā (Cornell University, 1975). Of
course, Europeanized grammar occurs not only in Bā Jīn's works but in the
works of almost all authors since around 1900.

Acknowledgements

This work would not have been possible without the help and advice
of very many people. First and above all, I must thank my first teacher of
Chinese, Mrs. Pei Shin Ni, who has been closely involved with this project
since its conception. She has gone over every vocabulary entry with me and
has made innumerable criticisms and suggestions. She has also taught Jiā
using these notes for three semesters in her Chinese 411-412 classes.
Furthermore, she contributed the Gaō Family Tree (p. 12) and did the calligraphy on the title page. Without her scholarship, wide teaching experience, meticulous nature, and friendship, I would never have been able to
complete this text.

I would also like to thank Professor John McCoy for his constant en-
couragement at every stage of the project and his many useful suggestions;
Dr. Hsiang-po Lee, who criticized an earlier draft of the notes to the
first few chapters; and Miss Chih-ling Kuo, who wrote out all the characters
in the body of the notes. Others who have offered advice and criticisms at
various times include: William Baxter, Nicholas C. Bodman, Richard Bodman,
David Feng, Stella Fessler, Charles Fowler, Y.Y. Lee, Timothy Light, Helen
Lin, Tsu-lin Mei, Ronald Walton, Pilwun Wang, Kam-ming Wong, and the members
of the 1973 and 1974 Cornell Chinese 411-412 classes. To all of the above,
and to many more unnamed, go the hearty thanks of the author.

Appreciative acknowledgement is also made here of financial assistance
received from the following sources: a small grant from the Ford Foundation
for various expenses related to the pilot run of the notes in the Cornell
Chinese classes; a small grant from the Agency for Educational Innovation

at Cornell for the reproduction of the preliminary version of these notes
for the Cornell students; and a grant from the Cornell China-Japan Program
which enabled me to type the final version of the notes this summer.

Although great pains have been taken to ensure the accuracy of these
notes, there will undoubtedly be some errors in them, both typographical
and factual. For these I alone take full responsibility. However, it would
be greatly appreciated if readers who find errors or have suggestions on
how this text could be improved would write to me, care of Department of
Modern Languages and Linguistics, Cornell University, Ithaca, New York
14853. 希望大家批評指正！

Cornelius C. Kubler

Ithaca, New York
July 19, 1975

ABBREVIATIONS AND CONVENTIONS EMPLOYED

Word Class Abbreviations

A	Adverb
ADJ	Adjunct
AV	Auxiliary Verb
BF	Bound Form
CV	Coverb
EV	Equative Verb
EX	Expression
FF	Free Form
FV	Functive Verb
I	Interjection
IE	Idiomatic Expression
M	Measure
N	Noun
ON	Onomatopoeic Term
P	Particle
PH	Phrase
PN	Pronoun
PT	Pattern
PW	Place Word
RC	Resultative Compound
RE	Resultative Ending
SV	Stative Verb
VO	Verb-Object Compound

For explanations of how the word classes above are used in Chinese, consult the introduction to Dictionary of Spoken Chinese (Yale University Press, New Haven, 1966, pp. xviii-xxxv) or the list of abbreviations in volume II of Intermediate Reader in Modern Chinese by Harriet C. Mills and P. S. Ni (Cornell University Press, Ithaca, New York, 1967, pp. xiv-xix).

Other Conventions

*   in the notes to the Preface and chapters 1-20, indicates that an item reoccurs three times or more in subsequent chapters and is consequently worth learning most and first; in the notes to chapters 21-40, indicates than an item re-occurs once or more

( )   used to enclose the traditional form of a preceding sim-plified character; or for English explanation which is not part of the definition; or to indicate chapter and number references of previous items that bear some relation to the present one

[ ]   used to enclose an alternate form of a preceding character

々   indicates reduplication of the preceding character

...   indicates characters or words that have been skipped between two parts of a construction

/   used to separate the abbreviations of different word classes and the glosses of different grammatical functions of a word

=   "equals"; used in explaining certain items in terms of Chinese equivalents

" "   used mostly for literal translations of Chinese four-character expressions and other phrases; a freer, more natural English equivalent usually follows

人名   name of a person

四川   indicates that an item is a feature of the Sìchuan subdialect and is not commonly so used in Standard Mandarin

文言   indicates that an item is a feature of Literary Chinese and is not ordinarily so used in Modern Mandarin

PREFACE

page 1

1. 激流   jīliú   N: turbulent stream, rapids

2. 总(總)序   zǒngxù   N: general introduction, preface

3. 托尔(爾)斯泰   Tuō'ěrsītài   N: Leo Tolstoy (1828-1910), Russian novelist and moral philosopher

*4. 复(復)活   Fùhuó   N: Resurrection (novel by Tolstoy, published in 1899)

5. 扉頁   fēiyè   N: flyleaf (blank page at the beginning of a book)

*6. 本身   běnshēn   N: itself, oneself (used in apposition to a preceding noun or pronoun)

*7. 悲剧(劇)   bēijù   N: tragedy

8. 搏斗(鬥、鬭)   bódòu   N/FV: fight, struggle

9. 罗(羅)曼·罗(羅)兰(蘭)   Luómán Luólán   N: Romain Rolland (1866-1944), French novelist, music critic, and dramatist (a dot is often used to separate the characters representing a foreign first name from those representing the last name)

*10. 征服   zhēngfú   FV: conquer, subdue

*11. 經历(歷)   jīnglì   FV/N: experience

12. 寒暑   hánshǔ   N: "winter and summer," year

*13. 度过(過)   dùguò   FV: pass through, spend (time)

*14. 周圍   zhōuwéi   N: circumference, surroundings, environment

*15. 黑暗   hēi'àn   N/SV: blackness, darkness/black, dark

*16. 孤独(獨)   gūdú   SV: isolated, alone

*17. 絶望   juéwàng   VO: give up hope, despair

*18. 股   gǔ   M: (for sudden surges of water, blasts of air, rays of light, strands of hair, etc.)

19. 动(動)蕩   dòngdàng   FV: move in agitation, undulate

*20. 道路   daòlu   N: road

21. 乱(亂)山碎石   luànshānsuìshí   EX: "confused mountains, broken rocks," rough terrain

*22. 途   tú   N: road

23. 發射   fāshè   FV: shoot forth, launch

24. 水花   shuǐhuā   N: foam, froth, spray

*25. 欢(歡)乐(樂)   huānlè   N: happiness, joy

26. 奔騰   bēnténg   FV: rush forth

27. 具(俱)   jù   FV: have (short for 俱有 jùyǒu)

28. 排山之势(勢)   paíshānzhìshì   EX: ability to overturn mountains

page 2

*29. 唯[惟]一   weíyǐ   ADJ: the only, sole

*30. 确(確)定   quèdìng   FV: decide, make sure

*31. 信仰   xìnyǎng   N/FV: belief, faith (usually religious or political)/believe in (something)

*32. 結束   jiéshù   FV/N: draw to a close, finish/ conclusion

*33. 根(概)念   gaìniàn   N: rough idea

*34. 沉(沈)默   chénmò   SV: silent, taciturn

35. 哑(啞)子   yǎzi   N: mute, person who cannot speak

36. 展开(開)   zhǎnkai   RC: open, spread out, unfold

37. 乃是   naǐshì   PH: is (= 就是 jiùshi)

*38. 幅   fú   M: (for scrolls, paintings, etc.)

*39. 如何   rúhé   A: "equals what," how

40. 説教者   shuōjiàozhě   N: preacher

41. 明确(確)   míngquè   SV: clear and definite (P-30)

42. 誰是誰非   sheíshìsheífeī   EX: "who is right and who is wrong"

43. 判断(斷)   pànduàn   FV: judge, decide

44. 且看   qiě kàn   PH: "let's see" (cf.且説,且問, 且聽., all of which have the general meaning 'Let's now...')

*45. 載   zaì   FV: carry, convey (of a vehicle or other means of transportation)

CHAPTER ONE

page 4

1. 刮（颳）	guā	FV:	blow (e.g., the wind)
2. 扯破	chěpò	RC:	tear apart, shred
3. 棉絮	miánxù	N:	cotton fluff
*4. 飄落	piāoluò	FV:	float downward
*5. 石板路	shíbǎnlù	N:	stone slab road (M: 條 tiáo)
6. 鑲边（邊）	xiāngbiān	VO:	fringe, border
*7. 轎子	jiàozi	N:	sedan chair
8. 畏縮	wèisuō	ADJ:	timid, shrinking from, cringing
*9. 茫々地	mángmángde	A:	far and wide, vast
10. 伞（傘）	sǎn	N:	umbrella (M: 把 bǎ)
11. 笠	lì	BF:	reed hat
12. 偏倒	piāndǎo	FV:	fall to one side
*13. 怒吼	nùhǒu	FV:	howl, roar
14. 凄（凄）厉（厲）	qīlì	SV:	sad, sorrowful
15. 混合	hùnhé	FV:	mix together, mingle
*16. 古怪	gǔguài	SV:	strange
*17. 刺痛	cìtòng	FV:	pierce and hurt, irritate
*18. 警告	jǐnggaò	FV:	warn
19. 明媚	míngmeì	SV:	bright and beautiful
*20. 傍晚	bàngwǎn	N:	time near evening, dusk
*21. 燃	rán	FV:	light a fire, burn
*22. 消失	xiāoshī	FV:	vanish, disappear

23. 暮色	mùsè	N: twilight
*24. 僻静	pìjìng	SV: out of the way, secluded
*25. 吃力	chīlì	SV: tired, tiring
26. 棉袍	miánpaó	N: cotton-wadded long gown (also 棉袍子 , cf. <u>Jiā</u> p. 312, l. 10; M: 件 jiàn)
27. 下幅	xiàfú	N: bottom hem, trouser cuff

page <u>4</u>

*28. 冻（凍）	dòng	FV: freeze
29. 鼻子	bízi	N: nose
*30. 金絲眼鏡	jīnsīyǎnjìng	N: gold wire-rimmed glasses(M: 副 fù)
*31. 身材	shēncaí	N: physical build (of a person)
*32. 瘦	shoù	SV: skinny, thin
33. 扮	bàn	FV: dress up as, play the part of
*34. 語調	yǔdiaò	N: tone of voice
*35. 濺	jiàn	FV: splash, splatter
36. 褲脚〔腳〕	kùjiaò	N: trouser legs
37. 黑狗	Heīgoǔ	N: "Black Dog" (name of the pirate in <u>Treasure Island</u>; 1-60)
*38. 嘞	lei	P: (四川 ; = 呢 ne)
*39. 責備（備）	zébeì	FV: reprove, rebuke
40. 慌	huāng	SV: agitated, frightened
*41. 恨不得	hènbudé	PH: "hate that one cannot," wish very much that one could (do something difficult)
42. 遺漏	yíloù	FV: leave out, omit
43. 旋轉	xuánzhuǎn	FV: turn around
*44. 閉	bì	FV: close (especially the mouth or eyes)

*45. 捏（揑）	niē	FV: knead with one's fingers, squeeze
46. 伞（傘）柄	sǎnbǐng	N: umbrella handle
*47. 堆积（積）	duījī	FV: pile up, collect
48. 融化	rónghuà	FV: melt
49. 白皑皑	baí'aí'aí	A: bright white
50. 重重叠〔疊〕	chóngchongdiédié	EX: layer upon layer
51. 脚〔腳〕迹〔跡,蹟〕	jiǎojī	N: footprint
52. 掩盖（蓋）	yǎn'gaì	FV: cover
*53. 踏	tà	FV: tread, step
54. 中断（斷）	zhōngduàn	FV: interrupt

page 5

55. 上演	shàngyǎn	FV: stage (a play)
*56. 严（嚴）肃（肅）	yánsù	SV: serious
*57. 软〔軟〕	ruǎn	SV: soft
*58. 轻松（鬆）	qīngsōng	SV: light, relaxed, carefree
*59. 道	daò	FV: say (old novel form for 说 shuō)
*60. 宝（寶,寶）岛	Baǒdaǒ	N: Treasure Island (popular adventure story by Robert Louis Stevenson, 1850-1894)
61. 剧（劇）本	jùběn	N: script for a play
*62. 博得	bódé	FV: receive, win
*63. 称（稱）赞〔讚〕	chēngzàn	N/FV: praise, acclaim
64. 讨得	taǒdé	FV: obtain
*65. 奇异（異）	qíyì	SV: strange, exotic
66. 境界	jìngjie	N: state of mind, condition
67. 彭保	Péngbaǒ	N: (transliteration of) Benbow
68. 毕尔（爾）	Bì'ěr	N: (transliteration of) Bill

69. 江湖气（氣）質　　jiānghúqìzhi　　EX: "rivers and lakes dispo-
　　　　　　　　　　　　　　　　　　　　　sition," inclined to wander
　　　　　　　　　　　　　　　　　　　　　in search of adventure
　　　　　　　　　　　　　　　　　　　　　(like Robin Hood)

*70. 变（變）故　　　　biàngù　　　　　N: accident, misfortune

71. 踪〔蹤〕跡〔蹟迹〕zōngjī　　　　N: footprint, traces　(of
　　　　　　　　　　　　　　　　　　　　　someone)

72. 交織　　　　　　jiāozhī　　　　FV: interlace, interweave

*73. 复（復）仇〔讎〕　fùchóu　　　　VO: take revenge

74. 莫名　　　　　　mòmíng　　　　　PH: "no name," inexpressable,
　　　　　　　　　　　　　　　　　　　　　indescribable

*75. 恐怖　　　　　　kǒngbù　　　　　N: terror, horror

76. 盘（盤）算　　　　pánsuàn　　　FV: make mental calculations,
　　　　　　　　　　　　　　　　　　　　　plan, figure

77. 弃（棄）信背盟　　qìxìnbeìméng　EX: "abandon a pledge, turn
　　　　　　　　　　　　　　　　　　　　　one's back on an agreement,"
　　　　　　　　　　　　　　　　　　　　　commit a breach of faith,
　　　　　　　　　　　　　　　　　　　　　betray

78. 隐（隱）匿　　　　yǐnnì　　　　FV: conceal, hide

79. 宝（寶、寳）藏　　baǒzàng　　　　N: collection of treasures

*80. 涌（湧）　　　　　yǒng　　　　　FV: well up, rush in (like a
　　　　　　　　　　　　　　　　　　　　　flood)

*81. 醒悟　　　　　　xǐngwù　　　　FV: come to one's senses, awake

*82. 惊（驚）訝　　　　jīngyà　　　　SV: surprised, startled

page 6

83. 奥妙　　　　　　aòmiaò　　　　N/SV: wonder, secret of how to
　　　　　　　　　　　　　　　　　　　　　do something/wonderful,
　　　　　　　　　　　　　　　　　　　　　mysterious

84. 幼稚　　　　　　yoùzhi　　　　　SV: childish, immature

*85. 得意　　　　　　déyì　　　　　　SV: "having obtained one's
　　　　　　　　　　　　　　　　　　　　　intention," satisfied,
　　　　　　　　　　　　　　　　　　　　　content, proud

86. 流露　　　　　　liúlù　　　　　FV: flow out

*87. 思索　　　　　　sīsuǒ　　　　　FV: search one's mind for an
　　　　　　　　　　　　　　　　　　　　　answer, ponder

88. 抖落	dǒuluò	FV: shake off
*89. 并（並）排	bìngpái	PH: in one row, side by side
*90. 肩	jiān	BF: shoulder (FF: 肩膀 jiānbǎng)
*91. 閃	shǎn	FV: flash, gleam
92. 灯（燈）烛（燭）輝〔輝〕煌	dēngzhúhuīhuáng	EX: "lamps and candles bright and dazzling," ablaze with lights
*93. 夹（夾）杂（雜）	jiāzá	FV: mix or blend with
*94. 漆	qī	N/FV: paint, lacquer
*95. 公館〔館〕	gōngguǎn	N: residence, living compound
96. 点（點）綴	diǎnzhuì	FV/N: decorate/decoration
*97. 寂寞	jímò	SV: lonesome, forlorn
*98. 發抖	fādǒu	FV: shudder, tremble (1-88)
*99. 激云力（動）	jīdòng	SV: aroused, excited, moved
100. 課堂	kètáng	N: classroom (M: 間 jiān)
*101. 哪一个（個）	nǎyíge	PN: who (四川；＝誰 shéi; also occurs as 哪個 nǎge)

page 7

*102. 挨	āi	FV: touch, be physically close
103. 忘却〔卻〕	wàngquè	FV: forget (＝忘記 wàngji)
*104. 天真	tiānzhēn	SV: natural, unaffected, innocent (like a child)
*105. 轉弯（彎）	zhuǎnwān	VO: make a turn
*106. 点（點）头（頭）	diǎntóu	VO: nod one's head
107. 加速	jiāsù	FV: increase the speed of, accelerate
*108. 玻璃	bōli	N: glass (the material)
109. 罩〔罩〕子	zhàozi	N: shade, cover (of a lamp)
*110. 清油	qīngyóu	N: vegetable oil

*111. 孤寂	gūjí	SV:	lonely (=1-97 寂寞 jímò)
112. 灯（燈）柱	dēngzhù	N:	lamppost or pillar
*113. 淡淡地	dàndànde	A:	weakly, lightly, mildly
*114. 寥々	liáoliáo	ADJ:	very few
*115. 匆〔忽〕忙地	cōngmángde	A:	in a hurry, quickly
*116. 默々地	mòmòde	A:	silently
*117. 疲倦	píjuàn	SV:	tired, exhausted
118. 一白無际（際）	yìbáiwújì	EX:	"uniformly white without limit," boundlessly white
*119. 静寂	jìngjí	SV:	quiet, tranquil
*120. 狮子	shīzi	N:	lion (M: 隻 zhī)
*121. 蹲	dūn	FV:	squat on the heels
122. 怪兽（獸）	guàishòu	N:	strange beast or wild animal
123. 更換	gēnghuàn	FV:	alter, change
124. 脱落	tuōluò	FV:	drop, fall off
125. 塗	tú	FV:	daub, smear
*126. 依旧（舊）	yījiù	A:	in the usual manner, as before

page 8

*127. 石阶（階）	shíjiē	N:	stone step
*128. 擦	cā	FV:	rub, brush, wipe
*129. 恢复（復）	huīfù	FV:	restore, revert back
130. 屋檐〔簷〕	wūyán	N:	eaves of a house, over-hanging lower part of a roof
*131. 灯（燈）籠	dēnglong	N:	lantern
132. 台（臺）阶（階）	táijiē	N:	steps leading to a building (1-127)
133. 石缸	shígāng	N:	stone vat or cistern

*134. 副刂   fù   M: (for sets or pairs of
                                              things, coffins, etc.)

*135. 对（對）联（聯）   duìlián   N: pair of scrolls or tablets
                                              on which is written a
                                              couplet of rimed, anti-
                                              thetical characters

136. 底子   dǐzi   N: background, foundation
                                              (here, the parts of an
                                              engraving or picture which
                                              are set furthest back)

137. 隶（隸）書   lìshū   N: clerical style of charac-
                                              ters in Chinese calligraphy

138. 国（國）恩家庆（慶）   guó'ēnjiāqìng EX: "country benevolent, family
                                              happy," "may our country's
                                              rulers be benevolent toward
                                              us, and our family be blessed
                                              with good fortune"

139. 人寿（壽）年丰（豐）   rénshòuniánfēng EX: "people long life, year
                                              abundant," "may the members
                                              of our family enjoy long
                                              life, and the yearly harvest
                                              be abundant"

*140. 扇   shàn   M: (for doors, gates, and
                                              windows)

*141. 执（執）   zhí   FV: hold, grasp

142. 顶天立地   dǐngtiānlìdì EX: "pushing against the sky
                                              (with one's head), standing
                                              on the ground (with one's
                                              feet," very large and tall

CHAPTER TWO

*1. 灰　　　　　　　huī　　　　　　ADJ: ash color, gray, drab

*2. 天井　　　　　　tiānjǐng　　　　N: courtyard, patio

3. 墊(墊)高　　　diàngāo　　　　FV: raise, elevate (by putting something under something else)

*4. 盆　　　　　　　pén　　　　　　BF: pot, bowl, basin (FF: 盆兒 pér or 盆子 pénzi) 盆

*5. 梅花　　　　　　méihuā　　　　　N: plum blossom (M: 朵 duǒ)

6. 厢(廂)房　　　xiāngfáng　　　N: side room or wing of a building

*7. 級　　　　　　　jí　　　　　　　M: (for steps, ranks, and grades)

*8. 跨　　　　　　　kuà　　　　　　FV: bestride, pass over

*9. 門檻　　　　　　ménkǎn　　　　　N: threshhold, doorsill

*10. 上房　　　　　shàngfáng　　　N: main rooms of a Chinese courtyard

*11. 少爷(爺)　　shàoyé　　　　　N: young lord

*12. 婢女　　　　　bìnǚ　　　　　　N: bondmaid, maidservant

*13. 鳴鳳　　　　　Míngfèng　　　　N: (人名)

*14. 垂　　　　　　chuí　　　　　　FV: fall, drop, dangle

15. 髮辮　　　　　fǎbiàn　　　　　N: pigtail, braids (M: 根 gēn)

16. 棉袄(襖)　　mián'ǎo　　　　N: cotton-padded Chinese jacket (M: 件 jiàn)

17. 苗条(條)　　miáotiáo　　　　SV: slim (of a woman's figure)

18. 臉龐(龐)　　liǎnpáng　　　　N: face, countenance

19. 丰(豐)潤　　fēngrùn　　　　　SV: abundant, full, healthy

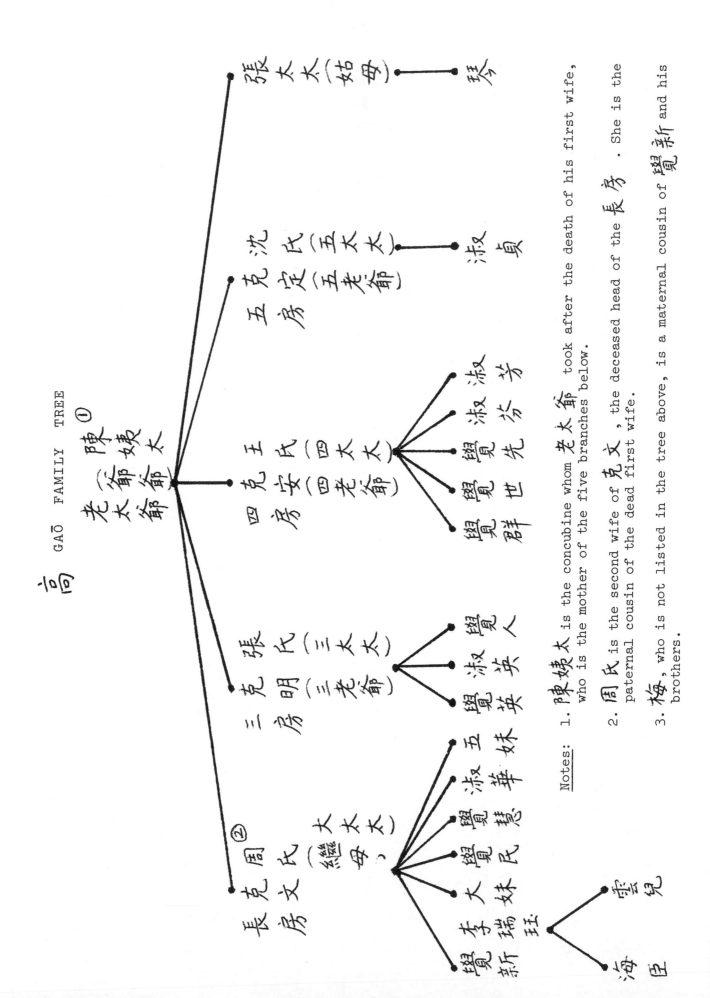

GAŌ FAMILY TREE

Notes: 1. 陳姨太 is the concubine whom 老太爺 took after the death of his first wife, who is the mother of the five branches below.

2. 周氏 is the second wife of 克文, the deceased head of the 長房. She is the paternal cousin of the dead first wife.

3. 梅, who is not listed in the tree above, is a maternal cousin of 覺新 and his brothers.

*20. 頰　　　　　　　　jiá　　　　　　　　BF: cheek (FF: 臉頰 liǎnjiá)

21. 酒窩　　　　　　　jiǔwō　　　　　　　N: dimple

*22. 琴　　　　　　　　Qín　　　　　　　　N: (人名)

page 10

*23. 晏　　　　　　　　yàn　　　　　　　　SV: late (四川; =晚 wǎn)

*24. 畢　　　　　　　　bì　　　　　　　　　RE: (indicates completion of action; = 完 wán)

*25. 好在　　　　　　　hǎozài　　　　　　A: fortunately

*26. 打湿 (濕, 溼)　　dǎshī　　　　　　RC: get wet (=弄濕 nòngshī)

27. 屢 (屢) 次　　　　lǚcì　　　　　　　PH: many times

28. 江山易改　　　　　jiāngshānyìgǎi　　EX: "rivers and mountains easy
　　本性难 (難) 移　　běnxìngnányí　　　　to change, basic nature
　　　　　　　　　　　　　　　　　　　　　　hard to move," it is easier
　　　　　　　　　　　　　　　　　　　　　　to change mountains and
　　　　　　　　　　　　　　　　　　　　　　rivers than to alter a man's
　　　　　　　　　　　　　　　　　　　　　　character

*29. 抱怨　　　　　　　bàoyuan　　　　　　FV: complain, grumble, blame

*30. 性情　　　　　　　xìngqing　　　　　N: temperament, disposition

31. 催　　　　　　　　cuī　　　　　　　　FV: urge, press, hasten on

*32. 耽擱　　　　　　　dān'ge　　　　　　FV: delay

33. 嘴硬　　　　　　　zuǐyìng　　　　　　SV: "mouth hard,"　sharp
　　　　　　　　　　　　　　　　　　　　　　tongued, argumentative

*34. 說不过 (過)　　　shuōbuguò　　　　RC: can't outtalk (also 講不過,
　　　　　　　　　　　　　　　　　　　　　　cf. p. 34, 1. 1)

35. 脑 (腦) 海　　　　nǎohǎi　　　　　　N: mind, memory

*36. 景象　　　　　　　jǐngxiàng　　　　N: scene, appearance, image

*37. 繼母　　　　　　　jìmǔ　　　　　　　N: stepmother

*38. 氏　　　　　　　　shì　　　　　　　　BF: family, clan (placed after
　　　　　　　　　　　　　　　　　　　　　　a married woman's maiden
　　　　　　　　　　　　　　　　　　　　　　name, somewhat like English--
　　　　　　　　　　　　　　　　　　　　　　originally French--née)

*39. 姑母　　　　　　　gūmǔ　　　　　　　N: aunt (father's sister)

*40. 表   biǎo   BF: (indicates second degree
                                          relatives, i.e., cousins,
                                          of a different surname)

*41. 嫂ㄠ   sǎosao   N: sister-in-law (older
                                          brother's wife)

*42. 瑞珏〔珏〕   Ruìjué   N: (人名)

*43. 淑华（華）   Shūhuá   N: (人名)

*44. 行礼（禮）   xínglǐ   VO: perform an act of courtesy,
                                          bow

*45. 招呼   zhāohu   FV: greet, wave to

*46. 女佣（傭）   nǚyōng   N: female servant

 47. 盛   chéng   FV: fill (a container)

page 11

*48. 端   duān   FV: carry with the hands

*49. 关（關、闗、関）心   guānxīn   FV: care for, be concerned
                                          about

*50. 素来（來）   sùlái   A: up to the present, always

*51. 人道主义（義）者   réndàozhǔyìzhě N: humanitarian

 52. 游艺（藝）会（會）   yóuyìhuì   N: exhibition of student's
                                          work, student night (at
                                          a school)

*53. 学（學）堂   xuétáng   N: school (四川; =學校 xuéxiào)

 54. 小名   xiǎomíng   N: childhood name

 55. 蕴华（華）   Yùnhuá   N: (人名)

*56. 活泼   huópo   SV: lively, vivacious

*57. 姑娘   gūniang   N: maiden, girl

 58. 省立一女师（師）   Shěnglì Yìnǚshī N: Provincial First Girls'
                                          Normal (name of a school)

 59. 走读生   zǒudúshēng   N: day student (as opposed to
                                          a boarding student)

 60. 经费   jīngfèi   N: funds; outlay (M: 笔 bǐ)

61. 挪　　　　　　　　nuó　　　　　FV: move, transfer

62. 充作〔做〕　　　　chōngzuò　　FV: act as, be used for

page 12

63. 薪水　　　　　　　xīnshuǐ　　　N: salary (for white-collar
　　　　　　　　　　　　　　　　　　　workers)

*64. 督軍　　　　　　　dūjūn　　　　N: highest military commander
　　　　　　　　　　　　　　　　　　　and provincial governor
　　　　　　　　　　　　　　　　　　　(in the early days of the
　　　　　　　　　　　　　　　　　　　Republic)

65. 筷　　　　　　　　kuài　　　　BF: chopsticks (FF: 筷子 kuàizi)

66. 絞　　　　　　　　jiǎo　　　　FV: bind, twist

67. 臉帕　　　　　　　liǎnpà　　　N: facecloth (M: 張 zhāng)

*68. 插嘴　　　　　　　chāzuǐ　　　FV: interrupt, put in a word
　　　　　　　　　　　　　　　　　　　edgewise

69. 外国(國)語　　　　Wàiguóyǔ　　N: Foreign Language Technical
　　　专(專)門学(學)校　Zhuānmén Xuéxiào　School

70. 和　　　　　　　　hú　　　　　FV: win a trick (in 麻將
　　　　　　　　　　　　　　　　　　　májiàng, a popular Chinese
　　　　　　　　　　　　　　　　　　　game; it is known in the
　　　　　　　　　　　　　　　　　　　West as mah-jong, which is
　　　　　　　　　　　　　　　　　　　the Cantonese pronunciation
　　　　　　　　　　　　　　　　　　　of the two characters)

*71. 揩　　　　　　　　kāi　　　　FV: wipe (=1-128 擦 cā)

72. 一齐(齊)　　　　　yìqí　　　　A: in unison, together

73. 招收　　　　　　　zhāoshōu　　FV: recruit and accept, admit

*74. 惊(驚)喜地　　　　jīngxǐde　　A: surprised and delighted

*75. 光輝〔煇〕　　　　guānghuī　　N: glow (here, of pleasure)

*76. 水汪々的　　　　　shuǐwāngwāngde　A: watery

*77. 盯　　　　　　　　dīng　　　　FV: fix one's eyes upon, stare
　　　　　　　　　　　　　　　　　　　at

78. 喜訊　　　　　　　xǐxùn　　　　N: good news

*79. 疑心　　　　　　　yíxīn　　　　FV: suspect

80. 説謊話   shuō huǎnghuà   PH: tell a lie

page 13

*81. 兴(興)奋(奮)   xīngfèn   SV: excited

*82. 含笑   hánxiào   A: smilingly

*83. 接口   jiēkǒu   A: joining in a conversation

*84. 衛道   weìdaò   VO: protect the traditional culture

85. 憤慨   fènkǎi   SV: indignant, angered by an injustice

*86. 下决〔決〕心   xià juéxīn   PH: make up one's mind, come to a decision

87. 报(報)名   baòmíng   VO: sign up

88. 投考   toúkaǒ   FV: take part in the entrance exam of a school

89. 鼓舞   gǔwǔ   FV: arouse, stir up

*90. 喚   huàn   FV: call, summon

91. 耍   shuǎ   FV: play, have fun (四川; = 玩 wán; distinguish from 要 yaò)

92. 慫恿〔慂〕   sǒngyǒng   FV: urge, egg on, incite

93. 麻将(將)牌   májiàngpaí   N: mah-jong piece (2-70)

94. 磨擦   mócā   FV/N: rub, click/friction (between people)

95. 圈   quān   M: round (of a mah-jong game)

CHAPTER THREE

1. 聘   pìn   FV: employ, engage, appoint

2. 吳又陵   Wú Yòulíng   N: the 號 or literary name of 吳虞 Wú Yú (1872-1949), Chinese scholar and poet whose intensely anti-Confucian writings contributed to the success of the May Fourth Movement (6-158)

*3. 新青年   Xīn Qīngnián   N: New Youth (monthly literary journal which began publication in 1915 and played an important role in the New Culture Movement of early Republican China)

4. 吃人的礼(禮)教   Chīrénde Lǐjiaò   N: "Cannibalistic Ethical Teachings" (of Confucius; the article was published in the November, 1919 issue of New Youth)

5. 只(隻)手打孔家店   zhǐ shǒu dǎ Kǒngjiādiàn   PH: single-handedly fight the "Confucian shops"

*6. 羨[羡]慕   xiànmù   FV: envy, admire

7. 举(舉)人   jǔrén   N: successful candidate in the provincial exam (somewhat like an M.A. here)

8. 秀才   xiùcaí   N: successful candidate in the district exam (somewhat like a B.A. here)

9. 古文观(觀)止   Gǔwénguānzhǐ   N: "old literature looking stops" (i.e., there is no need to look further), The Best Ancient Literature (title of a famous collection of classical prose essays)

10. 謙伯	Qiānbó	N:	(transliteration of) Chamber (author of an English text-book popular in China)
11. 老古董	laǒ gǔdǒng	N:	old antique
12. 巴不得	bābudé	PH:	hope very much (1-41)
*13. 开(開)放女禁	kaīfàng nǔjìn	PH:	lift the ban on girls
14. 詩人解頤語	Shīrén Jiěyíyǔ	N:	Smiles from the Poets (title of a book translated by the famous writer 林琴南 Lín Qínnán [3-16]; 解頤語 literally means "loosen the jaws speech," i.e., 'jokes, smiles')
15. 出于(於)…手笔(筆)	chūyú…shoǔbǐ	PH:	"from the pen of," written by
16. 林琴南	Lín Qínnán	N:	the 字 or courtesy name of 林紓 Lín Shū (1852-1924), famous early translator of Western literature into Classical Chinese
*17. 嘲笑	chaóxiaò	FV:	laugh at, ridicule
*18. 人家	rénjia	N:	(here) I (usually: 'others')
*19. 正經	zhèngjing	SV:	serious
*20. 故意	gùyì	A:	on purpose

page 15

*21. 堂屋	tángwū	N:	middle one of the main rooms of a Chinese house
22. 昏暗	hūn'àn	SV:	dark
23. 裝(裝)飾	zhuāngshì	FV:	decorate
*24. 純潔	chúnjié	SV/N:	pure, clean/purity
25. 昂头(頭)	ángtoú	VO:	raise the head high
*26. 張望	zhāngwàng	FV:	look round about
*27. 异(異)常	yìcháng	A:	extraordinarily, unusually
28. 輕快	qīngkuai	SV:	light-hearted, relaxed

*29. 揮动（動）　　　huǐdòng　　　FV: wave, fling

30. 手臂　　　　　　shǒubei　　　N: arm (from the wrist up)

31. 广（廣）阔[濶]　guǎngkuò　　SV: broad, wide, extensive

32. 束縛　　　　　　shùfú　　　　FV/N: bind up, restrain/restraint

*33. 阻碍（礙）　　　zǔ'ai　　　　FV/N: obstruct, impede, hinder/
　　　　　　　　　　　　　　　　　　　obstruction, impediment

34. 出場　　　　　　chūchǎng　　FV: go on stage (e.g., an
　　　　　　　　　　　　　　　　　　　actor)

35. 侍者　　　　　　shìzhě　　　N: waiter

36. 豪气（氣）　　　haóqi　　　　N: heroic air, exhilaration

37. 陡然　　　　　　doǔrán　　　A: suddenly, unexpectedly

*38. 心头（頭）　　　xīntou　　　N: mind, heart

*39. 明夕　　　　　　míngmíng　　A: clearly, distinctly

*40. 吃惊（驚）　　　chījīng　　　VO: become alarmed

*41. 顫抖　　　　　　zhàndoǔ　　　FV: tremble, shake (1-88)

42. 潑　　　　　　　pō　　　　　FV: spill

43. 茶盘（盤）　　　chápán　　　N: tea tray

44. 侧　　　　　　　cè　　　　　FV: turn to the side

45. 門框　　　　　　ménkuàng　　N: door frame

*46. 歇　　　　　　　xiē　　　　　FV: pause, rest

*47. 裝（装）　　　　zhuāng　　　FV: assume (an air), feign,
　　　　　　　　　　　　　　　　　　　pretend

*48. 总（總）之　　　zǒngzhī　　　A: in short, in a word (short
　　　　　　　　　　　　　　　　　　　form of 總而言之 "sum-
　　　　　　　　　　　　　　　　　　　marizingly to say it," 'to
　　　　　　　　　　　　　　　　　　　sum up, in conclusion')

page 16

49. 理睬　　　　　　lǐcai　　　　FV: notice, pay attention to

*50. 喊　　　　　　　hǎn　　　　　FV: call, cry, shout; tell
　　　　　　　　　　　　　　　　　　　(someone to do something;
　　　　　　　　　　　　　　　　　　　= 叫 jiaò)

51. 挨駡〔罵〕   aímà   PH: suffer scolding, be scolded

*52. 倘若   tǎngruò   A: if

*53. 惹、   rě   FV: stir up, cause, make

54. 發脾气（氣）   fā píqi   PH: get angry, lose one's temper

*55. 説不定   shuōbuding   A: can't say for sure, maybe

*56. 頓   dùn   M: (for scoldings, meals, etc.)

57. 装（裝）烟（煙）   zhuāngyān   VO: fill with tobacco

58. 哑（啞）巴   yǎba   N: mute, person who cannot speak (巴 is a noun suffix like 子 , e.g., 下巴 xiàba 'chin', 尾巴 weǐba (or yǐba) 'tail', 嘴巴 zuǐba 'mouth'; P-35)

*59. 清晰   qīngxī   SV: loud and clear

page 17

60. 鞭子   biānzi   N: whip (M: 根 gēn, 條 tiaó)

*61. 羞愧   xiūkuì   SV: ashamed

62. 辯护（護）   biànhù   FV: defend verbally

*63. 面龐（龐）   miànpáng   N: face, countenance (=2-18 臉龐 liǎnpáng)

*64. 毫不   haóbù   A: "not even by a piece of down," not the least bit, not at all

*65. 訴苦   sùkǔ   VO: complain, air grievances

*66. 吞   tūn   FV: swallow, gulp down

67. 吼声（聲）   hoǔshēng   N: sound of beasts howling (1-13)

*68. 不时（時）   bùshí   A: sometimes

69. 剛毅   gāngyì   SV: resolute, tough and determined

70. 指示   zhǐshì   FV: show, indicate

*71. 命運   mìngyun   N: fate, fortune

*72. 番   fān   M: (for acts or deeds; sometimes translatable as '[one] time')

*73. 哀求   aīqiú   FV: entreat, beseech, implore

*74. 無意間   wúyìjiān   A: unexpectedly, unintentionally (also 無意中 , cf. p. 44, 1. 6)

*75. 出世   chūshì   FV: be born

76. 浮現   fúxiàn   FV: "float in and become manifest," appear, come

77. 啞(啞)然失笑   è'ránshīxiaò   EX: "with the sound of laughter emit a laugh," laugh unconsciously

page 18

*78. 留恋(戀)   liúliàn   FV: be unwilling to leave, be reluctant to part with, be attached to

*79. 抛弃(棄)   paōqì   FV: abandon, throw away

*80. 疑問   yíwèn   N: question, doubt

*81. 处(處)   chǔ   FV: live (in a certain kind of circumstances; distinguish from 處 chù 'a place')

82. 决[決]断(斷)   juéduàn   FV: decide, conclude

83. 癡想   chīxiǎng   N: silly thoughts

84. 匈奴未灭(滅), 何以家为(為)   Xiōngnú weì miè héyǐ jiā weí   EX: "The Huns not yet defeated, how make a home?" to put one's country before one's personal affairs (attributed to 霍去病 Huò Qùbìng, a famous Hàn Dynasty general who won several brilliant battles over the Huns; when asked to look at a mansion the emperor had built for him, he answered with the phrase above, that he could not think of houses while the Huns were still undefeated)

85. 陳腐	chénfǔ	SV:	hackneyed, out-of-date
86. 妙法	miàofǎ	N:	perfect way, clever and wonderful method
87. 慷慨激昂	kāngkǎijī'áng	EX:	impassioned, greatly aroused, fervent (2-85)
*88. 寻(尋)常	xúncháng	SV:	ordinary
*89. 嚷	rǎng	FV:	shout, call out

page 19

90. 發瘋	fāfēng	VO:	go crazy, become insane
*91. 写(寫)字枱(檯)	xiězìtái	N:	writing table (M:張 zhāng)
*92. 藤[籐]椅	téngyǐ	N:	rattan chair (M:把 bǎ)
93. 發惱(惱)	fā'nǎo	VO:	be irritated or angry
*94. 紳士	shēnshi	N:	gentleman, member of the gentry
95. 憤恨	fènhèn	SV:	bitter, resentful
*96. 一时(時)	yìshí	A:	for a moment, for a time
*97. 适(適)当(當)	shìdàng	SV:	appropriate
98. 长(長)吁短嘆[歎]	chángxūduǎntàn	EX:	"long pant, short sigh," sigh incessantly
*99. 閑[閒]气(氣)	xiánqì	N:	needless abuse, groundless mistreatment
100. 五世同堂	wǔshìtóngtáng	EX:	"five generations same hall," five generations under one roof
101. 明争暗斗(鬥、鬥)	míngzhēng'àndòu	EX:	"openly quarrel, secretly wrangle," fight overtly and covertly

page 20

102. 堵塞	dǔsāi	FV:	stop up, (here) choke
103. 咽喉	yānhóu	N:	throat, larynx
*104. 接近	jiējìn	FV/SV:	become close (to someone)/ close (of relations between people)

105. 堵	dǔ	M:	(for walls; 3-102)
106. 光芒四射	guāngmángsìshè	EX:	"light ray four-ways shoots," shining in all directions
*107. 肩膀	jiānbǎng	N:	shoulder (1-90)
108. 怒气（氣）	nùqì	N:	anger
*109. 处（處）境	chǔjìng	N:	position one is in, circumstances one faces (3-81)
*110. 忧郁（鬱）	yōuyù	SV/N:	melancholy
*111. 荡〔盪〕漾	dàngyàng	FV:	be gently tossed about, drift along
112. 姿态（態）	zītai	N:	deportment, poise, manner
113. 沉思	chénsī	ADJ:	submerged in thought
114. 阴郁（鬱）	yīnyù	SV:	sorrowful (3-110)
*115. 苦恼（惱）	kǔ'nǎo	FV/N:	distress, trouble
*116. 念头（頭）	niàntou	N:	thought, idea
*117. 脑（腦）筋	nǎojīn	N:	mind, brains
*118. 忧愁	yōuchóu	SV/N:	sad, mournful/sadness
*119. 愿望	yuànwàng	N:	hope, wish
*120. 牺（犧）牲	xīshēng	FV/N:	sacrifice

page 21

121. 空泛	kōngfàn	SV:	containing only generalities, impractical
122. 有志者事竟成	yōuzhìzhě, shì jìng chéng	EX:	"he who has ambition, the matter will finally succeed," where there's a will there's a way
*123. 爷（爺）爷	yéye	N:	grandpa
124. 极端	jíduān	A:	to the highest degree, extremely
*125. 撑〔撐〕	chēng	FV:	prop up, support

*126. 摸   mō   FV: touch, feel, grope

*127. 額角   éjiǎo   N: temples (of the head)

*128. 呆〔獃〕   dāi   SV: stupid, silly

*129. 恳（懇）切   kěnqiè   SV: very sincere, earnest

*130. 补（補）習   bǔxí   FV: make up defects in one's learning, study on the side

*131. 外专（專）   Wàizhuān   N: "Foreign Tech." (school; abbreviation of 2-69)

*132. 挑   tiǎo   FV: push aside, adjust

*133. 髮鬢   fàbìn   N: hair on the temples

*134. 焦虑（慮）   jiāolǜ   N/SV: worry, concern/worried, concerned

*135. 婆   pó   N: grandma

*136. 闲〔閒〕話   xiánhuà   N: gossip

*137. 愤〔忿〕怒   fènnù   SV/N: angry, enraged/anger, rage (3-108)

138. 一女师（師）   Yìnǚshī   N: "First Girls' Normal" (school; abbreviation of 2-58)

139. 閨范（範）   guīfàn   N: (model of) feminine virtue

140. 舅母   jiùmǔ   N: aunt (wife of maternal uncle; 2-39)

*141. 当（當）面   dāngmiàn   A: to one's face, in one's presence

page 22

142. 高明   gāomíng   SV: enlightened, wise

143. 东（東）家长（長）西家短   dōng jiā cháng xī jiā duǎn   EX: "eastern house long, western house short," gossip incessantly, find fault with everything

144. 捏（揑）造   niēzaò   FV: fabricate (charges), invent, make up (1-45)

145. 堵住　　　　　dǔzhù　　　　RC: stop up (=3-102 堵塞 dǔsaī)

*146. 横竖〔豎〕　　héngshù　　　A: anyway, in any case (=反正 fǎnzhèng)

147. 取笑　　　　　qǔxiaò　　　　FV: laugh at, make fun of

*148. 代价（價）　　daìjià　　　　N: price, cost

page 23

*149. 赞〔讚〕叹〔歎〕　zàntàn　　　FV: praise, admire

*150. 下　　　　　　xià　　　　　M: (for strikes of a clock or of anything else)

151. 理　　　　　　lǐ　　　　　　FV: put in order, straighten up

*152. 齐（齊）声（聲）qíshēng　　　A: in one voice, together (2-72)

*153. 不觉（覺）　　bùjué　　　　A: unaware, unconsciously

154. 冲（衝）口　　chōngkoǔ　　　A: bursting out, blurting out

*155. 吐　　　　　　tǔ　　　　　　FV: spit, spew forth

*156. 沉溺　　　　　chénnì　　　　FV: indulge in, sink into

*157. 幻想　　　　　huànxiǎng　　N: daydream, vision (contrast 幻 with 约 yuē as in 纽约 Niǔyuē 'New York')

*158. 分辩　　　　　fēnbiàn　　　FV: make excuses, explain

*159. 说着玩　　　　shuōzhe wán　PH: kid around (verbally)

*160. 疑惑　　　　　yíhuò　　　　FV/N: doubt

*161. 清脆　　　　　qīngcuì　　　SV: clear and crisp, sharp and loud

*162. 仆人　　　　　púren　　　　N: servant

*163. 袁成　　　　　Yuánchéng　　N: (人名); contrast 袁 with 3-73 哀 aī and 衣 yī)

164. 带〔帶〕沙　　daìshā　　　　VO: "carry sand," hoarse, raspy (of the voice)

*165. 乘   chèng   M: (for vehicles; distinguish 乘 chéng 'to ride')

*166. 鑼   luó   N: gong (M: 面 miàn)

*167. 沉重   chénzhòng   SV: heavy, deep, serious

168. 悲愴   bēichuàng   SV: sad, mournful

169. 更   gēng   M: (for the two hour periods of the night watch in old China between 7:00 P.M. and 5:00 A.M.; 二更鑼 here marks the beginning of the period from 9:00 to 11:00; contrast with 更 gèng 'even more'; 1-123)

CHAPTER FOUR

*1. 凄〔淒〕惨（慘） qīcǎn SV: tragic, heartbreaking

2. 無所不在 wúsuǒbúzài EX: "there is no place where it is not present," everywhere, ubiquitous

3. 哭泣 kūqì N/FV: crying, weeping/cry, weep

4. 面具 miànjù N: mask

5. 結算 jiésuàn FV: put in order, settle (e.g., financial accounts)

6. 总（總）賬 zǒngzhàng N: overall account, record of wins and losses

7. 隅 yú N: corner, nook

8. 角落 jiǎoluò N: corner, nook

*9. 悔恨 huǐhèn FV/N: feel remorse for, regret/ remorse, regret

*10. 剩 shèng FV: have left, be left

11. 被窩 bèiwō N: quilt for sleeping folded like a sleeve, bedding

12. 僕婢室 púbìshì N: servants' room (2-12, 3-162)

*13. 盏 zhǎn M: (for lamps)

14. 瓦油灯（燈） wǎyóudēng N: lamp consisting of an earthen pot filled with oil

15. 惨（慘）淡〔澹〕 cǎndàn SV: lacking brightness, dull, feeble

16. 灯（燈）芯 dēngxīn N: lamp wick

17. 灯（燈）花 dēnghuā N: snuff (of a candle; i.e., the charred and partly consumed portion of a candle wick)

18. 黑魆魆 heīxùxù A: very dark

*19. 光景 guāngjǐng N: approximate appearance (here, of age)

20. 孙(孫)少爷(爺) sūnshaòyé N: "grandson little lord" (i.e., 海兒 Haǐ'ér, the infant son of 覺新 Juéxīn and 瑞珏 Ruìjué)

*21. 伺候 cìhou FV: wait upon, serve

22. 粗促 cūcù SV: hoarse and short

23. 鼾声(聲) hānshēng N: sound of snoring

page 25

*24. 床[牀]沿 chuángyán N: edge of a bed

*25. 癡癡地 chīchīde A: stupidly, listlessly, without expression (3-83)

26. 照理 zhaòlǐ A: according to custom, usually

*27. 才[纔]是 caí shì PH: "would only be proper" (occurs at the end of the sentence to which it refers; = 才對 caí duì)

28. 尊重 zūnzhòng FV: respect, esteem, cherish

29. 輕易 qīngyì A: lightly, easily, recklessly

30. 清閑[閒] qīngxián N/SV: leisure, free time/without work, leisurely

*31. 責罵[駡] zémà FV: scold, blame

32. 忙碌 mánglù SV: busy

*33. 折磨 zhémó FV/N: torment, torture

*34. 奇怪 qíguaì FV/SV: feel that something is strange/strange

35. 吃打罵[駡] chī dǎmà PH: get hit and scolded (3-40)

36. 畢竟 bìjìng A: in the long run, ultimately

37. 平凡 píngfán SV: ordinary

38. 万(萬)能 wànnéng ADJ: all-powerful, omnipotent

39. 神明	shénmíng	N:	god
40. 注〔註〕定	zhùdìng	FV:	destine, predestinate
41. 作怪	zuòguaì	FV:	act up, be mischievous
42. 煽	shān	FV:	"fan the fire," stir up, bring up
*43. 渴望	kěwàng	N/AV:	yearning, craving/yearn, crave

page 26

44. 年头（頭）	niántou	N:	year (= 年 nián)
45. 罗（囉）	luo	P:	(sometimes indicates slight disagreement with one's interlocutor)
46. 单（單）調	dāndiaò	N/SV:	monotony/monotonous
47. 归（歸）宿	guīsù	N:	final settling place, marriage
48. 荒野	huāngyě	N:	wilderness, barren area
49. 去处（處）	qùchù	N:	place, place where one is heading (3-81)
*50. 面孔	miànkǒng	N:	face, visage (M: 張 zhāng; 孔 kǒng 'hole'; the face is said to have seven openings)
*51. 晃动（動）	huàngdòng	FV:	quaver, sway, move
52. 自言自語	zìyánzìyǔ	EX:	"self talk, self speak," talk to oneself
*53. 情景	qíngjǐng	N:	conditions, circumstances
54. 凶（兇）恶（惡）	xiōngè	SV:	wicked, mean
55. 領	lǐng	FV:	take away
*56. 一刹〔剎〕那間	yíchànàjiān	PH:	in an instant, in a moment (originally a Buddhist term; from Sanskrit kṣaṇa, a word for the smallest measure of time)
57. 冷酷	lěngkù	SV:	cold-blooded, merciless, ruthless

58. 精美	jīngměi	SV:	delicate and beautiful, exquisite
59. 玩具	wánjù	N:	toy, bauble
60. 华(華)丽(麗)	huálì	SV:	beautiful
*61. 服侍	fúshì	FV:	serve, wait on

page 27

62. 宠爱(愛)	chǒngài	N/FV:	exaggerated love/dote, love to excess
63. 俊美	jùnměi	SV:	handsome
*64. 接	jiē	FV:	take (as a wife)
65. 收敛	shōuliǎn	FV:	contract, draw together
*66. 嫁	jià	FV:	marry, get married (of women only)
67. 打冷噤	dǎ lěngjin	PH:	"give a shudder," shiver
*68. 辫子	biànzi	N:	pigtail, braids (M: 根 gēn; 2-15)
69. 髮髻	fǎjì	N:	hair tied in a knot, bun
*70. 诉说	sùshuō	FV:	air grievances, complain (3-65)
71. 预[豫]报(報)	yùbaò	FV:	forecast, predict
*72. 因了	yīnle	A:	because
*73. 懒洋々	lǎnyángyáng	PH:	indolent, listless
74. 拨	bō	FV:	move, adjust
75. 去掉	qùdiaò	RC:	remove, do away with

page 28

*76. 略[畧]	lüè	A:	slightly, a little bit
77. 宽松(鬆)	kuānsōng	SV:	loose and comfortable, relaxed
*78. 肥胖	féipàng	SV:	fat, obese
79. 被褥	beìrù	N:	quilt and bedding (M: 床 chuáng)

*80. 冒   mào   FV: emit, give off (smoke, gas, or fluids)

81. 悶住   mēnzhù   RC: suffocate, smother, muffle

82. 臃肿（腫）   yōngzhǒng   SV: fat and swollen, massive

*83. 摆（擺）   bǎi   FV: place, put

84. 死   sǐ   A: "like dead," soundly (asleep)

*85. 四面八方   sìmiànbāfāng   EX: "four sides, eight regions," all directions

*86. 隐（隱）約   yǐnyuē   A: indistinctly

87. 獰笑   níngxiào   PH: laugh with malignant intent

88. 歪   wāi   SV: crooked, askant (notice the structure of this character: 不 bù 'not' + 正 zhèng 'straight')

*89. 畏怯   wèiqiè   SV: fearful

*90. 遮住   zhēzhù   RC: obstruct, cover, protect

91. 搖[搖]撼   yáohàn   FV: shake violently

92. 窗格   chuānggé   N: window frame

93. 糊   hú   FV: paste

94. 驟然   zòurán   A: abruptly, suddenly

95. 哼   hng   I: (grunt of disapproval or contempt)

96. 招牌   zhāopái   N: name of a person enjoying popularity, good name

*97. 吓（嚇）   xià   FV: frighten

*98. 唉   ai   I: (sound of sighing)

*99. 没精打彩   méijīngdǎcǎi   EX: "not have energy to work up one's colors," listless, lacking energy (also 無精打彩 wújīngdǎcǎi)

100. 紐[鈕]扣   niǔkoù   N: button (M: 顆 kē)

101. 汗衫   hànshān   N: sweatshirt, undershirt (M: 件 jiàn)

102. 柔軟〔輭〕	róuruǎn	SV:	soft, yielding
103. 凸	tú	FV:	stick out, protrude (a good example of an ideographic character)
104. 面顏	miànyán	N:	countenance, face
105. 心灵（靈）	xīnlíng	N:	mind, spirit

page 29

106. 开（開）展	kāizhǎn	FV:	expand, spread out
*107. 綫〔線〕	xiàn	M/N:	thread (M: 條 tiáo, 根 gēn)
*108. 盼望	pànwàng	FV:	wish, hope, look forward to
109. 拯救	zhěngjiù	FV:	save, rescue
*110. 一下子	yí xiàzi	PH:	all of a sudden, in a moment
111. 灰塵	huīchén	N:	dust
112. 敞开（開）	chǎngkai	FV:	open, unfold
*113. 胸膛	xiōngtáng	N:	breast
*114. 揉	róu	FV:	rub
*115. 场〔場〕	chǎng	M:	(for events that take place over a period of time, such as dreams, movies, illnesses, etc.)
116. 恋（戀）乀不舍（捨）	liànliànbùshě	EX:	"very fond of and not giving up," unwilling to part with (3-78)
117. 鑽进（進）	zuānjìn	RC:	bore in, creep in, crawl in
118. 打轉	dǎzhuǎn	VO:	turn, move in a circle
119. 薄命	bómìng	N/SV:	wretched fate/ill-fated (of pretty girls)
*120. 惊（驚）醒	jīngxǐng	FV:	cause (someone) to wake up
*121. 黯淡〔澹〕	àndàn	SV:	gloomy, somber
*122. 嘆〔歎〕息	tànxī	FV:	sigh

CHAPTER FIVE

page 30

1. 庄(莊)严(嚴)　　zhuāngyán　　SV: dignified, solemn

2. 伴侣　　bànlǚ　　N: companion

*3. 惋惜　　wǎnxī　　FV: regret, feel sorry for

*4. 余(餘)音　　yúyīn　　N: remaining sound, echo

5. 引路　　yǐnlù　　VO: lead the way

6. 缩头(頭)　　suōtóusǒngjiān　　EX: "contract head, raise shoul-
   簹肩　　　　　　　　　　　ders," with the head bunched
   　　　　　　　　　　　　　up between the shoulders

*7. 偶尔(爾)　　oǔ'ěr　　A: sometimes, from time to time

8. 短促　　duǎncù　　SV: short, brief

*9. 咳嗽　　késou　　FV/N: cough

*10. 在意　　zàiyì　　FV: pay attention

11. 赤脚[脚]　　chìjiǎo　　PH/A: bare feet/barefoot

*12. 规律　　guīlǜ　　N: regularity

13. 呵　　hē　　FV: blow

14. 循环(環)　　xúnhuán　　FV: circulate, rotate (遍biàn
   　　　　　　　　　　　　is here a RE meaning 'all
   　　　　　　　　　　　　over, all around')

15. 出汗　　chūhàn　　VO: sweat

page 31

16. 衰老　　shuāilǎo　　FV: be very old, be senile

*17. 痕迹[跡、蹟]　　hénjī　　N: sign, trace

18. 搓　　cuō　　FV: rub or roll with the hand

19. 昏沉沉的　　hūnchénchénde　　A: drowsily

*20. 帘（簾）   lián   BF: curtain, blinds (FF: 簾子 liánzi, 簾兒 liár)

21. 光彩夺（奪）目   guāngcǎiduómù EX: "bright color seizes the eyes," so bright as to dazzle the eyes

22. 拦（攔）阻   lánzǔ   FV: impede, obstruct

*23. 仍旧（舊）   réngjiù   A: still, as before (short for 仍然依舊 réngrányījiù; 1-126)

24. 顾虑（慮）   gùlü   N/FV: concern, worry/be concerned about (something)

*25. 时（時）而…   shí'ér...shí'ér PT: sometimes...other times, now...then
    时（時）而

*26. 往常   wǎngcháng   A: heretofore, in the past, usually

27. 折（摺）   zhé   FV: fold

28. 衣柜（櫃）   yīguì   N: clothes closet, cabinet

*29. 湖绉   Húzhoù   ADJ: made from a kind of silk produced at 湖州 Húzhoū, Zhèjiang province

30. 皮袄（襖）   pí'ǎo   N: fur-lined jacket (M: 件 jiàn; 2-16)

31. 感叹（歎）   gǎntàn   FV: exclaim

*32. 斜对（對）面   xiéduìmiàn   PW: place across from or diagonally opposite

33. 亏（虧）得   kuīde   A: fortunately (here, sarcastic)

34. 诵经念佛   sòngjīngniànfó EX: "recite scriptures, chant Buddhist prayers," recite the Buddhist scriptures

page 32

*35. 层   céng   M: (here, for levels of meaning; refers to the fact, just stated by 琴 Qín, that playing mah-jong too much wastes one's energy)

36. 和蔼   hé'ǎi   SV: gentle, warm

37. 煨	wēi	FV:	stew slowly, simmer
38. 五更鷄[鷄]	wǔgēngjī	N:	lamp shade woven from bamboo inside of which is placed a pot of oil, used to boil tea
*39. 討厭	taǒyàn	FV/SV:	"invite loathing," dislike/ annoying, disgusting
40. 交叉[义]	jiaōchā	FV:	intersect, cross
41. 鐘擺(擺)	zhōngbǎi	N:	pendulum (of a clock)
42. 滴答	dīdá	ON:	"tick-tock" (sound of clocks ticking; cf. the Cantonese pronunciation of these two characters: dihkdaap)
*43. 睜开(開)	zhēngkaī	RC:	open (the eyes)
44. 茶几	chájī	N:	small tea table
45. 茶壺(壺)	cháhú	N:	teapot (M: 把 bǎ)
46. 斟	zhēn	FV:	pour, fill a cup with
47. 釅	yàn	SV:	strong (in taste, of tea or liquor)
*48. 凳[櫈]	dèng	BF:	bench, stool (FF: 凳子 dèngzi; M: 張 zhāng)

page 33

49. 亲(親)热(熱)	qīnrè	SV:	warm, loving
*50. 玩弄	wánnòng	FV:	toy with, play with
51. 希[稀]奇	xīqí	SV:	rare, strange, uncommon
52. 著名	zhùmíng	SV:	famous, renowned
53. 男女同学(學)	nánnǚtóngxué	EX:	"male and female together study," coeducation
54. 万(萬)々	wànwàn	A:	absolutely, by all means (before negative expressions)
55. 名堂	míngtang	N:	mischief, shenanigans
56. 瓢	piaó	N:	ladle made from a gourd
*57. 隔	gé	FV:	be apart from, be separated by

page 34

58. 駁   bó   FV: contradict, disprove

59. 老腐敗   laǒfǔbai   N: corrupt old fellow, corrupt
                                             old hag

*60. 央求   yāngqiú   FV: beg, plead

*61. 尼姑庵   nígū'ān   N: Buddhist nunnery or convent

62. 拿定主意   nádìng zhúyi   PH: make up one's mind, be de-
                                             termined

63. 頹唐   tuítáng   SV: dispirited, disconcerted

*64. 胆(膽)量   dǎnliàng   N: bravery, fortitude

*65. 絲毫不   sīhaóbù   A: not the tiniest or least
                                             bit (3-64)

*66. 体(體)貼   tǐtiē   FV: be kind or considerate to

*67. 爹   diē   N: papa, daddy (=爸ㄚ bàba)

*68. 肩头(頭)   jiāntou   N: shoulder (1-90, 3-107)

69. 纏(纏)脚[腳]   chánjiaǒ   VO: bind the feet

70. 外公   waìgōng   N: maternal grandfather
                                             (=外祖父 waìzǔfù)

page 35

71. 疲乏   pífá   SV: weary, exhausted (1-117)

72. 穿   chuān   FV: pass, cross

*73. 凄(淒)涼   qīliáng   SV: desolate and sorrowful (4-1)

74. 遺容   yíróng   N: portrait of a dead person

*75. 裙子   qúnzi   N: skirt (M: 條 tiaó)

76. 錫灯(燈)盞   xídēngzhǎn   N: tin or pewter lamp

*77. 映   yìng   FV: reflect light, shine

78. 易卜生   Yìbǔshēng   N: (transliteration of) Henrik
                                             Ibsen (1828-1906), Norwegian
                                             playwright and poet

79. 娜 拉   Nàlā   N: (transliteration of) Nora (main character in Ibsen's play <u>A</u> <u>Doll's</u> <u>House</u>)

80. 启〔啟〕示   qǐshì   N/FV: revelation/reveal

*81. 顿时（時）   dùnshí   A: immediately, promptly

*82. 倩如   Qiànrú   N: （人名 ）

page 36

83. 开（開）辟（闢）   kāipì   FV: open up, build

84. 有暇   yǒuxiá   PH: have free time

85. 家母   jiāmǔ   N: "my mother" (家 jiā precedes certain kinship terms to re- fer to senior members of one's own family)

*86. ✕ ✕   (mǒumǒu)   PH: so-and-so, such-and-such (the symbol ✕ can sometimes be read for the character 某 mǒu 'a certain [person, thing, date]')

87. 标（標）点（點）   biāodiǎn   N: punctuation

88. 拖长（長）   tuōcháng   FV: lengthen

89. 俗不可耐   súbùkě'nài   EX: "vulgar not can endure," unbearably vulgar

90. 工整   gōngzhěng   SV: neat (of calligraphy or writing)

91. 通信栏（欄）   tōngxìnlán   N: "letters to the editor" column (of a magazine or newspaper)

CHAPTER SIX

1. 长（長）子 — zhǎngzǐ — N: eldest son

2. 长（長）房 — zhǎngfáng — N: branch of the family tree descending from the first-born son

3. 长（長）孙（孫） — zhǎngsūn — N: eldest grandson

4. 相貌清秀 — xiàngmàoqīngxiù — EX: "facial features clear and beautiful," handsome

5. 聪（聰）慧 — cōnghuì — SV/N: intelligent/intelligence

6. 双（雙）亲（親） — shuāngqīn — PH: both parents

7. 鍾爱（愛） — zhōngài — N/FV: great love (for children)/ love very much

8. 私塾 — sīshú — N: home school with a private tutor (in old China)

*9. 成就 — chéngjiù — N: achievement, accomplishment

*10. 庆（慶）幸 — qìngxìng — FV: congratulate oneself, rejoice

11. 宁（寧）馨兒 — níngxīn'ér — N: lovely and perfect child

12. 优（優）良 — yōuliáng — SV: excellent

13. 名列第一 — mínglièdìyī — EX: "name arranged in first place (on roster of examinees)," be graduated at the top of one's class

14. 化学（學） — huàxué — N: chemistry

15. 恶（惡）运（運） — èyùn — N: bad luck, misfortune

16. 肄業 — yìyè — FV: learn, study (at school)

*17. 娶 — qǔ — FV: marry (only of a man marrying a woman; 4-66)

18. 堂 — táng — BF: (indicates cousins of the same surname)

*19. 样（樣）   yàng   M: kind, sort (= 種 zhǒng)

page 38

*20. 显（顯）著   xiǎnzhù   SV: clear, obvious, evident

*21. 伤（傷）痕   shānghén   N: scar

22. 前程   qiánchéng   N: "road ahead," future

*23. 美妙   meǐmiaò   SV: exquisite, beautiful

*24. 幻梦（夢）   huànmèng   N: daydream, fantasy

25. 残酷   cánkù   SV: cruel, heartless

26. 师（師）友   shīyoǔ   N: teachers and friends

27. 赞（讚）誉（譽）   zànyù   N/FV: praise

28. 文憑   wénping   N: diploma (M: 張 zhāng)

*29. 門   mén   M: (for marriages, courses, lines of work, etc.)

*30. 亲（親）事   qīnshi   N: marriage

31. 重孙（孫）   chóngsūn   N: great-grandson

32. 抱孙（孫）   baòsūn   VO: have a grandson

33. 接亲（親）   jiēqīn   VO: take a wife (4-64)

34. 了結   liaǒjié   FV: bring to a conclusion

35. 桩（椿）   zhuāng   M: (for affairs, matters, business, etc.)

36. 积（積）蓄   jīxù   N: savings

37. 愁   chóu   FV/SV: worry (about something)/ worried, depressed

38. 休养（養）   xiūyǎng   FV: rest and recuperate

*39. 料理   liaòlǐ   FV: manage, take care of

40. 少不掉   shaǒbudiaò   RC: cannot do without

41. 内助   neìzhù   N: wife

42. 下定   xiàdǐng   FV: give engagement presents (of the groom's family to the bride's family)

*43.	順从（從）	shùncóng	FV: obey
*44.	鋪盖（蓋）	pūgaì	N: bedding (M: 床 chuáng)
*45.	蒙〔蒙〕	méng	FV: cover

page 39

46.	傳言	chuányán	N: rumor, unfounded talk
47.	好学（學）	haòxué	N/SV: love of learning/fond of learning and scholarship
*48.	待	daì	FV: await, wait for
*49.	做媒	zuòmeí	VO: "act as matchmaker," arrange a marriage match
50.	芳名	fāngmíng	N: honorable name (of a woman; 芳 BF 'fragrant, virtuous')
51.	淘汰	taótaì	FV: eliminate (undesirable elements), weed out
52.	适（適）宜	shìyí	SV: suitable, appropriate
53.	配偶	peì'oǔ	N: spouse, mate
54.	情面	qíngmiàn	N: prestige, face
55.	拈鬮	niānjiū	VO: draw lots
56.	祖宗	zǔzōng	N: ancestor
57.	神主	shénzhǔ	N: wooden tablet used as a symbol of the deceased
*58.	禱告	daǒgaò	FV/N: pray/prayer
59.	才子佳人	caízǐjiārén	EX: "man of talent, woman of beauty," ideal couple, perfect match
60.	心目中	xīnmùzhōng	PH: in the mind's eye
61.	中意	zhòngyì	SV/VO: "hit one's intention," suit one's fancy, be agreeable
62.	祈禱	qídaǒ	FV/N: pray/prayer (6-58)
63.	姨表兄妹	yíbiaǒxiōngmeì	N: maternal cousins
64.	挑选（選）	tiaōxuǎn	FV: select, pick

*65. 升学（學）　　　shēngxué　　　VO: advance to the next higher level in one's education

66. 泡影　　　　　　paòyǐng　　　　N: "shadow of bubbles," unreality

*67. 断（斷）送　　　duànsòng　　　FV: throw away, lose for good

*68. 意志　　　　　　yìzhì　　　　　N: wish, desire, will

69. 怨言　　　　　　yuànyán　　　　N: complaint (2-29)

page 40

*70. 傀儡　　　　　　kuǐleǐ　　　　　N: puppet

71. 珍爱（愛）　　　zhēn'aì　　　　FV: treasure, love dearly

72. 宝（寶、寶）貝　baǒbeì　　　　N: precious and cherished thing, darling

*73. 悲哀　　　　　　beī'aī　　　　N/SV: sadness, woe/sad, grieved

74. 应（應）尽（盡）yīngjìn　　　　PH: ought to fulfill

*75. 把戏（戲）　　　baǐxì　　　　　N: performance, show (usually in a derogatory sense)

76. 贺客　　　　　　hèkè　　　　　N: guests who come to offer congratulations

77. 书籍　　　　　　shūjí　　　　　N: books

*78. 整齐（齊）　　　zhěngqí　　　　SV: neat, tidy, well-arranged

79. 书橱　　　　　　shūchú　　　　N: bookcase

*80. 吩咐　　　　　　fēnfu　　　　N/FV: instructions, directions/ give someone instructions (to do something)

81. 搭　　　　　　　dā　　　　　　FV: add on, raise up

*82. 仪（儀）式　　　yíshì　　　　　N: rites, ceremonies

83. 一连　　　　　　yìlián　　　　A: successively, continuously

84. 孙（孫）媳　　　sūnxí　　　　　N: granddaughter-in-law

*85. 媳妇（婦）　　　xífu　　　　　N: daughter-in-law

86. 一无所得　　　　yìwúsuǒdé　　　EX: "uniformly without anything obtained," completely without gain

*87. 温（溫）柔	wēnroú	SV:	warm and tender
88. 料想	liaòxiǎng	FV:	imagine, reckon
89. 女郎	nǔláng	N:	young girl

page 41

90. 陶醉	taózuì	FV:	be intoxicated with happiness, be greatly pleased
*91. 陪伴	peíbàn	FV:	keep company
92. 挣錢过（過）活	zhèngqiánguòhuó	EX:	"struggle for money, pass life," earn money to make one's living
*93. 下面	xiàmian	PW:	(here) down-river, area to the east of Sìchuan (in this case probably Shànghaǐ)
*94. 一则…二则	yìzé…èrzé	PT:	first of all...secondly
95. 分家	fēnjiā	VO:	divide the family property
96. 賬	zhàng	N:	account, bill (4-6)
97. 位置	weìzhi	N/FV:	position
98. 西蜀实（實）業公司	Xīshǔ Shíyè Gōngsī	N:	West Sìchuan Industrial Corporation
99. 零用	língyòng	FV/N:	use (money) for everyday purposes/sundry expenses, pocket money
100. 出头（頭）	chūtoú	VO:	make good, succeed
*101. 事务（務）所	shìwùsuǒ	N:	business office (e.g., of a company)
102. 股子	gǔzi	N:	share (of stock)
103. 董事	dǒngshì	N:	member of the board of directors (of a company)
*104. 照料	zhaòliao	FV/N:	take care of/care
105. 平板	píngbǎn	SV:	even (of the voice)
*106. 藏	cáng	FV:	hide, store away, be hidden

*107. 待   dai   FV: treat or deal with (people; 6-48)

*108. 一一   yīyī   A: one by one, each separately

page 42

109. 八字鬚   bázìxū   N: mustache shaped like the character 八

110. 駝背   tuóbeì   ADJ/N: hunchbacked/hunchback

111. 老太婆   laǒtaìpó   N: old woman

112. 会（會）計   kuaìji   N: accountant, bookkeeper; accounting, bookkeeping

113. 职（職）員   zhíyuán   N: employee, staff member (of a company)

*114. 举（舉、擧）动（動） jǔdòng   N: behavior, conduct, action

*115. 惶恐   huángkǒng   SV: afraid

116. 世兄   shìxiōng   N: brother, comrade (very respectful term of address between friends whose fathers were also friends)

117. 囚犯   qiúfàn   N: criminal

118. 遇赦   yùshè   VO: meet with pardon

119. 訓話   xùnhuà   N: teachings, instructions

120. 問长（長）問短   wènchángwènduǎn EX: "ask the long, ask the short (of it)," question at great length

121. 学（學）識   xuéshi   N: learning, erudition

*122. 陌生   mòshēng   SV: strange, unfamiliar, unaccustomed

123. 領到   lǐng   FV: receive (something issued or distributed; 4-55)

124. 現金   xiànjīn   N: ready money, cash

page 43

125. 平淡   píngdàn   SV: smooth

126. 特殊　　　　　tèshū　　　　SV: special

127. 呆〔獃〕板　　　daībǎn　　　SV: dull, boring

*128. 平静　　　　　píngjìng　　SV: quiet, calm

*129. 安稳（穩）　　ānwěn　　　 SV: secure and stable

130. 时（時）疫　　shíyì　　　　N: epidemic

131. 棺木　　　　　guānmù　　　N: coffin

*132. 清春　　　　　qīngchūn　　N: "clear spring," prime of life

133. 箭　　　　　　jiàn　　　　 N: arrow (M: 枝 zhī, 根 gēn)

*134. 射　　　　　　shè　　　　　FV: shoot (P-23)

*135. 面目　　　　　miànmù　　　N: aspect, feature

136. 仇〔讎〕恨　　chóuhèn　　　N: enmity, hatred

page 44

*137. 正当（當）　　zhèngdang　 SV: legitimate, proper

138. 烦恼（惱）　　fánnǎo　　　N/SV: troubles, anguish/troubled, vexed

*139. 叔　　　　　　shū　　　　　BF: uncle (father's younger brother; FF: 叔叔，叔父）

*140. 嬸　　　　　　shěn　　　　 BF: aunt (father's younger brother's wife; FF: 嬸母，嬸子，嬸兒）

*141. 得罪　　　　　dézuì　　　　FV: offend, wrong

142. 挑拨　　　　　tiǎobō　　　 N/FV: provocation/provoke, incite

143. 跟...作对（對）gēn...zuòduì PH: pair off against, oppose

*144. 陈（陳）姨太　Chén Yítai　 N: concubine Chén

145. 说服　　　　　shuōfú　　　 FV: overcome by talking

*146. 寻（尋）　　　xún　　　　　FV: search for (找 zhǎo)

*147. 精力　　　　　jīnglì　　　 N: physical and mental strength, energy, vigor

148. 处(處)世方法 chǔshìfāngfǎ N: way of dealing with the world, way of conducting oneself in life

*149. 敷衍 fūyǎn FV: go through the necessary courtesies without sincerity, discharge responsibility in a perfunctory manner

*150. 恭敬 gōngjìng SV/FV: respectful/respect

151. 欢(歡)心 huānxīn N: love, contentment, favors

152. 淑蓉 Shūróng N: (人名)

153. 肺病 fèibìng N: "lung disease," tuberculosis

154. 嬰兒 yīng'ér N: infant

page 45

155. 遺留 yíliú FV: hand down

*156. 教养(養) jiàoyǎng FV: educate and rear, bring up

157. 抱負 bàofu N: aspirations, ambition

158. 五四运(運)动(動) Wǔsì Yùndong N: May Fourth movement (the Chinese intellectual revolution of the late teens and early twenties of this century, dated from the student demonstrations in Beǐjing on May 4, 1919)

159. 如火如荼 rúhuǒrútú EX: "like fire, like bitterweed," fiery, bitter (contrast 荼 and 茶 chá)

*160. 貪婪 tānlán SV: greedy, longing (for something)

161. 罢(罷)市 bàshì VO: close down shops

162. 每周(週)評論 Meǐ Zhoū Pínglùn N: Weekly Review (a magazine published at Beǐjing University from 1918 to 1919, more political in content than 3-3 新青年 Xīn Qīngnián)

163. 出售 chūshoù FV: sell

164. 流通处(處) liútōngchù N: circulation place

*165. 刊 物   kānwù   N: periodical, publication
                                     (M: 期 qī, 份 fèn)

166. 火 星   huǒxīng   N: spark

*167. 点 (點) 燃   diǎnrán   FV: light (a fire; 1-21)

168. 新 奇   xīnqí   SV: new, novel

*169. 議 論   yìlùn   N/FV: discussion, argument/discuss

*170. 抗 拒   kàngjù   FV: resist, oppose

171. 信 服   xìnfú   FV: believe in, trust

172. 新 潮   Xīn Cháo   N: New Tide (also entitled
                                     Renaissance; a magazine pub-
                                     lished by the students of
                                     Běijīng University from 1919
                                     to 1922; the most influential
                                     student magazine of the period)

173. 星期評論   Xīngqī Pínglùn N: Weekly Critic (published in
                                     Běijīng from 1918 to 1919,
                                     especially concerned with
                                     political problems of the
                                     time)

174. 少年中国 (國)   Shaònián Zhōngguo N: Young China (a monthly pub-
                                     lished from 1919 to 1931 first
                                     in Běijīng, later in Shànghǎi,
                                     by the Young China Association;
                                     very popular among young readers)

175. 輪 流   lúnliú   A/FV: in turns/rotate, take turns

176. 通 訊 栏 (欄)   tōngxùnlán   N: "letters to the editor" col-
                                     umn (of a magazine or news-
                                     paper; 5-91)

page 46

177. 刘 (劉) 半农 (農) Liú Bànnóng   N: courtesy name of 劉復 Liú
                                     Fù [1889-1934], Chinese teacher,
                                     linguist, and man of letters

*178. 作 揖主义 (義)   zuōyīzhǔyì   N: "compliant bow philosophy"
                                     (according to this philosophy,
                                     formulated by 劉復 Liú Fù in
                                     a September, 1918 article in 3-3
                                     新青年 Xīn Qīngnián, one
                                     should not waste one's time and
                                     effort on discussion, but rather

outwardly agree with one's adversary and greet his statements with a bow, all the time keeping one's own convictions; 作揖 'make a bow')

*179. 拥（擁）护（護） yǒnghù FV: protect, support

180. 呆〔獃〕子伊凡 的故事 Dāizi Yīfánde Gùshi N: "The Story of Ivan the Fool" (a short story by Tolstoy; P-3)

181. 顺应（應） shùnyìng FV: conform, adjust (to a certain kind of circumstances)

*182. 矛盾 maódùn SV/N: "spear and shield," contradictory/contradiction

183. 重 chóng M: level, layer (1-50)

184. 暮气（氣）十足 mùqìshízú EX: "setting sun air (i.e., declining), ten feet (i.e., 十分之十 —— completely, extremely)," completely lacking energy, supine and spineless

185. 责难（難） zénàn FV: reprimand, upbraid

186. 坦然 tǎnrán SV: composed, placid

187. 阅读 yuèdú FV: read

188. 爬 pá FV: crawl, climb

189. 注 zhù FV: fix upon, concentrate on

*190. 奶妈 nǎimā N: wet nurse, amah

191. 喂〔餵〕奶 weinǎi VO: "feed milk," nurse (a baby) with milk

192. 抚养（養） fǔyǎng FV: bring up, rear

193. 奶汁 naǐzhī N: mother's milk

page 47

194. 创举（舉） chuàngjǔ N: new or unprecedented undertaking

195. 体（體）会（會） tǐhuì FV: understand, comprehend

*196. 心思　　　　　xīnsī　　　　N: idea, intention, motive, mood

*197. 迟（遲）　　　chí　　　　　SV: late (=晚, 2-23 晏 yàn)

*198. 临（臨）　　　lín　　　　　BF: about to, just before

199. 手腕　　　　　shǒuwàn　　　N: wrist

*200. 俯　　　　　　fǔ　　　　　　FV: bend down

*201. 吻　　　　　　wěn　　　　　FV: kiss

*202. 喃々地　　　　nánnánde　　　A: mumbling, murmuring

*203. 含糊　　　　　hánhu　　　　SV: "containing confusion," vague, unclear

204. 喷泉　　　　　pēnquán　　　N: fountain

205. 管　　　　　　guǎn　　　　　BF: tube, pipe (FF: 管子 , 管兒; M: 根 gēn)

page 48

*1. 照常	zhàocháng	A:	habitually, as usual (4-26)	
2. 例假	lìjià	N:	legal holiday, customary holiday	
3. 办(辦)公室	bàngōngshì	N:	office (M: 間 jiān)	
4. 商場[塲]	shāngchǎng	N:	market place, shopping arcade	
5. 鋪[舖]面	pùmiàn	N:	shopfront, store (contrast 鋪 pù BF 'a store' and 鋪 pū 'to spread (a mat, road, etc.)'; 6-44)	
6. 附設	fùshè	FV:	attach to, be affiliated with	
7. 小型	xiǎoxíng	ADJ:	small scale	
8. 發电(電)厂(廠)	fādiànchǎng	N:	electric power plant	
9. 租户	zūhù	N:	tenant	
10. 經租	jīngzū	FV:	manage rentals	
11. 銷售	xiāoshòu	FV/N:	sell/sales	
12. 开(開)設	kāishè	FV:	establish, set up	
*13. 期	qī	M:	issue (of a publication)	
14. 十六开(開)本	shíliù kāiběn	N:	sextodecimo (printer's technical term for the size of a page)	
*15. 捧	pěng	FV:	hold in both hands	
16. 老板	lǎobǎn	N:	boss, manager (of a store; also written 老闆)	
*17. 嘱咐	zhǔfù	FV:	instruct (someone to do something), charge (someone) with a task	

18. 翻閱   fānyuè   FV: read by turning pages,
                                    look over (6-187)

19. 賬目   zhàngmù   N: account book, details of
                                    accounts

page 49

20. 訂閱   dìngyuè   FV: subscribe (7-18)

21. 津々有味   jīnjīnyǒuwèi   EX: "it overflows (with saliva),
                                    there is taste," mouth wa-
                                    tering; with great interest
                                    and relish

22. 邮(郵)包   yóubāo   N: postal parcel

23. 加快   jiākuài   ADJ: (here) special delivery mail

24. 間隔   jiàn'gé   FV/N: intersperse, set apart with
                                    space in between/interval of
                                    space or time

25. 活动(動)   huódòng   SV/FV/N: moveable, active/move about/
                                    activity

26. 圓椅   yuányǐ   N: swivel chair (M: 把 bǎ)

27. 算盘(盤)   suànpán   N: abacus

*28. 透   tòu   FV: pass through, penetrate

29. 淡青   dànqīng   ADJ: pale blue

30. 窗帷   chuāngwéi   N: window curtain or screen

31. 三合土   sānhétǔ   N: mortar, cement (also written
                                    三和土)

32. 掀   xiān   FV: lift up, raise

*33. 劍云(雲)   Jiànyún   N: (人名)

page 50

34. 茶园(園)   cháyuán   N: "tea garden," opera theater

35. 筹(籌)款[欵]   chóukuǎn   VO: raise money

36. 殷勤   yīnqin   SV: polite, civil

*37. 留心   liúxīn   FV/SV: pay attention/attentive

38. 主动（動）　　　zhǔdòng　　　FV: initiate, back (an under-
　　　　　　　　　　　　　　　　　　　　　　　　taking)

39. 脚〔腳〕色　　　jiǎosè　　　　N: character, role (in a play)

40. 扮演　　　　　　bànyǎn　　　　FV: portray, play (a character)

41. 終身大事　　　Zhōng Shēn Dà Shì N: "of a whole lifetime the
　　　　　　　　　　　　　　　　　　　　great event," Marriage
　　　　　　　　　　　　　　　　　　　　(title of a one-act play
　　　　　　　　　　　　　　　　by 胡適 Hú Shì; this
　　　　　　　　　　　　　　　　is a common four-character
　　　　　　　　　　　　　　　　phrase referring to marriage)

*42. 担（擔）心　　　dānxīn　　　　VO/SV: worry/worried

*43. 闔　　　　　　　hé　　　　　　FV: close

*44. 膝　　　　　　　xī　　　　　　BF: knee (FF: 膝蓋 xīgài)

45. 算賬　　　　　　suànzhàng　　　VO: settle accounts

46. 局促不安　　　júcùbù'ān　　　EX: nervous and ill at ease

page 51

47. 远（遠）房　　　yuǎnfáng　　　N: distant branch of the family
　　　　　　　　　　　　　　　　　　　　　　tree (6-2)

48. 平輩　　　　　　píngbei　　　　N: same generation

49. 寄养（養）　　　jìyǎng　　　　FV: send (children) to another
　　　　　　　　　　　　　　　　　　　　　family for temporary care

50. 伯父　　　　　　bófù　　　　　N: uncle (father's elder brother)

51. 無力　　　　　　wúlì　　　　　PH: (here) not to have the where-
　　　　　　　　　　　　　　　　　　　　　withal, cannot afford

52. 餬口　　　　　　húkoǔ　　　　FV: eke out a living

53. 算学（學）　　　suànxué　　　　N: arithmetic (distinguish 數學
　　　　　　　　　　　　　　　　　　　shùxué 'mathematics')

54. 保养（養）　　　baǒyǎng　　　　FV: take care of one's health

55. 陰沉　　　　　　yīnchén　　　　SV: gloomy, downcast

*56. 勉强　　　　　　miǎnqiǎng　　　SV/FV/A: forced, unnatural/force,
　　　　　　　　　　　　　　　　　　　　　compel/barely

*57. 嘴唇〔脣〕　　　zuǐchún　　　　N: lip

*58. 单（單）   dān   A: only, solely

59. 不以为（為）然   bùyǐweírán   EX: "not to take it to be so," disagree

*60. 道   daò   M: (for rays of light, streets, courses of food, air currents, rivers, etc.)

*61. 掠   lüè   FV: sideswipe, pass over

page 52

*62. 系（繫）   jì   FV: be attached or fastened

63. 我鳥蛋形   édànxíng   ADJ: "goose egg shape," oval

64. 恰到好处（處）   qiàdaòhaǒchù EX: "opportunely arrives at a good place," just right, not too much and not too little

65. 刘（劉）海   liúhaǐ   N: bangs, hair on the forehead

66. 修眉   xiūmeí   PH: trimmed eyebrows

67. 根   gēn   M: (for noses; 四川)

*68. 嵌   qiàn   FV: be inlaid or inset

69. 深透   shēntoù   SV: penetrating (7-28)

*70. 添   tiān   FV: add, increase

71. 視綫［線］   shìxiàn   N: line of vision

*72. 們   men   BF: (plural suffix; here, 覺新們 means 'Juéxīn and the rest [i.e., his two brothers]')

73. 打招呼   dǎ zhaōhu   PH: greet (2-45)

74. 讓座位   ràng zuòwei PH: offer or give up one's seat

75. 按鈴   ànlǐng   VO: ring a bell

76. 泡茶   paòchá   VO: make tea

77. 明軒   Míngxuān   N: (the 字 zì or style [name] of 覺新 Juéxīn)

78. 新發祥   Xīn Fāxiáng N: "New Prosperity" (name of a department store)

79.	衣料	yīliào	N: clothing material
80.	毛葛	máogé	N: silk or linen cloth
*81.	迟(遲)疑	chíyí	FV: hesitate
*82.	等候	děnghòu	FV: await

page 53

*83.	搶	qiǎng	FV: seize, snatch
*84.	遞給	dìgeǐ	FV: give, hand over
*85.	免得	miǎnde	FV: avoid, save (someone from an inconvenience); lest

page 54

86.	賬簿	zhàngbù	N: account book (4-6, 6-96)
87.	女性	nǔxìng	N: (here) member of the female sex, female
88.	挖苦	wākǔ	FV: tease, mock
89.	姨媽	yímā	N: maternal aunt (6-144)
90.	守寡	shǒuguǎ	VO: become a widow
*91.	惊(驚)奇	jīngqí	SV: surprised
*92.	憔悴	qiáocuì	SV: worn, haggard
*93.	問話	wènhuà	VO/N: ask questions/question
94.	宜寅(賓)	Yíbīn	PW: (name of a city in Sìchuan)
95.	風土人情	fēngtǔrénqíng	EX: "wind, soil, and human feelings," people and places, local customs and practices

page 55

96.	直率	zhíshuài	SV: frank, straightforward
97.	感伤(傷)	gǎnshāng	SV: sad, sentimental (also 傷感)
*98.	不見得	bújiànde	A: not necessarily
99.	保定	baǒdìng	FV: guarantee
100.	慎重	shènzhòng	SV: careful and serious

101.	美滿	měimǎn	SV: happy, perfect

page 56

*102.	祝福	zhùfú	FV: bless
103.	回味	huíwèi	FV: recollect the pleasant "flavor" (of some past event), savor
104.	作梗	zuògěng	FV: be stubborn (like the prickly 梗 tree), obstruct, hinder
*105.	气﹝氣﹞憤	qìfèn	SV: angry, furious (also written 氣忿)
*106.	調子	diàozi	N: tone of voice (1-34)
107.	舅	jiù	BF: maternal uncle (FF: 舅ㄣ jiùjiu, 舅父 jiùfu) 舅ㄣ jiùjiu
*108.	托﹝託﹞	tuō	FV: request
109.	允意	yǔnyì	N: intention to permit (something)
110.	八字	bázì	N: (Chinese equivalent of our horoscope; a term for the Celestial Stems ﹝天干 tiāngān﹞ and the Terrestrial Branches ﹝地支 dìzhī﹞, which denote the time of a person's birth; used by fortunetellers as a reference to see if the betrothed are well matched)
111.	两﹝兩﹞造	liǎngzào	N: the two people involved in something (such as a contract or lawsuit), the two parties or sides
112.	相尅	xiāngkè	FV: to be mutually destructive
113.	牌桌子	páizhuōzi	N: card table (M: 張 zhāng)
114.	跟...有意見	gēn...yǒu yìjian	PH: have a quarrel or disagreement with (someone)
115.	受委屈	shòu wěiqū	PH: suffer a wrong or humiliation
116.	报﹝報﹞复﹝復﹞	bàofu	FV/N: revenge

117. 鬧〔閙〕翻 naòfān FV: have an upset, become very pieved at each other

118. 恍然大悟 huǎngrándàwù EX: "in a wild manner greatly comprehend," come to understand suddenly

119. 錯怪 cuòguaì PH: wrongly blame

120. 抱不平 baòbupíng PH: be indignant at an injustice

121. 糊里（裏）糊塗 húlihútu EX: all mixed up, muddle-headed (also 糊塗 ; in both expressions 糊 is sometimes written 胡)

page 57

*122. 起勁 qǐjìn SV: get worked up about, be enthusiastic

123. 天經地乂（義） tiānjīngdìyì EX: "principles of heaven and earth," very appropriate, a matter of course

124. 説不上 shuōbushàng RC: cannot speak of, not fit a description

125. 性情投合 xìngqíngtóuhé EX: personalities match (often used in reference to marriage; 2-30)

*126. 覺（覺）察 juéchá FV: discover, realize, detect

*127. 躲避 duǒbì FV: avoid, hide from

*128. 思念 sīniàn FV: remember fondly, think about

*129. 豈不是 qǐbúshì PH: "if it isn't," "how could it not be," "doesn't it" (implies an affirmative response)

*130. 冷淡 lěngdàn SV: cold, indifferent

131. 反駁 fǎnbó FV: retort (5-58)

page 58

132. 否定 fǒudìng FV: deny

133. 光明正大 guāngmíngzhèngdà EX: honest and upright

134. 無須乎　　　wúxūhū　　PH: there's no need to (=不必 búbì)

135. 隐（隱）諱　　yǐnhuì　　FV: conceal, hide

*136. 神情　　　　shénqíng　　N: facial expression, appearance

*137. 为（為）难（難）weínán　FV/VO: make trouble, trouble

138. 窘相　　　　jiǒngxiàng　N: embarrassed or hard-pressed expression

*139. 舌头（頭）　shétou　　N: tongue (M: 根 gēn)

140. 迟（遲）鈍　chídùn　　SV: stupid, awkward (6-197)

*141. 凄〔凄〕然　qīrán　　SV: very sad and sorrowful (1-14, 5-73)

142. 謙虚　　　　qiānxū　　SV: modest

143. 比不得　　　bǐbudé　　RC: cannot be compared with, be unlike

144. 外人　　　　wairen　　N: strangers, outsiders

page 59

145. 誠摯　　　　chéngzhì　SV: sincere

*146. 猝然　　　　cùrán　　A: suddenly, abruptly

*147. 話題　　　　huàtí　　N: topic of conversation or discussion

148. 細心　　　　xìxīn　　SV: careful, meticulous, cautious

149. 猜透　　　　caitoù　　RC: guess through (7-28)

150. 改天　　　　gǎi tiān　PH: "change day," another day

*151. 毅然　　　　yìrán　　A: firmly, determinedly

*152. 沉吟　　　　chényín　A: heavy and hesitating, in a deep voice

page 60

153. 刺激　　　　cìji　　N/FV/SV: irritation, upset, shock/ upset, shock, stimulate/ exciting

*154. 誠恳 (懇)　　　chéngkěn　　　SV: sincere

155. 辩解　　　　　　biànjiě　　　　FV: explain in an argument, justify

*156. 認真　　　　　　rènzhēn　　　　SV: serious, conscientious

157. 伤 (傷) 心人　　　shāngxīnrén　　EX: "heartbroken person ad-
     别有怀 (懷) 抱　　bié yǒu huáibaò　　ditionally has thoughts,"
                                          harbor a secret heartbreak

158. 生错了时 (時) 代　shēngcuòle　　　PH: born in the wrong age
                       shídaì

159. 膝头 (頭)　　　　xītou　　　　　N: area above the knee, lap,
                                         thigh (7-44)

160. 管得全　　　　　guǎndequán　　RC: be able to deal with all

161. 师 (師) 爷 (爺)　shīyé　　　　　N: "Master"

162. 正色　　　　　　zhèngsè　　　　N: stern and serious facial
                                         expression

163. 哪兒有不肯的　　nǎr yǒu bùkěnde　PH: "where is there a logical
     道理　　　　　　daòlǐ　　　　　　basis for not wanting to?"
                                         "of course (I) want to"

*164. 欣喜　　　　　　xīnxǐ　　　　　A: happily, with delight

165. 开 (開) 头 (頭)　kaītoú　　　　　VO: begin

page 61

*166. 揭　　　　　　　jiē　　　　　　FV: raise up, lift off

page 62

*1. 气（氣）咻咻   qìxiūxiū   A: breathing heavily

*2. 抓   zhuā   FV: grab

3. 認不得   rènbudé   RC: not able to recognize (verb 認得 rènde plus negative infix 不 bù)

4. 三角臉   sānjiǎoliǎn   N: triangular face

*5. 顆   kē   M: (for beads, teardrops, hearts, and other small objects)

6. 汗珠   hànzhū   N: beads or drops of sweat (5-15)

*7. 喘气（氣）   chuǎnqì   VO: pant

*8. 惊（驚）惶   jīnghuáng   SV: alarmed

*9. 呼吸   hūxī   N/FV: breathing, breath/breathe

10. 平順   píngshùn   FV/SV: become even and smooth/even, smooth, calm

11. 發顫   fāzhàn   FV: tremble, quaver (3-41)

12. 丘八   qiūbā   N: soldier (term of contempt; from the upper and lower components of the character 兵 bīng 'soldier')

13. 左臂   zuǒbei   N: left arm (3-30)

page 63

*14. 憎恨   zēnghèn   FV: hate intensely, abhor

15. 侵犯   qīnfàn   FV: encroach (on the rights of others)

16. 异（異）样（樣）   yìyàng   ADJ: unusual, extraordinary

17. 不由自主   bùyoúzìzhǔ   EX: "not from self mastered," cannot control self

18. 渾身	húnshēn	PH:	whole body
19. 看客	kànkè	N:	spectator
20. 看白戏（戲）	kàn báixì	PH:	see a play for free (without paying admission)
21. 不可理喻	bùkělǐyù	EX:	"cannot (use) reason to explain," unreasonable
*22. 約	yuē	FV:	invite, ask
23. 同伴	tóngbàn	N:	companion
24. 搗乱（亂）	daǒluàn	VO:	make trouble
25. 息事宁（寧）人	xīshìníngrén	EX:	settle a matter and soothe the concerned, bring to peace
26. 放肆	fàngsi	SV:	unruly, reckless, without restraint
27. 妨碍（礙）	fáng'ai	FV:	interfere with, hinder, obstruct
28. 胡闹〔鬧〕	hú'naò	FV:	be wildly reckless, raise a ruckus
29. 干涉	gānshè	FV:	interfere, intervene
30. 闹〔鬧〕乱（亂）子	naò luànzi	PH:	cause a disturbance, make trouble
31. 城防司令部	chéngfángsīlìngbù	N:	city garrison command
*32. 連	lián	M:	company, battery (of soldiers; usually consists of 126 men)
33. 弹压（壓）	tányā	FV:	put down, suppress
34. 不成样（樣）子	bùchéng yàngzi	PH:	not be the way something is supposed to be, wild, in a shambles
35. 肇事	zhaòshì	FV:	stir up trouble
36. 逃光	taóguāng	RC:	flee away to the very last man, disappear completely (the RE 光 guāng indicates the use of something to the

			point where nothing is left, e.g., 飯吃光了 'The food was eaten up (to the very last bit)', 錢花光了 'The money was completely spent')
37. 徒手	túshǒu	ADJ:	empty-handed, unarmed
38. 哪个(個)舅子才相信	nǎge jiùzi caí xiāngxìn	PH:	"What fool would believe it?" (7-107)
39. 預先	yùxiān	A:	beforehand
40. 怒火直往上冒	nùhuǒ zhí wǎng shàng maò	PH:	"fury fire keeps on proceeding to the top and being emitted," extremely angry (4-80)
41. 炸裂	zhàliè	FV:	burst apart, explode

page 64

42. 謠傳	yaóchuán	FV/N:	spread a rumor/rumor
43. 当(當)局	dāngjú	N:	the authorities
44. 仇[讎]貨	choúhuò	N:	enemy (here, Japanese) goods
45. 游[遊]行	yoúxíng	VO/N:	parade (often as part of a demonstration)
46. 示威	shìweī	VO:	hold a demonstration
47. 气(氣)焰(燄)	qìyàn	N:	arrogance, pride
48. 严(嚴)加管束	yánjiā guǎnshù	PH:	strictly control
49. 少城公园(園)	Shaòchéng Gōngyuán	PW:	Shaòchéng Park (in 城都 Chéngdū, capital of Sìchuan province)
50. 紧(緊)急	jǐnjí	SV:	urgent, of an emergency
51. 召集	zhaòjí	FV:	summon, call together
52. 督軍署	dūjūnshǔ	N:	office of the military commander (2-64)
53. 請願	qǐngyuàn	FV/N:	petition, demand
54. 操場	caōchǎng	N:	training ground, athletic field

55. 漕杂（雜）	caózá	SV: noisy and confused
56. 高一班	gāo yìbān	PH: one class higher (=比他 高一班 bǐ tā gāo yìbān)
57. 發言	fāyán	VO: speak
58. 出發	chūfā	FV: set out, set forth, leave
59. 实（實）数（數）	shíshù	N: actual number (here, of students enrolled in the schools)

page 65

*60. 好奇	haòqí	SV: curious
*61. 胆（膽）怯	dǎnqiè	SV: timid
62. 倒霉	daǒméi	SV/VO: be out of luck, be unfortunate (also written 倒楣)
63. 奸猾	jiānhuá	SV: crafty and cunning
*64. 眉毛	meímao	N: eyebrow
65. 竖〔豎〕	shù	FV: stand erect
66. 漠不关（關、関）心	mòbuguānxīn	EX: pay no attention at all, completely indifferent (2-49)
67. 市民	shìmín	N: city resident, citizen
68. 广（廣）場	guǎngchǎng	N: plaza, city square
69. 鋒利	fēnglì	SV: sharp (e.g., a blade)
70. 搶刺	qiāngcì	N: bayonet
71. 爭持不下	zhēngchíbuxià	RC: argue without result, not be able to bring something to a settlement
72. 推举（舉、擧）	tuījǔ	FV: elect forth
*73. 拦（攔）住	lánzhù	RC: obstruct
74. 督座	Dūzuò	N: "His Honor the Commander" (2-64)
75. 回府	huífǔ	PH: return to one's residence (polite term)

page 66

76. 交涉   jiāoshè   N/FV: negotiation, discussion/ negotiate, discuss

*77. 騷 动（動）   saōdòng   FV/N: become restless, cause commotion or disturbance/ commotion, disturbance

78. 三七二十一   sānqī'èrshiyī   N: "3 X 7 = 21," end result, consequence

79. 迴 响（響）   huíxiǎng   FV/N: echo, reverberate/echo

80. 擋 住   dǎngzhù   RC: obstruct

*81. 雨点（點）   yǔdiǎn   N: raindrop

82. 叫 啞（啞）   jiaòyǎ   RC: shout (until) hoarse (P-35, 3-58)

page 67

83. 一 致   yízhì   SV: unanimous, uniform

84. 上 当（當）   shàngdàng   VO: be swindled, fall into a trap

85. 轉达（達）   zhuǎndá   FV: transmit (a message) through another person, convey

86. 緩 和   huǎnhé   SV/FV: calm, moderate/appease, pacify

87. 据（據）理力争   jùlǐlìzhēng   EX: "according to reason strongly contend," argue vigorously on the basis of sound reason or justice

*88. 人丛（叢）   réncōng   N: "clump of people," group, throng

89. 刺 刀   cìdaō   N: bayonet (8-70)

90. 黑 压（壓）々   heīyāyā   A: very crowded

91. 憋   biē   FV: suffer a breathing obstruction, suffocate

92. 風 傳   fēngchuán   N: rumor

93. 出之于（於）   chūzhīyú   PH: end up, result in

94. 卑鄙	beǐbǐ	SV:	underhanded, dishonorable, despicable
95. 罪名	zuìmíng	N:	criminal charge (brought against a person), crime
96. 真誠	zhēnchéng	SV:	sincere
97. 禍害	huòhaì	N/FV:	evil, disaster, harm/injure, harm

page 68

*98. 煩躁	fánzaò	SV:	annoyed, impatient
99. 浸	jìn	FV:	seep into, soak
100. 抄手	chaōshoǔ	VO:	place one's hands into the sleeves of the hand opposite
*101. 挺	tǐng	FV:	straighten up, stretch out (usually a part of the body)
102. 箕起肩膀	sǒngqǐ jiānbǎng	PH:	shrug one's shoulders (3-107)
103. 坐牢	zuòlaó	VO:	go to jail
*104. 模粘月	móhu	SV:	indistinct, blurred (also written 模糊)
105. 赴湯蹈火	fùtāngdaòhuǒ	EX:	"go through hot water, tread on fire," go through fire and water, do anything
*106. 难(難)堪	nánkān	SV:	hard to tolerate

page 69

*107. 理	lǐ	FV:	pay attention to, notice
108. 肃(肅)静	sùjìng	SV:	solemnly silent
109. 科长(長)	kēzhǎng	N:	department chief
110. 兄弟	xiōngdi	N:	I, me (in speeches only)
*111. 抱歉	baòqiàn	FV:	feel sorry, regret
*112. 方才[纔]	fāngcaí	A:	just now, a moment ago (= 剛才 gāngcaí)

113. 自有办（辦）法　　zì yǒu bànfa　　PH: "of course there's a way"
(here, 自 is short for
自然 and means 'naturally,
of course')

114. 慰 問　　weìwèn　　FV: show sympathy by making
inquiries

*115. 爱（愛）护（護）aìhu　　FV: show concern for, be kind
to

*116. 意 外　　yìwaì　　SV/N: unintentional, accidental/
something unanticipated

117. 滑 头（頭）　　huátou　　N: slick or cunning fellow

118. 玩 味　　wánweì　　FV: digest food for thought,
ponder

page 70

*119. 縱 然　　zòngrán　　A: even if

120. 耗 费　　haòfeì　　FV: waste, squander, spend

121. 响（響）应（應）xiǎngyìng　　FV: echo in support, answer
favorably

CHAPTER NINE

page 71

*1. 諾言　　　　nuòyán　　　　N: pledge, promise

2. 履行　　　　lǚxíng　　　　FV: fulfill, bring about

3. 罢(罷)課　　bàkè　　　　VO: strike from school, not attend classes (6-161)

4. 高师(師)　　Gāoshī　　　N: Higher Normal School (abbreviation of 高級師範學校 Gāojí Shīfàn Xuéxiaò)

*5. 主持　　　　zhǔchí　　　N/FV: sponsorship, direction/ sponsor, manage

*6. 兵士　　　　bīngshì　　　N: soldier (also 士兵)

7. 居民　　　　jūmín　　　　N: resident, inhabitant

8. 吃亏(虧)　　chīkuī　　　VO: have trouble, be at a disadvantage, suffer loss

9. 做寿(壽)　　zuòshoù　　　VO: celebrate a birthday

10. 伤(傷)兵　　shāngbīng　　PH: wounded soldiers

11. 威風　　　　weīfēng　　　N: awe-inspiring reputation, domineering influence

12. 任意　　　　rènyì　　　　A: at will, as one wants, arbitrarily

13. 橫行　　　　hèngxíng　　　FV: do evil, act outrageously (3-146)

page 72

14. 制服　　　　zhìfú　　　　FV/N: control/uniform (e.g., for policemen, soldiers, nurses)

15. 尊严(嚴)　　zūnyán　　　N/SV: dignity, respect/dignified

16. 發傳單(單)　fā chuándān　PH: give out handbills or leaf- lets

17. 活躍	huóyuè	SV:	active
18. 通电（電）	tōngdiàn	PH:	cable all concerned
19. 公道	gōngdaò	N/SV:	justice/just
*20. 外州县（縣）	waìzhoūxiàn	N:	regions and districts outside
21. 联（聯、聧）絡	liánluò	FV/N:	contact, get in touch (with someone)/contact (between people)
22. 風潮	fēngchaó	N:	"wind and tide," upheaval, unrest
23. 撇	piě	N:	stroke made in the lower left direction, e.g. ノ (in calligraphy)
24. 花白	huābaí	ADJ:	white with streaks of dark, gray, graying (hair)
25. 光秃	guāngtū	ADJ:	completely bald
26. 鼻孔	bíkǒng	N:	nostril(1-29, 4-50)
27. 声（聲）息	shēngxī	N:	sound, noise
28. 定睛	dìngjīng	A:	fixing the eyes upon, with a stare
29. 假寐	jiǎmeì	FV/N:	take a nap, doze/nap
30. 敬畏	jìngweì	FV:	fear and respect, revere
31. 凛然	lǐnrán	ADJ:	stern, forbidding, awe-inspiring

page 73

*32. 神气（氣）	shénqi	N:	expression, air
*33. 請安	qǐng'ān	VO:	pay respects, inquire after (an elder)
34. 拘束	jūshù	SV:	restrained, uncomfortable
*35. 衰弱	shuaīruò	SV:	weak, feeble (5-16)
36. 口水	koǔshuǐ	N:	saliva
37. 頷下	hànxià	N:	chin, jaws

38. 古板   gǔbǎn   SV: ultraconservative, old-
                                                fashioned, "square"

39. 不近人情   bújìnrénqíng   EX: "not approach human feeling,"
                                                inconsiderate of others,
                                                unreasonable

40. 不爱濃牰爱淡牰

Bú'ai nóngzhuāng ai dànzhuāng

I don't like heavy make-up, I like light make-up

天然丰韵压群芳

Tiānrán fēngyùn yā qúnfāng

Natural appearance wins over all the other beautiful ladies

果然我見犹怜汝

Guǒrán wǒ jiàn yóu lián rǔ

And so I see you and even I still like you

爭怪檀郎兴欲狂

Zhēngguai tánláng xìng yù kuáng

No wonder that your male lovers go crazy over you

41. 濃牰（牪）   nóngzhuāng   PH: heavy make-up
42. 淡牰（牪）   dànzhuāng   PH: light make-up
43. 丰韵〔韻〕   fēngyùn   PH: charming appearance
44. 压（壓）   yā   FV: "oppress," win over, excell
45. 群〔羣〕芳   qúnfāng   PH: multitude of beautiful la-
                                          dies
46. 犹（猶）   yóu   A: still（文言）
47. 怜（憐）   lián   BF: to love
48. 汝   rǔ   N: you（文言）
49. 爭怪   zhēngguai   PH: "how blame," no wonder that
                                          （文言）
50. 檀郎   tánláng   N: male lover (literary allu-
                                          sion; 6-89)

51. 兴（興）   xìng   BF: interest

52. 欲   yù   FV: will be (= 要; 文言)

*53. 狂   kuáng   SV: mad, violent, furious

54. 亡故   wánggù   ADJ: dead, deceased

55. 校書   jiàoshū   N: "(one who) collates books,"
                                         (euphemism for) high-class
                                         prostitute, courtesan

56. 荒唐   huāngtáng   SV: wild; given to wine,
                                         women, and song

57. 道貌儼然   dàomàoyǎnrán   EX: "educated appearance,
                                         dignified manner," digni-
                                         fied in appearance

58. 仁义（義）   rényì   N: humanity and righteousness

59. 頑固   wán'gù   SV: stubborn, conservative

60. 便   biàn   A: even

61. 小旦   xiǎodàn   N: actor who plays the role
                                         of young girls in Chinese
                                         opera

62. 戏（虘戈、戲）子   xìzi   N: actor (derogatory)

*63. 化装（裝）   huàzhuāng   VO: dress up, disguise oneself

*64. 梳头（頭）   shūtóu   VO: comb one's hair

65. 拚   pàn   FV: risk, disregard recklessly

66. 殘年   cánnián   PH: remaining years (of life)

67. 重責   zhòngzé   N: great responsibility

68. 自任   zìrèn   PH: take (a burden) upon one-
                                         self

69. 遺老   yílǎo   N: ministers under the pre-
                                         ceding emperor, old-timers

70. 大吹大擂   dàchuīdàleī   EX: "greatly blow (horn), greatly
                                         beat (drum)," brag about
                                         one's success, make much ado

71. 梨园（園）榜   líyuánbǎng   N: ranked list of actors in
                                         Beijing opera

72. 点（點）　　　diǎn　　　　　FV: mark, check off (e.g., names on a list)

73. 花旦　　　　　huādàn　　　　N: female role in Chinese opera

74. 状（狀）元　　zhuàngyuán　　N: highest scorer in a competition (usually the national exam)

75. 風雅　　　　　fēngyǎ　　　　SV: refined, cultured

76. 名士　　　　　míngshì　　　　N: celebrated scholar

77. 遯斋（齋）　　Dùnzhāi　　　　N: (the grandfather's first name)

78. 收藏　　　　　shōucáng　　　　FV: collect

79. 免俗　　　　　miǎnsú　　　　PH: forego customary routine, go against the fashion

page 74

80. 并（並）存不悖　bìngcúnbúbèi　EX: "together exist and not be opposed," carry on several things at the same time without conflict, coexist

81. 濃妝（粧）艳（艷）抹　nóngzhuāngyànmǒ　EX: "thick make-up, beautiful smears," wear heavy make-up (9-41)

82. 爱（愛）娇　　aìjiaō　　　　N: (here) attractiveness, beauty

83. 尖声（聲）尖气（氣）　jiānshēngjiānqì　EX: "sharp voice, sharp breath," in a very high-pitched voice

*84. 扭々捏（揑）々　niǔniǔniēniē　PH: twisting and turning from side to side

*85. 将（將）近　jiāngjìn　　　A: approaching, nearly, approximately

86. 賞玩　　　　shǎngwán　　　FV: enjoy, appreciate

87. 謎　　　　　mí　　　　　N: riddle, puzzle

88. 多嘴　　　　duōzuǐ　　　　FV: talk too much, have a big mouth

89. 招骂（罵）　zhaōmà　　　　PH: invite scolding

*90. 静悄々　jìngqiāoqiāo　A: very quietly

*91. 老　lǎo　BF: (used before numerals in designating sons, daughters, brothers, and sisters; here, 老三 lǎosān or 'son number three' indicates 覺慧 Juéhuì)

*92. 先前　xiānqián　A: before (a given time)

93. 干（乾）燥　gānzào　SV: dry

*94. 严（嚴）厉（厲）　yánlì　SV: harsh, severe

95. 窘住　jiǒngzhù　RC: embarrass, distress (7-138)

page 75

*96. 扫（掃）　sǎo　FV: sweep

97. 扯谎　chěhuǎng　VO: tell a lie (2-80)

98. 嚣張　xiāozhāng　SV: bossy, pushing people around

99. 游［遊］街　yóujiē　VO: demonstrate in the streets, hold a procession (8-45)

100. 目無法紀　mùwúfǎjì　EX: "in one's eyes are neither laws nor rules," disregard all laws

101. 風声（聲）　fēngshēng　N: news, information

102. 条（條）　tiáo　M: (for 性命 xìngmìng; 你這条小命 nǐ zhèitiáo xiǎo mìng 'this little life of yours')

103. 脂粉　zhǐfěn　N: face powder or cream, cosmetics

104. 香　xiāng　N: fragrance, aroma

*105. 捶　chuí　FV: pat, beat

*106. 子弟　zǐdì　N: children, young people

107. 吟詩作对（對）　yínshīzuòduì　EX: chant poems and compose couplets

page 76

108. 無緣無故　wúyuánwúgù　EX: "without cause, without reason," for no reason at all

109.	强辩	qiángbiàn	FV: argue (7-155)
*110.	説	shuō	FV: scold
*111.	居然	jūrán	A: actually, surprisingly (contrary to expectation)
112.	顫巍巍	zhànweǐweǐ	A: shaking, quivering (3-41, 8-11)
113.	痰	tán	N: phlegm, mucus
*114.	气（氣）	qì	FV/SV: make (someone) angry/angry
*115.	好	haǒ	A: so that, in order that
116.	将（將）息	jiāngxī	FV: rest
117.	板臉	bǎnliǎn	VO: make a "wooden" or long face, look grim
118.	發作	fāzuò	FV: go into action, let loose, have a fit of anger

page 77

119.	顴骨	quángu	N: cheekbone
120.	晃	huǎng	FV: flash, dazzle
*121.	瞥	piē	M/FV: glimpse
*122.	律师（師）	lǜshī	N: lawyer
123.	打官司	dǎ guānsi	PH: bring up a lawsuit
124.	我就問你要人	wǒ jiù wèn ni yaò rén	PH: "I'll ask you about him and want him back," "I'll hold you responsible for him"
*125.	唯唯	weǐweǐ	IE: "yes, yes"
*126.	恭順	gōngshùn	SV: respectful and obedient
*127.	半晌	bànshǎng	A: for some time, a while
128.	有气（氣）無力	youǐqìwúlì	EX: "there is breath but no vigor" (used to describe a feeble voice)
*129.	手势（勢）	shoǔshì	N: hand gesture

page 78

*130.	摊(攤)开(開)	tānkai	FV: spread out, unfold
131.	轟々烈々	hōnghōnglièliè	EX: "booming and fiery," in a great way
132.	他老人家	tā laǒ rénjiā	PH: "the old gentleman" (a polite reference to old people, male or female; 3-18)
133.	处(處)之	chǔzhī	FV: deal with or settle (a matter; 6-148)
134.	基督徒	Jīdūtú	N: follower of Jesus Christ, Christian (2-64)
*135.	發泄(洩)	fāxiè	FV: give vent to, let out
*136.	性子	xìngzi	N: temper, disposition (2-30)
137.	看他把我怎样(樣)	kàn tā bǎ wǒ zěnyàng	PH: "(Let's) see what he will do about me!"
*138.	頓脚[腳]	dùnjiaǒ	VO: stamp one's feet

page 79

139.	不声(聲)不响(響)	bùshēngbùxiǎng	EX: "not sounding, not echoing," completely silent
140.	九霄云(雲)外	jiǔxiaōyúnwaì	EX: "beyond the nine misty clouds," very far away
141.	飞(飛)馳	feīchí	FV: fly by, drift
142.	烏云(雲)	wūyún	PH: dark clouds (distinguish 烏 'black' from 鳥 niaǒ)
*143.	欣慰	xīnweì	SV: comforted, relieved (8-114)
144.	恰好	qiàhaǒ	A: just by chance (7-64)
145.	鼻端	bíduān	N: nostril (1-29, 9-26)
146.	摘	zhaī	FV: pick off (fruit, etc.)
147.	手掌心	shoǔzhǎngxīn	N: palm (of one's hand)
148.	花瓣	huābàn	N: flower petal
149.	潤湿(濕、溼)	rùnshī	ADJ: moist and fresh

CHAPTER TEN

1. 囚禁   qiújìn   FV: imprison, lock up (6-117)

2. 告示   gaòshi   N: announcement, proclamation (佈告 bùgaò is more common)

3. 道歉   daòqiàn   FV: apologize (8-111)

4. 毆打   oūdǎ   FV: fight with the fist, strike

5. 供認   gòngrèn   FV: confess

6. 处（處）罰   chǔfá   N/FV: punishment/punish

7. 囚籠   qiúlóng   N: cage for prisoners (1-131)

8. 帳頂   zhàngdǐng   N: top of a bed canopy

*9. 出神   chūshén   VO: be absorbed in, appear occupied in thought

10. 甜蜜   tiánmì   SV: sweet, pleasant

11. 气（氣）忿   qìfèn   SV: angry, furious (=氣憤 qìfèn)

12. 恼（惱）怒   naǒnù   FV: become angry or indignant

*13. 相干   xiānggān   N/FV: relation, connection/be related to, be connected with

14. 狹的籠   Xiáde Lóng   N: "Narrow Cage" (title of a story by V.I. Eroshenko [1889-1952], Russian author who lived and wrote in Japan)

*15. 踱   duò   FV: walk slowly, stroll

16. 月洞門   yuèdòngmén   N: moon-gate

*17. 曲折   qūzhé   SV: turning and twisting (e.g., a road)

18. 尽（盡）处（處）jìnchù — N: end, extremity (of a place)

*19. 扑（撲） pū — FV: rush against, bang into, beat

page 83

20. 豁然开（開）朗 huòránkāilǎng — EX: "in a clearing up manner to open up and be clear," suddenly clear or open up

21. 披开（開） pīkai — FV: push aside

22. 弯（彎）曲 wānqū — ADJ: bent, curved (10-17)

23. 亭子 tíngzi — N: pavilion

24. 紫 zǐ — SV/N: purple/purple color

*25. 朝 chao — FV: face (in some direction, or some object)

*26. 逼近 bījìn — FV: approach, draw near

*27. 丫头（頭） yātou — N: bondmaid, slave girl

*28. 倩兒 Qiàn'ér — N: （人名 ）

*29. 隐 yǐn — FV: hide, conceal (1-78)

30. 唧里（哩）咕噜 jīligūlū — EX: talk in an indirect manner, grumble

page 84

31. 端 duān — N: end, bend, side (of a garden, pole, cloth, etc.; 2-48)

32. 迈（邁）步子 mai bùzi — PH: take steps, walk

33. 松（鬆）手 sōngshoǔ — VO: let one's hand go (of something)

34. 踮脚〔腳〕 diǎnjiaǒ — VO: stand tiptoe

35. 脚〔腳〕尖 jiaǒjiān — N: tip of the foot, tiptoe

page 85

*36. 讥笑 jīxiaò — FV: make fun of, ridicule

37. 颇 pō — A: rather

38. 含苞未放   hánbaōweìfàng   EX: "containing a bud but not yet opened," in bud

39. 注目   zhùmù   FV: look at attentively, gaze at

40. 树〔樹〕身   shùshēn   N: tree trunk

41. 打量   dǎliàng   FV: size up, measure

42. 使不得   shǐbudé   IE: "that won't do," "don't do that" (=作不得 zuòbudé)

43. 看   kàn   A: (here) if

44. 跌   diē   FV: stumble, fall down

*45. 株   zhū   M: (for trees)

46. 棉紧〔緊〕身   miánjǐnshēn   N: close-fitting padded jacket (M: 件 jiàn)

page 86

47. 纷纷   fēnfēn   A: in great numbers, in large groups

*48. 当〔當〕心   dāngxīn   FV/SV: be careful

*49. 挽   wǎn   FV: hold, grasp, seize

*50. 纏〔纏〕   chán   FV: bind up, wrap around tightly, entangle (5-69)

51. 披   pī   FV: drape, put something over one's shoulders (10-21)

52. 钓台〔臺〕   diaòtaí   N: fishing pier

page 87

*53. 噗嗤   pūchī   ON: (sound of gurgling laughter)

page 88

54. 端详   duānxiáng   FV/N: study or examine in detail/details (of how something happened)

55. 剔除   tīchú   FV: separate out, eliminate (undesirable elements)

*56. 湖濱   húbīn   N: edge of a lake, lakeshore

57. 花台〔臺〕	huātaí	N: flower terrace
58. 流泉	liúquán	N: spring, fountain
59. 砂土	shātǔ	N: sandy soil, gravel
60. 淙々	cóngcóng	ON: (gurgling sound of flowing water)
61. 縫隙	fèngxì	N: crack, fissure
62. 碎石	suìshí	N: gravel
63. 幽靜	yōujìng	SV: tranquil, serene
*64. 手帕	shǒupà	N: handkerchief (M: 條 tiaó; 2-67)
65. 拂拭	fúshì	FV: wipe (clean)

page 89

66. 重新	chóngxīn	A: anew, all over again
67. 成人	chéngrén	N: adult
68. 晶瑩	jīngyíng	ADJ: sparkling, radiant
69. 睫毛	jiémaó	N: eyelash
*70. 当（當）真的	dàngzhēnde	IE: really
*71. 过（過）火	guòhuǒ	SV: overdone, excessive
72. 無非	wúfeī	PH: be no other than, be only this
73. 試探	shìtàn	FV: test, sound out

page 90

*74. 后（後）悔	hòuhuǐ	FV: regret
*75. 愛（愛）怜（憐）地	aìliánde	A: lovingly, fondly
76. 反复（覆）無常	fǎnfùwúcháng	EX: "backward and forward without a constant," not dependable, ever changing
77. 嗚咽	wūyè	FV: sob
*78. 抽泣	choūqì	FV: weep

79. 撫摩   fǔmó   FV: pass one's hand over, stroke

page 91

*80. 尽（盡）   jìn   A: entirely, totally

81. 居多   jūduō   PH: be most, be in the majority

82. 豺狼   cháiláng   N: ferocious wolf (豺 and 狼 are the names of two different kinds of wolves)

83. 山腰   shānyāo   N: "waist" or mid-slope of a mountain

84. 救星   jiùxīng   N: "saving star," savior

*85. 一輩子   yíbeìzi   PH: in one's whole lifetime, one's whole life long (7-48)

page 92

*86. 照应（應）   zhàoying   FV: take care of, look after

*87. 惭愧   cánkuì   SV: ashamed (3-61)

88. 遺憾   yíhàn   N/FV: regret

page 93

89. 一生一世   yìshēngyíshì   EX: "one lifetime, one generation," one's whole life, always

90. 欺負   qīfu   FV: oppress, insult, take advantage of

91. 倾听（聽）   qīngtīng   FV: listen carefully

92. 搀（攙）杂（雜）   chānzá   FV: be mingled or blended in with and made impure

93. 开（開）飯   kāifàn   VO: serve a meal

94. 石壁   shíbì   N: stone wall

page 94

*95. 占（佔）据（據）   zhànjù   FV: occupy forcibly, take possession of

96. 肘   zhǒu   BF: elbow (FF: 胳臂肘 gēbezhǒu)

*97. 忽々地   cōngcōngde   A: hurriedly (1-115)

*98. 舍(捨)不得   shěbudé   AV: cannot bear to, hate to
                                      (do something)

*99. 輪   lún   M: "wheel" (for round things)

100. 一碧無际(際) yíbìwújì   EX: "uniformly jade-green with-
                                      out boundary," vast, bound-
                                      less (1-118)

101. 撒   sǎ   FV: sprinkle, scatter

*102. 瓦   wǎ   N: roof tile (M: 塊 kuaì,
                                      片 piàn)

*103. 染   rǎn   FV: dye

104. 月如霜   yuè rú shuāng PH: "moonlight like frost," very
                                      bright and white

page 95

105. 更正   gēngzhèng   FV: correct, put right (1-123)

*106. 膀子   bǎngzi   N: shoulder (3-107)

107. 瀰漫   mímàn   FV: overflow, pervade

108. 渗(滲)透   shèntòu   FV: seep through, infiltrate
                                      (7-28)

109. 哀鳴   aīmíng   PH: mournful cry

110. 高亢   gaōkàng   SV: loud and ringing, rever-
                                      berating (of sounds)

111. 婉轉   wǎnzhuǎn   SV: gentle, graceful, suave
                                      (also written 宛轉)

112. 哀訴   aīsù   PH: plaint, lament

113. 震蕩   zhèndàng   FV: vibrate (P-19)

page 96

114. 攪动(動)   jiaǒdòng   RC: move, stir

115. 惊(驚)疑   jīngyí   SV: fearful and apprehensive

116. 簫   xiaō   N: bamboo flute (M: 管 guǎn)

117. 不由得   bùyoúde   PH: cannot help but

*118. 果真   guǒzhēn   A: actually, really

119. 皎潔   jiaǒjié   SV: bright

page 97

1. 平息	píngxī	FV:	come to an end, subside
2. 旧(舊)历(曆)年	jiùlìnián	N:	Chinese Lunar New Year
3. 补(補)考	bǔkǎo	VO:	make up or repeat an exam
4. 学(學)潮月	xuéchaó	N:	student uprising (9-22)
5. 监(監)牢	jiānlaó	N:	prison, jail (8-103)
6. 咒骂[罵]	zhoùmà	N/FV:	curse
7. 单(單)独(獨)	dāndú	A:	all alone (7-58)
*8. 似...非...	sì...feī...	PT:	seemingly...but not really...

page 98

9. 翻转	fānzhuǎn	FV:	turn around
10. 报(報)仇[讎]	baòchoú	VO:	gain revenge (6-136)
*11. 抛	paō	FV:	throw away, abandon (3-79)
12. 搁置	gēzhì	FV:	shelve, put aside
13. 信笔(筆)	xìnbǐ	A:	writing freely and aimlessly (here, 信 means 'free and easy'; cf. 信口说」 'speak freely and randomly', 信步行 'wander aimlessly')
14. 描写(寫)	miaóxiě	FV/N:	describe/description
15. 堂	táng	M:	(for sets of things, such as scrolls, porcelain, and furniture)
16. 寿(壽)屏	shoùpíng	N:	long vertical scroll inscribed with wishes for a long life (given to someone on his birthday)
17. 寿(壽)诞	shoùdàn	N:	birthday, birthday feast (of an older person)

18. 寿（壽）序   shòuxù   N: literary composition wishing another longevity on his birthday

19. 起草   qǐcǎo   VO: prepare a draft, write

20. 綫［線］裝（裝）書   xiànzhuāngshū   N: book bound in traditional Chinese style with stitches in the back (M: 本 běn)

page 99

21. 批改   pīgǎi   FV: criticize and correct

*22. 榜样（樣）   bǎngyàng   N: example, model

*23. 溜   liū   FV: slip out, leave

*24. 暢快   chàngkuai   SV: cheerful, exuberant

25. 衙門   yámen   N: yamen, office of an official in the government

26. 伪（偽）君子   wěijūnzi   N: "false gentleman," hypocrite

27. 签（籤）条（條）   qiāntiáo   N: slip of paper pasted on a book, label

28. 題名   tímíng   N: title (of a literary composition)

29. 刘（劉）芷唐   Liú Zhǐtáng   N: （人名）

30. 教孝戒淫淺訓   Jiàoxiào Jièyín Qiǎnxùn   N: <u>Simple Teachings on the Instruction of Filial Piety and the Shunning of Lewdness</u> (title of a book)

*31. 丰（豐）满   fēngmǎn   SV: healthy, full

32. 灵（靈）活   línghuo   SV: limber, lively

33. 自家   zìjia   N: oneself

*34. 善意、   shànyì   PH: good intentions (7-109)

35. 帳檐［簷］   zhàngyán   N: flap along the edge of a canopy (M: P-38 幅 fú; 1-130)

page 100

36. 快活   kuàihuo   SV: happy

37. 愁悶   chóumèn   SV/N: sad and depressed,
                                             melancholy/melancholy

38. 悶   mèn   FV/SV: cause (something to happen)
                                             because one is depressed/
                                             depressed, lonely

39. 下棋〔萁〕   xiàqí   VO: play chess

*40. 犹（猶）如   yóurú   A: as if, like (= 好像 haǒxiàng)

41. 长（長）姐   zhǎngjiě   N: older sister (6-1, 6-2)

*42. 信賴   xìnlaì   FV: trust

43. 倾心   qīngxīn   FV: "slant one's heart out for,"
                                             be in love with (10-91)

44. 担（擔）憂   dānyoū   SV: be anxious, worry

page 101

*45. 譬如   pìrú   A: for example (=比方 bǐfang)

46. 羞耻   xiūchǐ   SV/N: shameful/shame (3-61)

47. 写（寫）照   xiězhaò   N: written representation,
                                             portrait

48. 主人公   zhǔréngōng   N: main character (of a novel
                                             or play)

49. 賴克留道甫   Laìkèliúdaòfǔ   N: Nekhlyudov (name of the main
                                             character in Tolstoy's novel
                                             Resurrection; P-4)

*50. 結局   jiéjú   N: outcome, end

page 102

51. 君 要 臣 死 不 死 不 忠

Jūn yaò chén sǐ, bù sǐ bù zhōng

If a lord wishes his minister to die and he does not, he is not loyal

父要子亡，不亡不孝

Fù yaò zǐ wáng, bù wáng bú xiaò

If a father wishes his son to die and he does not, he is not filial

52. 万（萬）恶（惡）淫为（為）首

Wàn è yín weí shoǔ

Of the ten thousand vices, lewdness is the first

百善孝为（為）先

Baǐ shàn xiaò weí xiān

Of the one hundred virtues, filial piety is the first

*53. 撕	sī	FV:	tear
54. 翅膀	chìbǎng	N:	wing (3-107)
*55. 呻吟	shēnyín	FV/N:	moan, groan
56. 用意	yòngyì	N:	intention
57. 解闷	jiěmèn	VO:	dispel loneliness, get rid of boredom (11-37, 11-38)
58. 拂意	fúyì	VO:	thwart or go against someone's wishes (10-65)
59. 象棋〔綦〕	xiàngqí	N:	Chinese chess (11-39)
60. 不及	bùjí	PH:	not reach, not be so good as
61. 局	jú	M:	(for a game of chess)
62. 逗着…玩	dòuzhe…wán	PH:	play with, tease

page 103

63. 画（畫）理	huàlǐ	N:	principles of art
64. 聚精会（會）神	jùjīnghuìshén	EX:	"collect one's energy, assemble one's spirit," concentrate very hard
65. 红晕	hóngyùn	N:	red mist or tinge
66. 三弟妹	sāndìmèi	N:	"third little brother's wife" (the future wife of 覺慧 Juéhuì)

67. 瓷〔磁〕瓶	cípíng	N:	porcelain vase
*68. 插	chā	FV:	stick in, insert (something into something)
69. 分割	fēn'gē	FV:	split apart
70. 荒疏	huāngshū	FV:	neglect **the practice** (of some skill)
71. 俗	sú	SV:	unrefined, vulgar (5-89)
72. 彩虹	cǎihóng	N:	rainbow (M: 道 dào)
73. 处（處）女	chǔnǚ	N:	maiden, virgin

page 104

74. 大方	dàfang	SV:	open, relaxed (of a person's personality)
75. 娇羞	jiāoxiū	ADJ:	bashful, modest (of women; 3-61, 9-82)
76. 兴（興）致	xìngzhi	N:	mood (for doing something)
77. 嗯	ng	I:	(sound of musing)
78. 她大我三岁（歲）	tā dà wǒ sānsuì	PH:	"She's three years older than me" (= 她比我大三歲 Tā bǐ wǒ dà sānsuì)
79. 广（廣）元县（縣）	Guǎngyuán Xiàn	PW:	(name of a district in Sìchuan province)
80. 知县（縣）	zhīxiàn	N:	county magistrate
81. 坝子	bàzi	N:	level area, embankment (四川)
82. 桑树（樹）	sāngshù	N:	mulberry tree (M: 棵 kē)
83. 喜鹊	xǐquè	N:	magpie (M: 隻 zhī)
*84. 尖锐	jiānruì	SV:	sharp
85. 吹哨	chuīshào	VO:	blow a whistle
86. 跑文书	pǎo wénshu	PH:	carry official dispatches
87. 紧（緊）要	jǐnyào	SV:	important (here,= 要緊)

88. 信函　　　　　　　xìnhán　　　　　N: letter, epistle (M: 封 fēng)

89. 专（專）差　　　zhuānchāi　　　N: special messenger

90. 馬驛站　　　　　　yìzhàn　　　　　N: postal relay station

91. 奍（蠶）　　　　cán　　　　　　　N: silkworm (M: 條 tiáo)

page 105

92. 稀少　　　　　　　xīshǎo　　　　　SV: few, scarce

93. 辛亥革命　　　　　Xīnhài Gémìng　N: Chinese Revolution of 1911

94. 辞（辭）官　　　cíguān　　　　　VO: resign an official post

95. 可以　　　　　　　kéyi　　　　　　IE: "good enough," "O.K."

96. 扇庄（莊）　　　shànzhuāng　　　N: fan shop

*97. 扇子　　　　　　　shànzi　　　　　N: hand fan (M: 把 bǎ; 1-140, 4-42)

98. 酬金　　　　　　　chóujīn　　　　　N: cash reward, recompense

99. 顏料　　　　　　　yánliào　　　　　N: pigments, paints (for use in painting)

100. 小产（產）　　　xiǎochǎn　　　　FV/N: have a miscarriage/miscarriage

101. 将（將）就　　　jiāngjiu　　　　FV: (here) let someone have his way

102. 嬌养（養）　　　jiāoyǎng　　　　FV: rear a child in a spoiling and pampering way (6-156)

103. 笨拙　　　　　　　bènzhuó　　　　　SV: clumsy, awkward

104. 太亲（親）母　　Tàiqīnmǔ　　　　N: (term of address used by the members of 覺新 Juéxīn's generation for 李瑞玨 Lǐ Ruìjué's mother)

page 106

*105. 战（戰）略〔畧〕 zhànlüè　　　　N: strategy

106. 黑尽（盡）　　　hēijìn　　　　　PH: become completely dark

*107. 婉兒　　　　　　　Wǎn'ér　　　　　N: (人名)

*108. 屈服　　　　　　　qūfú　　　　　　FV: submit, give in

CHAPTER TWELVE

page 107

1. 負債　　　　　　　fùzhài　　　　VO: be in debt

2. 过(過)多　　　　　guòduō　　　　PH: be too much, excessive

3. 佳节(節)　　　　　jiājié　　　　N: festival, carnival

4. 气(氣)象　　　　　qìxiàng　　　　N: atmosphere

5. 爆竹　　　　　　　baòzhú　　　　N: firecracker

6. 喇叭　　　　　　　lǎba　　　　　N: horn, trumpet

7. 坐落　　　　　　　zuòluò　　　　FV: be located or situated
　　　　　　　　　　　　　　　　　　　at (of a building)

8. 礼(禮)节(節)　　　lǐjié　　　　　N: rites, ceremonies, etiquette

*9. 主子　　　　　　　zhǔzi　　　　　N: master

10. 賞錢　　　　　　　shǎngqián　　　N: gift of cash, gratuity

11. 娛乐(樂)　　　　　yúlè　　　　　N: amusement, entertainment

12. 年糕　　　　　　　nián'gāo　　　N: glutinous rice cakes
　　　　　　　　　　　　　　　　　　　(eaten at New Year's)

13. 折(摺)金銀錠　　　zhéjīnyíndìng　EX: "fold gold and silver (paper
　　　　　　　　　　　　　　　　　　　into the shape of) ingots"

14. 供奉　　　　　　　gòngfèng　　　FV: offer sacrifice to

15. 剪紙花　　　　　　jiǎn zhǐhuā　　PH: cut designs out of paper

16. 九老会(會)　　　　Jiǔlǎohuì　　　N: Nine Old Men's Club

17. 宴客　　　　　　　yànkè　　　　　VO: entertain guests at a party
　　　　　　　　　　　　　　　　　　　(2-23)

18. 鑒[鑑]賞　　　　　jiànshǎng　　　FV: "examine and appreciate,"
　　　　　　　　　　　　　　　　　　　appreciate, enjoy (also 賞鑒)

19. 古玩　　　　　　　gǔwán　　　　　N: curios, antiques

*20. 指揮　　　　　zhǐhuī　　　　FV/N: direct, command/instruction, command; conductor (of a musical group)

*21. 布（佈）置　　bùzhi　　　　　FV: arrange, decorate (11-12)

page 108

22. 灯（燈）彩　　　dēngcǎi　　　　N: lamps and colorful decorations

*23. 緞子　　　　　duànzi　　　　　N: satin

*24. 繡[繡]花　　　xiùhuā　　　　　VO: embroider (often flowers)

*25. 屏　　　　　　píng　　　　　　BF: screen, covered frame serving as a partition (FF: 屏風　píngfeng)

26. 高臥　　　　　gāowò　　　　　PH: lie, be placed

*27. 除夕　　　　　chúxì　　　　　N: lunar New Year's Eve

28. 年飯　　　　　niánfàn　　　　N: large family dinner on Chinese New Year's Eve

29. 前夜　　　　　Qián Yè　　　　N: On The Eve (novel by Ivan Turgenev [1818-1883])

*30. 眉头（頭）　　méitou　　　　N: eyebrow region (8-64)

*31. 皺皮　　　　　zhoù　　　　　　FV: wrinkle, crease

page 109

32. 爱（愛）恋（戀）aìliàn　　　　FV: love (romantically)

33. 热（熱）望　　rèwàng　　　　N/FV: fervent hope/hope for earnestly, wish for ardently

34. 畸人　　　　　jīrén　　　　　N: odd or strange person, freak

35. 愚人　　　　　yúrén　　　　　N: silly or foolish person, fool

36. 枯涩（澀）　　kūsè　　　　　　SV: dry and rasping, rough

page 110

37. 宇宙　　　　　yǔzhoù　　　　　N: universe

38. 宁（寧）静　　níngjìng　　　　SV: quiet, calm

*39. 片刻　　　　　piànkè　　　　　A: for a moment, for a while

40. 飞（飛）翔	fēixiáng	FV:	fly, soar
41. 沉〔沈〕悶	chénmèn	SV:	heavy at heart, miserable (7-55, 11-38)
42. 高山大水	gāoshāndàshuǐ	EX:	"tall mountains, big waters," many different places
43. 奇幻	qíhuàn	ADJ:	strange and dreamlike (3-157, 6-24)
*44. 一旦	yídàn	A:	"one morning," once
45. 下人	xiàren	N:	servant

page 111

46. 触（觸）怒、	chùnù	FV:	offend and cause anger, infuriate
47. 童年	tóngnián	N:	childhood years
48. 烟〔煙〕灯（燈）	yāndēng	N:	lamp for roasting opium before smoking
49. 大烟〔煙〕	dàyān	N:	opium
50. 席地	xídì	A:	"with the ground for a mat" (席地而坐 xídì'érzuò 'sitting on the ground' is a common four-character phrase)
51. 劍仙	jiànxiān	N:	knight-errant, wandering swordsman
52. 侠客	xiákè	N:	swordsman, fencing master
53. 事迹	shìjī	N:	accomplishments, exploits (of a person during his life)
54. 劫富济（濟）貧	jiéfùjìpín	EX:	"steal from the rich and aid the poor"
55. 飄風游	piāoyóu	FV:	drift about without any fixed destination
56. 培养（養）	péiyǎng	FV:	cultivate (either minds or plants)

57. 梁 任 公   Liáng Rèngōng   N: the 號 haò or courtesy name of 梁啟超 Liáng Qǐchaǒ (1873-1929), major advocate of political reform in China during the late nineteenth and early twentieth centuries

58. 煽动（動)性   shāndòngxìng   N: "flaming instigation," agitation

59. 中国（國）云魂   Zhōngguo Hún   N: The Soul of China (collection of essays by 梁啟超 Liáng Qǐchaǒ on Chinese and Western culture, and on the future of China

60. 飲冰室丛（叢）著   Yǐnbīngshìcōngzhù   N: Collection of Stories from the Yǐnbīng Studio (written by 梁啟超 Liáng Qǐchaǒ)

61. 国（國）民淺訓   Guómín Qiǎnxùn   N: Simple Teachings for Citizens (a work by 梁啟超 Liáng Qǐchaǒ on government)

62. 征兵制   zhēngbīngzhì   N: system of military conscription

63. 投笔（筆）从（從）戎   toúbǐcóngróng   EX: "throw away one's pen and follow the military," join the military service voluntarily (of a student or intellectual)

64. 粉碎   fěnsuì   RE/FV: broken into many small pieces, pulverized/smash to pieces, ruin

65. 激进（進）   jījìn   SV: radical

66. 人生真义（義）   Rénshēng Zhēnyì   N: "The True Meaning of Human Life" (title of an essay by 陳獨秀 Chén Dúxiù, published in 新青年 Xīn Qīngnián in February, 1918)

67. 人生問題發端   Rénshēng Wèntí Fāduān   N: "Introduction to the Problems of Human Life" (title of an essay by 傅斯年 Fù Sīnián, published in 新青年 Xīn Qīngnián in January, 1919)

68. 理解   lǐjiě   FV: comprehend, understand

69. 幽禁   yōujìn   FV: imprison, confine

page 112

70. 眼界   yǎnjiè   N: field of vision, outlook

71. 宽广（廣）   kuānguǎng   SV: wide and extensive, broad

72. 栅栏（欄）   zhàlan   N: fence, railing

*73. 摆（擺）脱   bǎituō   RC: shake off, free oneself
                                                 from, get rid of

74. 詛咒   zǔzhòu   FV/N: curse (11-6)

75. 討生活   tǎo shēnghuo   PH: try to get along in life,
                                                 make a living

page 113

76. 弃（棄）   qì   FV: reject, throw away (3-79)

77. 奢侈家   shēchǐjiā   N: sybarite, someone fond of
                                                 luxury and extravagance

78. 爱（愛）子   aìzǐ   N: beloved son, favorite son

79. 烈士   lièshì   N: martyr

80. 圍裙   weíqun   N: apron (5-75)

81. 照耀〔燿〕   zhaòyaò   FV: shine, illuminate

*82. 驕傲   jiaō'aò   N/SV: pride; arrogance/proud;
                                                 arrogant (the original
                                                 meaning of this word was
                                                 'arrogant, haughty, con-
                                                 ceited'; due to influence
                                                 from translations from Eng-
                                                 lish, however, the word has
                                                 now acquired the meaning
                                                 'proud' as in 我為你很
                                                 驕傲 Wǒ wei nǐ hěn jiaō'-
                                                 aò 'I'm very proud of you')

83. 折（摺）痕   zhéhén   N: dog-ear (turned down corner
                                                 of a page)

page 114

84. 憤激   fènjī   SV: bitter and excited

85. 日趨（趨）妥协   rìqūtuǒxié   EX: "daily tending toward
    （協）   compromise or appeasement"

*86. 嘆〔歎〕口气(氣) tàn kǒu qì   PH: heave a sigh (usually 嘆一口氣 tàn yìkǒu qì)

*87. 完結   wánjié   FV: come to an end

88. 剝奪(奪)   bōduó   FV: deprive, strip (a person of his rights or property)

89. 殮具   liànjù   N: articles for preparing a body for a coffin

page 115

90. 笔(筆)記   bǐjì   FV/N: write, note down/notes

91. 遺囑   yízhǔ   N: will (of a deceased person) (6-155, 7-17)

92. 烛(燭)台〔臺〕 zhútaí   N: candlestick

93. 墨盒   mòhé   N: ink box

*94. 結ㄅ巴ㄅ   jiéjiebābā   EX: stuttering, stammering

95. 大足县(縣)   Dàzú Xiàn   PW: (name of a district in Sìchuan province)

96. 典史   diǎnshǐ   N: district police-master and jail warden (old term)

97. 太平   taìpíng   SV: peaceful

98. 嗑   kè   FV: bite or crack open with one's front teeth (usually seeds; cf. next two items)

99. 松子   sōngzǐ   N: pine seeds

100. 瓜子   guāzǐ   N: melon seeds (a favorite Chinese snack)

101. 一搭一搭   yìdāyìdā   EX: reply in turn to questions in a conversation

102. 發狠   fāhěn   A: making a tremendous effort, exerting oneself (contrast 狠 and 10-82 狼 láng 'wolf')

103. 爭一口气(氣) zhēng yìkǒu qì   PH: "fight for a mouthful of air," do something to make someone feel proud, not let someone down

104. 逗笑　　　　　　　dòuxiaò　　　　FV: make laugh, cheer up (11-62)

*105. 才 [纔] 罢 (罷) caí bà　　　　PH: then and only then stop (4-27)

106. 八府巡 [巡] 按 bāfǔxún'àn　　　N: "eight prefectures patrol and examine," civil governor (old term)

107. 揚眉吐气 (氣) yángméitǔqì　　　EX: "raise eyebrows, spit out breath," feel proud (after one has suddenly attained fame or wealth)

108. 愁腸　　　　　　　chóucháng　　　N: grief, sadness (3-118, 6-37)

109. 委　　　　　　　　weǐ　　　　　FV: appoint, put in charge of

110. 着愁　　　　　　　zhaōchóu　　　VO: become anxious, worry

111. 以 … 身份 [分] yǐ...shēnfèn　　PH: in the capacity of …

112. 过 (過) 班知县 (縣) guòbānzhīxiàn　N: county magistrate who was promoted in rank because of official recommendation or a monetary contribution

113. 进 (進) 京　　　　jìnjīng　　　VO: enter the capital, go to Beǐjing

114. 引見　　　　　　　yǐnjiàn　　　FV: present a person to the emperor

115. 焦急　　　　　　　jiaōjí　　　　SV: very anxious, worried

116. 驗看　　　　　　　yànkàn　　　FV: examine, take a close look at (before an audience with the emperor could be granted, one had to pass a special personal inspection)

117. 陷居　　　　　　　xiànjū　　　FV: live in a place without being able to leave

118. 揶揄　　　　　　　yéyú　　　　FV: ridicule, jeer at

119. 中秋　　　　　　　Zhōngqiū　　　N: Mid-Autumn Festival (full form is 中秋節 Zhōngqiūjié)

120. 期望　　　　　　　qīwàng　　　FV: have hopes for

page 117

121. 报（報）答　　　bàodá　　　　FV: repay (someone a kindness)

122. 甘願　　　　　　gānyuàn　　　AV: be gladly willing (to do something)

123. 志願　　　　　　zhìyuan　　　N: will and desire, ambition

124. 衣袋　　　　　　yīdai　　　　N: pocket of a piece of clothing

*125. 埋葬　　　　　　máizàng　　　FV: bury

*126. 挖　　　　　　　wā　　　　　FV: dig (7-88)

127. 坟（墳）墓　　　fénmù　　　　N: grave (M: 座 zuò)

page 118

128. 棉鞋　　　　　　miánxié　　　N: padded cotton shoes (M: 隻 zhī, 雙 shuāng; 1-26, 2-16)

129. 服从（從）　　　fúcóng　　　FV: obey

130. 封閉　　　　　　fēngbì　　　FV: close and seal (1-44)

page 119

1. 一百支烛（燭）光　yìbǎizhǐ zhúguāng PH: 100 candle power (unit of light intensity)

2. 灯（燈）泡　dēngpaò　N: electric light bulb

3. 悬（懸）　xuán　FV: be suspended, hang

4. 中梁［樑］　zhōngliáng　N: central beam (of a ceiling)

5. 长（長）明灯（燈）　chángmíngdēng　N: eternal flame lamp (oil lamp lit day and night; M: 4-13 盏 zhǎn)

6. 煤油挂［掛］灯（燈）　meíyoúguàdēng　N: hanging kerosene lamp (M: 4-13 盏 zhǎn)

7. 繪　huì　FV: draw (pictures, etc.)

8. 宫灯（燈）　gōngdēng　N: decorative lantern (with picture glass panels, usually of hexagonal shape; M: 4-13 盏 zhǎn)

9. 画（畫）屏　huàpíng　N: screen decorated with paintings (M: 1-134 副 fù; 12-25)

10. 神龕　shénkān　N: altar, ancestral shrine

11. 朝服　chaófú　N: court dress

12. 磚［塼］　zhuān　N: brick (M: 块 kuaì)

13. 鋪 砌　pūqì　FV: pave

14. 接痕　jiēhén　N: crack (in the floor where bricks meet; 5-17)

15. 象牙　xiàngyá　N: "elephant tooth," ivory

16. 匙　chí　BF: spoon (FF: 匙子; M: 把 bǎ)

17. 碟子　diézi　N: dish, small plate

*18. 纸条（條）　　zhǐtiáo　　N: slip of paper (M: 張 zhāng)

19. 杏仁　　xìngrén　　N: almond

*20. 领头（頭）　　lǐngtóu　　VO: start, be the first to do something, lead

21. 说声（聲）入座　　shuōshēngrùzuò　　EX: "say a sound, enter seats," say one word and everyone sits down

22. 坐齐（齊）　　zuòqí　　FV: sit down in unison (3-152, 6-78)

page 120

*23. 恰々　　qiàqià　　A: just exactly (7-64, 9-144)

24. 觉（覺）字辈　　Juézìbèi　　N: generation whose names begin with the character 覺 ; it is a custom in Chinese families to give all male children one character, and sometimes female children another, as a character of their names)

*25. 淑芬　　Shūfēn　　N:（人名）

*26. 淑贞　　Shūzhēn　　N:（人名）

27. 旧（舊）历（曆）　　jiùlì　　N: lunar calendar (traditional Chinese calendar; 11-2)

28. 上了桌〔棹〕子　　shàngle zhuōzi　　PH: "came to the table" (not "climbed on"!)

*29. 怀（懷）　　huái　　N: (here) lap (usually: 'bosom')

*30. 挤（擠）　　jǐ　　FV: crowd, squeeze

31. 四世同堂　　sìshìtóngtáng　　EX: "four generations same hall," four generations under one roof (3-100)

32. 吃酒　　chījiǔ　　VO: drink wine (in some dialects of Mandarin, 吃 is used in the sense of 'drink' as well as 'eat'; cf. also 吃奶 chīnǎi 'drink milk' and 吃烟 chīyān 'to smoke')

33. 壶（壺）　　hú　　N: jug, pot (M: 把 bǎ)

34. 呷   xiā   FV: sip, drink a little at
                                               at time

page 121

*35. 端正   duānzhèng   SV: correct and proper
                                               (2-48, 10-31)

36. 酒意、   jiǔyì   N: symptoms of drunkenness
                                               (7-109)

37. 嘛   ma   P: (indicates a suggestion,
                                               or that what precedes is
                                               an obvious fact)

38. 搳拳   huáquán   VO: play a finger-guessing
                                               game where two people
                                               each put out their right
                                               hand and guess their total
                                               number of fingers (usually
                                               written 划拳)

39. 勤   qín   SV: frequent

40. 出身   chūshēn   FV: come from (a particular
                                               kind of a background)

41. 功名   gōngmíng   N: success as a scholar,
                                               glory, honor

42. 造就   zaòjiù   FV: achieve, accomplish

43. 广（廣）置   guǎngzhì   PH: buy up on a large scale

44. 兴（興）盛   xīngshèng   SV: prosperous, flourishing

45. 繁盛   fánshèng   SV: prosperous, thriving

page 122

*46. 不多儿（幾）时（時） bùduōjǐshí   PH: not a long time, soon
                                               (= 不久 bùjiǔ)

*47. 挾   jiā   FV: pick up (something with
                                               chopsticks, pincers, tongs,
                                               etc.)

48. 跪   guì   FV: kneel

49. 調羹   tiáogēng   N: spoon (M: 隻 zhī, 把 bǎ)

50. 男子家   nánzǐjiā   N: men folk, males

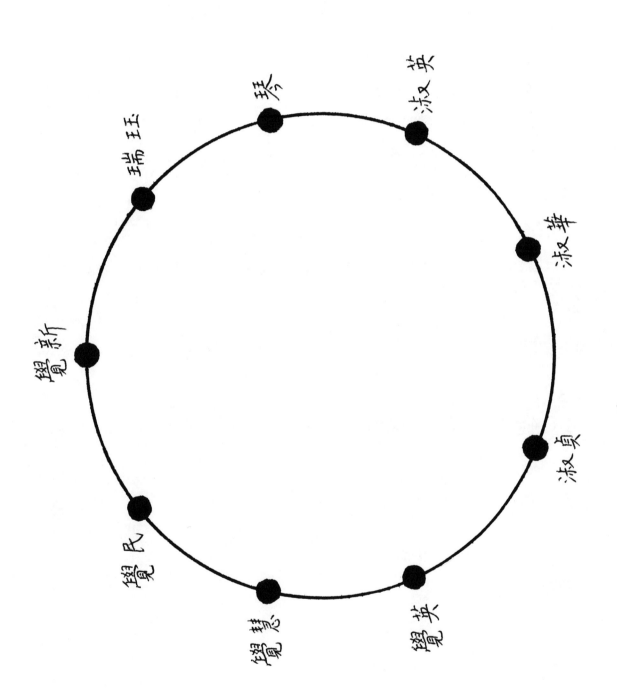

SEATING ARRANGEMENT OF THE YOUNGER 高 GAŌ'S DURING THEIR WINE DRINKING GAME (13–61)

51. 斯文　　　　　　　sīwén　　　　　SV: cultured, refined

52. 火會鮑魚片　　　　huì baòyú piàn　N: braised abalone slices
　　　　　　　　　　　　　　　　　　　　　（鮑魚、'abalone'）

*53. 目光　　　　　　　mùguāng　　　　N: "eye light," attention

54. 自来（來）　　　　zìlaí　　　　　A: heretofore, up to now

55. 海味　　　　　　　haǐweì　　　　N: "sea taste," seafood

56. 罰酒　　　　　　　fájiǔ　　　　　VO: punish someone by making
　　　　　　　　　　　　　　　　　　　　　him drink wine (10-6)

*57. 附和　　　　　　　fùhè　　　　　FV: follow another's lead in
　　　　　　　　　　　　　　　　　　　　　voicing an opinion, agree
　　　　　　　　　　　　　　　　　　　　　with what someone else says

58. 行酒令　　　　　　xíng jiǔlìng　PH: play a wine drinking game

59. 签（簽）　　　　　qiān　　　　　N: bamboo slip used in
　　　　　　　　　　　　　　　　　　　　　drawing lots (M: 根 gēn)

*60. 提議　　　　　　　tíyì　　　　　FV/N: suggest, propose/suggestion,
　　　　　　　　　　　　　　　　　　　　　proposal

page 123

61. 飞（飛）花令　　　feīhuālìng　　N: type of wine drinking game
　　　　　　　　　　　　　　　　　　　　　played by well educated
　　　　　　　　　　　　　　　　　　　　　people (rules are as follows:
　　　　　　　　　　　　　　　　　　　　　a group of people, usually--
　　　　　　　　　　　　　　　　　　　　　as here--limited to nine,
　　　　　　　　　　　　　　　　　　　　　sit at a round table; one of
　　　　　　　　　　　　　　　　　　　　　them, called the 令官
　　　　　　　　　　　　　　　　　　　　　lìngguān [13-87], begins by
　　　　　　　　　　　　　　　　　　　　　citing a line from a Táng
　　　　　　　　　　　　　　　　　　　　　poem, or sometimes a line
　　　　　　　　　　　　　　　　　　　　　from the Four Books, or a
　　　　　　　　　　　　　　　　　　　　　famous saying, which contains
　　　　　　　　　　　　　　　　　　　　　the word 花 ; beginning
　　　　　　　　　　　　　　　　　　　　　with himself, he "flies" [飛]
　　　　　　　　　　　　　　　　　　　　　or counts the characters of
　　　　　　　　　　　　　　　　　　　　　the line of poetry around the
　　　　　　　　　　　　　　　　　　　　　table until he comes to 花 ;
　　　　　　　　　　　　　　　　　　　　　the person whom the word 花
　　　　　　　　　　　　　　　　　　　　　falls on must then drink a
　　　　　　　　　　　　　　　　　　　　　cup of wine as "punishment"
　　　　　　　　　　　　　　　　　　　　　and himself recite a line)

62. 我不来（來）　　　wǒ bùlaí　　　PH: "I won't (do it)"

63. 拾   shí   FV: pick up

64. 出門俱是看花人

Chū mén jū shì kànhuārén

Those going outdoors will all be going to look at the flowers

(from the poem 城東早春 Chéngdōng Zǎochūn by 楊巨源 Yáng Jùyuán)

65. 作弄   zuónòng   FV: make fun of, play jokes on

*66. 違抗   weíkàng   FV: defy and oppose, disobey

*67. 催促   cuīcù   FV: hasten, urge, press

68. 春風桃李花开(開)日

Chūn fēng taó lǐ huā kaī rì

The day the peach and plum flowers open in the spring wind

(from 長恨歌 Chánghèn'gē by 白居易 Baí Jūyì, poem #72 in 唐詩三百首)

page 124

69. 桃花乱(亂)落如紅雨

Taóhuā luàn luò rú hóng yǔ

Peach flowers fall in confusion like red rain

(from 將進酒 Jiāngjìn Jiǔ by 李賀 Lǐ Hè)

70. 落花时(時)节(節)又逢君

Luò huā shíjié yoù féng jūn

At the time of the falling flowers I come upon you once again

(from 江南逢李龜年 Jiāngnán Féng Lǐ Guīnián by 杜甫 Dù Fǔ, #269 in 唐詩三百首)

71. 若待上林花似錦

Ruò daì Shànglín huā sì jǐn...

If you wait until the flowers in the Imperial Garden look like brocade...

(line before 13-64, same poem)

72. 桃花潭水深千尺

Taóhuātán shuǐ shēn qiān chǐ

The water of Peach Flower Pool is a thousand feet deep

(from 贈汪倫 Zèng Wānglún by 李白 Lǐ Baí)

73. 賞花归(歸)去馬蹄香

Shǎng huā guīqù mǎtí xiāng

After returning from enjoying the flowers, the horses' hoofs are
fragrant (source unknown)

74. 去年花里(裏)逢君別

Qùnián huālǐ féng jūn bié...

Last year I happened upon you in the flowers as you were leaving...

(from 寄李儋元錫 Jì Lǐ Dān Yuán Xī by 韋應物 Weí Yīngwù,
#184 in 唐詩三百首)

75. 今日花开(開)又一年

Jīnrì huā kaī yòu yìnián

Today the flowers are blooming and another year has passed
(continuation of 13-74)

76. 牧童遥指杏花村

Mùtóng yaó zhǐ xìnghuācūn

The little cowherd points out a tavern in the distance

(from 清明 Qīngmíng by 杜牧 Dù Mù)

77. 东(東)風無力百花殘

Dōngfēng wú lì baǐhuā cán

The East Wind has no strength, all the flowers have withered

(from 無題 Wútí by 李商隱 Lǐ Shāngyǐn, #210 in 唐詩三百首)

78. 感时(時)花濺泪(淚)

Gǎn shí huā jiàn leì

The flowers, which are affected by the times, splash tears

(from 春望 Chūnwàng by 杜甫 Dù Fǔ, #132 in 唐詩三百首)

79. 五言詩   wǔyánshī   N: poem where each line has five characters or syllables (the most common form for Chinese poems is either five or seven syllables per line; M: 首 shǒu)

80. 算数（數）   suànshù   FV: be of importance, "count"

81. 依   yī   FV: agree with (someone)

82. 不耐煩   búnàifán   SV: impatient

83. 揀（揀）   jiǎn   FV: select, choose

84. 急口令   jíkǒulìng   N: tongue twister

85. 九紋龙（龍）史进（進）   Jiǔwénlóng Shǐjìn   N: Nine-striped Dragon Shǐjìn (this and several items below are all the nicknames and names of characters in the novel 水滸傳 Shuǐhǔ Zhuàn, translated by Pearl Buck as All Men Are Brothers)

86. 解圍   jiěwéi   VO: "lift a siege," resolve difficulties, save someone from embarrassment

87. 令官   lìngguān   N: game leader (of a wine drinking game)

88. 認定   rèndìng   FV: conclude, decide

89. 充当（當）   chōngdāng   FV: assume the role of, be (2-62)

90. 豹子头（頭）林冲   Bàozitóu Línchōng   N: Leopard Head Línchōng

page 125

91. 行者武松   Xíngzhě Wǔsōng   N: Mendicant Priest Wǔsōng

92. 玉麒麟卢（盧）俊义（義）   Yùqílín Lújùnyì   N: Jade Unicorn Lújùnyì

93. 小旋风柴进（進）   Xiǎo Xuánfēng Cháijìn   N: Small Whirlwind Cháijìn

94. 母夜叉孙（孫）二娘   Mǔyèchā Sūn'èrniáng   N: Female Ogre Sūn'èrniáng

95. 逗引   dòuyǐn   FV: make (someone do something), rouse, stir (12-104)

96. 绰号（號）	chuòhaò	N:	nickname
97. 智多星吴用	Zhìduōxīng Wúyòng	N:	Star of Cunning Wúyòng
98. 异（異）口同声(聲)	yìkǒutóngshēng	EX:	"different mouths, same voice," in unison
99. 认、错	rèncuò	VO:	admit a fault or mistake

page 126

100. 散席	sànxí	VO:	disperse, break up (after a meeting or party)
101. 打扫（掃）	dásao	FV:	sweep, clean up
102. 万（萬）馬奔騰	wànmǎbēnténg	EX:	"ten thousand horses stampede" (used to describe a thundering or roaring noise; P-26)
*103. 信步	xìnbù	A:	wandering aimlessly (11-13)
*104. 鞭炮	biānpaò	N:	long string of firecrackers (3-60)
105. 散炮	sǎnpaò	PH:	individual firecrackers scattered here and there
106. 硫磺	liúhuáng	N:	sulphur
107. 气（氣）味	qìwei	N:	odor
*108. 尸（屍）体（體）	shītǐ	N:	corpse (M: 具 jù)
*109. 蜡（蠟）烛（燭）	làzhú	N:	candle (M: 支 zhī, 根 gēn; 12-92)
*110. 朦胧	ménglóng	ADJ:	dim, hazy (like the moon just before setting)
111. 爆裂	baòliè	FV:	explode to pieces
112. 残骸	cánhaí	N:	remains, wreckage
113. 凌乱（亂）	língluàn	SV:	in total disorder or disarray, untidy

page 127

114. 讨饭	taǒfàn	VO:	beg for food

115. 飄風蓬	piāopéng	ADJ:	scattered, disheveled (1-4, 12-55)
*116. 急促	jícù	SV:	hurried, excited
117. 銀圓	yínyuán	N:	silver dollar (also written 銀元」)
118. 控制	kòngzhi	FV/N:	control
119. 銀幣	yínbì	N:	silver currency
120. 飲食	yǐnshí	N:	food and drink
121. 伪（偽）善	wěishàn	ADJ:	"falsely good," hypo-critical (11-26, 11-34)
122. 愚蠢	yúchǔn	SV/N:	foolish, stupid/foolish-ness, stupidity (distin-guish 蠢 and 11-91 蠶 cán 'silkworm'; 12-35)
123. 頹然地	tuíránde	A:	despondently, depressed (5-63)

CHAPTER FOURTEEN

page 128

1. 棉被   miánbeǐ   N: cotton quilt (M: 床 chuáng, 條 tiaó)

2. 胡乱(亂)地   húluànde   A: recklessly, carelessly

*3. 翻身   fānshēn   VO: turn the body over, make a somersault

4. 香   xiāng   A: soundly (used here to describe a person's sleep; 9-104)

5. 咕噜   gūlu   A: muttering, grumbling (10-30)

*6. 皺紋   zhoùwén   N: wrinkle, crease (12-31)

page 129

7. 凶(兇)神恶(惡)煞   xiōngshén'èshà   EX:"wicked spirit, evil devil," with an evil expression

8. 逢年过(過)节(節)   féngniánguòjié   PH: New Year's and other holidays

*9. 鋪   pū   FV: spread out or over (7-5)

10. 放心不下   fàngxīnbúxià   PH: cannot relax or be at ease (四川 ; = 放不下心)

11. 渾水   húnshuǐ   PH: turbid water (清水 qīngshuǐ and 渾水 here refer, figuratively, to the "good days" and the "bad days" of the 高 Gaō family's life; 8-18)

12. 过(過)世   guòshì   FV: "pass from this earth," die

13. 少奶々   Shaònaǐnai   N: "younger madam" (refers to 瑞玨 Ruìjué)

14. 保佑   baǒyoù   FV: protect and bless

15. 时(時)节(節)   shíjié   N: time, occasion

16. 慈祥   cíxiáng   SV: kind, benevolent

page 130

17. 譏諷　　　　　　　jīfěng　　　　　　　FV: ridicule, make fun of

18. 迴〔迴〕廊　　　huíláng　　　　　　N: winding corridor

19. 粉白　　　　　　　fěnbaí　　　　　　ADJ: whitewashed

20. 大理石　　　　　　dàlǐshí　　　　　N: marble (M:塊 kuaì)

*21. 杆（欄）杆　　　lán'gān　　　　　N: railing, balustrade

22. 牡丹　　　　　　　mǔdān　　　　　　N: peony (type of shrub with
　　　　　　　　　　　　　　　　　　　　large, showy flowers)

*23. 枯枝　　　　　　kūzhī　　　　　　PH: dried and withered branch

*24. 包扎　　　　　　baōzā　　　　　　FV: wrap, cover

25. 棉花　　　　　　　miánhua　　　　　N: cotton (1-26, 10-46)

26. 霜　　　　　　　　shuāng　　　　　N: frost (10-104)

27. 枯萎　　　　　　　kūweǐ　　　　　　FV: wither

page 131

28. 熬过（過）　　　aóguo　　　　　　RC: endure, suffer through

29. 剪刀　　　　　　　jiǎndaō　　　　　N: scissors, shears (M:把 bǎ)

30. 躬腰　　　　　　　gōngyaō　　　　　VO: bend the waist (10-83)

31. 咆哮　　　　　　　baòxiaō　　　　　FV: roar (often pronounced
　　　　　　　　　　　　　　　　　　　　paóxiaō)

32. 长（長）頸　　　chángjǐng　　　　ADJ: long-necked

33. 白鶴　　　　　　　baíhè　　　　　　N: white crane (M:隻 zhī)

34. 竹篱（籬）　　　zhúlí　　　　　　N: bamboo fence

35. 羊腸小徑　　　　yángchángxiǎojǐng　N: "sheep intestine small
　　　　　　　　　　　　　　　　　　　　path," narrow and twisting
　　　　　　　　　　　　　　　　　　　　path (M:條 tiaó)

36. 小溪　　　　　　　xiaǒqī　　　　　　N: small stream or creek
　　　　　　　　　　　　　　　　　　　　(M:道 daò, 條 tiaó)

37. 清徹　　　　　　　qīngchè　　　　　SV: clear and penetrating,
　　　　　　　　　　　　　　　　　　　　transparent

*38. 引   yǐn   FV: lead (5-5)

39. 茅草   máocǎo   N: straw (as in thatched
                              rooves)

40. 凉亭   liángtíng   N: pavilion (10-23)

41. 桂树（樹）   guìshù   N: cassia or laurel tree

42. 茶花   cháhuā   N: camellia (flower)

43. 波涛   bōtāo   N: breaker, large wave

44. 迷陣   mízhèn   N: maze, disarray

45. 弯（彎）来（來）wānláiwānqù PH: twist and turn back and
    弯（彎）去   forth

46. 稀疏   xīshū   SV: scattered, dispersed

47. 弯（彎）   wān   M: (for the crescent moon; 10-99)

48. 圍抱   wéibào   FV: encircle, embrace

49. 湖心亭   húxīntíng   N: pavilion in the middle of
                              a lake (10-23)

page 132

*50. 湖畔   húpàn   N: edge or shore of a lake

51. 波动（動）   bōdòng   FV: undulate

*52. 擲   zhì   FV: throw, fling

53. 劝（勸）阻   quànzǔ   FV: dissuade

*54. 圆拱桥（橋）yuángǒngqiáo N: round arched bridge (M: 座
                              zuò)

*55. 玉兰（蘭）树（樹）yùlánshù N: magnolia tree (M: 株 zhū,
                              棵 kē)

56. 瓷[磁]凳   cídèng   N: glazed earthen stool (5-48)

57. 新近   xīnjìn   A: recently, lately

58. 油漆   yóuqī   FV/N: paint (1-94)

59. 朱（硃）红色 zhūhóngsè   N: vermilion color

60. 鲜艳（豔色） xiānyànduómù EX: "fresh, beautiful, and
    夺（奪）目   catching the eyes," at-
                              tractively bright colored
                              (5-21)

*61. 檐 [簷] 下   yánxià   PW: under the eaves (1-130)

62. 匾 額   biǎné   N: horizontal wooden tablet
                                         inscribed with characters
                                         that is hung above a door
                                         (M: 塊 kuài)

*63. 晚 香 楼 (樓)   Wǎnxiānglóu   N: "Evening Fragrance Building"

*64. 推 辞 (辭)   tuīcí   FV: decline, reject (an offer)

*65. 陈 (陳) 設   chénshè   N: decorations, furnishings

page 133

66. 楼 (樓) 梯   lóutī   N: staircase

67. 匤 床 (牀)   kàngchuáng   N: divan, couch

*68. 惊 (驚) 愕   jīng'è   SV: astonished, dumbfounded

69. 通 夜   tōngyè   PH: whole night

*70. 支 持   zhīchi   FV/N: support, sustain/support

71. 何 苦   hékǔ   A: "why trouble yourself?" why

72. 规 劝 (勸)   guīquàn   FV: admonish, give friendly
                                         advice

*73. 承 認   chéngrèn   FV: acknowledge, admit

page 134

74. 懦 夫   nuòfu   N: coward

75. 面 对 (對)   miànduì   FV: face up to

76. 糊 塗   hútu   SV: confused, befuddled (7-121)

77. 遺 忘   yíwàng   N/FV: forgetting/forget

*78. 怜 (憐) 憫   liánmǐn   FV: pity

page 135

*79. 闖 进 (進)   chuǎngjìn   FV: intrude, rush in

80. 再 ... 不过 (過)   zaì...búguò   PT: "could not be more..." (this
                                         construction surrounds a SV
                                         and implies the superlative;
                                         thus 再好不過 zaì haǒ
                                         búguò means 'couldn't be
                                         better')

81. 怨恨   yuànhèn   FV: hate, bear a grudge against (2-29, 6-69)

82. 負   fù   FV: turn one's back on (someone)

83. 娘家   niángjia   N: maiden home, home of a girl before she marries (2-57)

*84. 偏々   piānpiān   A: against expectations, perversely, contrarily

85. 居孀   jūshuāng   VO: become a widow

page 136

86. 寬恕   kuānshù   FV: forgive, pardon

87. 麻醉   mázuì   FV: anesthetize

88. 痛悔   tònghuǐ   N: deep regret, bitter remorse (10-74)

*89. 懦弱   nuòruò   SV: weak and cowardly (14-74)

90. 咎有应(應)得   jiùyǒuyīngdé   EX: "if there is misfortune, one should receive it," get what one deserves, be someone's own fault

91. 可悲   kěbēi   SV: sad, mournful

92. 入迷   rùmí   VO: become captivated or bewitched (by something)

*93. 爭辯   zhēngbiàn   FV: argue (9-109)

94. 寿(壽)命   shòumìng   N: life, life-span

95. 几(幾)时(時)   jǐshí   PH: little while, short time

page 137

96. 結   jié   N: knot

97. 襲击(擊)   xíjī   FV: attack by surprise

98. 挽救   wǎnjiù   FV: rescue, save (10-49)

99. 死尸(屍)   sǐshī   N: corpse (M: 具 jù; 13-108)

100. 腐烂(爛)   fǔlàn   N/FV: rottenness, putrefaction/ rot, spoil

101. 預言   yùyán   N: prophecy, premonition (4-71)

*102. 橫   héng   FV: be at right angles to, be across from (3-146, 9-13)

*103. 深淵 (淵)   shēnyuān   N: deep abyss (M: 道 dào)

104. 援救   yuánjiù   FV: rescue

105. 踢毽 [毽] 子   tī jiànzi   PH: kick a shuttlecock (popular game among Chinese children; the shuttlecock is made of a skin covering, a copper coin inside, and bird feathers which are tied in a tuft on top by a leather cord)

page 138

106. 本能地   běnnéngde   A: instinctively

107. 鈎 [鉤]   gōu   FV/N: hook onto/hook

108. 塔   tǎ   ON: (describes the sound of something falling, like English "thud")

109. 欢 (歡) 呼   huānhū   FV: cheer

110. 賠償 (償)   péicháng   FV: recompense, make up a loss

111. 仇 [讎]   chóu   N: enmity, spite (1-73, 6-136, 8-44)

112. 粉臉   fěnliǎn   PH: powdered face (9-103)

page 139

113. 能手   néngshǒu   N: expert, master, "whiz"

114. 吸住   xīzhù   RC: attract (8-9)

115. 听 (聽) 話   tīnghuà   SV/VO: obedient/obey

116. 吸力   xīlì   N: power of attraction (8-9)

*117. 孤零々   gūlínglíng   A: alone and forsaken (P-16, 1-111)

118. 熟悉   shúxī   FV/SV: be familiar with (something)

119. 游 [遊] 戏 (戲)   yóuxì   N: recreation, games

120. 畸形   jīxíng   ADJ: strange shaped (12-34)

121. 嬌弱   jiaōruò   ADJ: delicately weak (9-82)

page 140

*122. 槍彈痕   qiāngdànhén   N: rifle bullet scar (5-17)

123. 哀泣   aīqì   FV: cry, weep (4-3)

124. 越过 (過)   yuèguo   FV: pass over, cross

*125. 分明地   fēnmíngde   A: clearly, distinctly

126. 嗔怒   chēnnù   ADJ: angry, enraged

127. 擰   nǐng   FV: twist, pinch

128. 桥 (橋)头(頭)   qiaótoú   N: end of a bridge

page 141

*129. 拔   bá   FV: pluck up, raise

130. 旁观 (觀)   pángguān   FV: look on, watch from the side lines

131. 健忘   jiànwàng   SV: forget things easily, forgetful

132. 掘开(開)   juékaī   FV: dig open

CHAPTER FIFTEEN

page 142

1. 怒潮狂涌（湧） nùcháokuángyǒng EX: "angry tide madly rushes up," roaring tidal wave (1-80, 3-108)

2. 齐（齊）集 qíjí FV: assemble together

3. 敬神 jìngshén VO: offer sacrifice to the gods

4. 正中 zhèngzhōng PW: in the middle (=當中 dāngzhōng)

*5. 正門 zhèngmén N: main door (M: 1-140 扇 shàn)

*6. 供桌〔棹〕 gòngzhuō N: offering table, altar (M: 張 zhāng)

7. 絨 róng N: velvet

8. 桌〔棹〕帷 zhuōwéi N: veil which covers an offering table, altar cloth

9. 火盆架子 huǒpénjiàzi N: frame containing a flaming basin (used in religious ceremonies)

10. 熊々 xióngxióng ADJ: bright and brilliant, flaming

11. 炭圓 tànyuán N: charcoal briquet

*12. ...也似地 ...yě shìde PT: as if, like (follows a N or FV; here, 山也似地 shān yě shìde means 'like a mountain'; cf. also 他飛也似地跑出去了 Tā fēi yě shìde pǎochūqùle 'He ran out [so fast] it seemed as though he were flying')

13. 柏枝 bǎizhī N: cedar branch

14. 吱々 zhīzhī ON: (describes squeaking or crackling sounds; also pronounced zīzī)

15. 刺眼触(觸)鼻 cìyǎnchùbí   EX: "stab the eyes, butt against the nostrils," be irritating to one's eyes and nose (1-17, 1-29)

*16. 霧 wù   N: fog, mist

17. 大幅 dà fú   PH: (here) big (P-38)

18. 毡(氈)子 zhānzi   N: carpet, rug (M: 張 zhāng)

19. 随(隨)处(處) suíchù   A: in various places, everywhere

20. 拜垫(墊) bàidiàn   N: cushion for kneeling during rites (2-3)

21. 香爐 xiānglú   N: incense burner

page 143

22. 拜賀 bàihè   N/FV: greetings, congratulations/ send greetings (6-76)

23. 长(長)袍馬褂 chángpaómǎguà   PH: long gown and short outer jacket (formal apparel for men in old China; 1-26)

24. 紹兴(興)酒 Shaòxīng jiǔ   N: Shaòxīng wine (famous mild rice wine of golden color)

25. 侧門 cèmén   N: side door (3-44, 15-5)

26. 叩头(頭) kòutóu   VO: kowtow (knock one's forehead on the ground while kneeling as a sign of reverence; an example of a Chinese loan word in English)

27. 拈 niān   FV: take hold of with one's fingers (6-55)

28. 灶(竈)神 zaòshén   N: kitchen god

*29. 厨[廚]房 chúfáng   N: kitchen (M: 間 jiān)

*30. 女眷 nǔjuàn   N: female members of a family, "womenfolk"

*31. 其次 qícì   A: second in order, next

32. 从(從)容不迫 cōngróngbúpò   EX: "calmly and not pressed," in an unhurried or leisurely manner

33. 半点（點）鐘　　　bàndiǎnzhōng　　PH: half an hour (= 半個鐘頭
　　　　　　　　　　　　　　　　　　　　　　bàn'ge zhōngtou)

34. 迟（遲）缓　　　　chíhuǎn　　　　SV: slow, dilatory (6-197)

page 144

35. 慌忙　　　　　　huāngmáng　　　SV: hurried and flustered,
　　　　　　　　　　　　　　　　　　　　panicky (1-40)

36. 一字形　　　　　yízìxíng　　　N/ADJ: "in the form of the char-
　　　　　　　　　　　　　　　　　　　　acter 一 ," a straight
　　　　　　　　　　　　　　　　　　　　line/in a straight line

37. 道贺　　　　　　daòhè　　　　　VO: offer congratulations

*38. 个（個）别　　　gèbié　　　　　A: individually

*39. 聚拢来（來）　　jùlǒnglai　　　RC: assemble, come together

40. 吉庆（慶）　　　jíqìng　　　　ADJ: happy, auspicious

41. 带（帶）头（頭）　daìtóu　　　　VO: lead the way, be first
　　　　　　　　　　　　　　　　　　　　(=13-20 領頭　lǐngtóu)

page 145

42. 作揖　　　　　　zuōyǐ　　　　　VO: bow with one's hands clasped
　　　　　　　　　　　　　　　　　　　　in front and moving up and
　　　　　　　　　　　　　　　　　　　　down before one's face (6-178)

43. 还（還）礼（禮）　huánlǐ　　　　VO: return a bow or greeting

44. 雇[僱]用　　　　gùyòng　　　　FV: hire, employ

45. 光油々　　　　　guāngyóuyóu　　A: shining and glossy, lustrous

*46. 罩[罩]　　　　zhaò　　　　　FV: cover (1-109)

47. 滚[滾]边（邊）　gǔnbiān　　　VO: put a border or hem (on a
　　　　　　　　　　　　　　　　　　　　garment)

48. 竹布衫　　　　　zhúbùshān　　　N: short coat made of cotton
　　　　　　　　　　　　　　　　　　　　(M: 件　jiàn)

49. 圍墙（牆）　　　weíqiáng　　　N: enclosing wall (M: 道　daò)

50. 花兒　　　　　　huār　　　　　N: type of silent fireworks
　　　　　　　　　　　　　　　　　　　　(四川)

51. 火花　　　　　　huǒhuā　　　　N: spark (M: 根　gēn)

52. 金光 灿（燦）
火兰（爛）   jīnguāngcànlàn   EX: "golden light very brilliant,"
bright and dazzling

53. 引 綫［線］   yǐnxiàn   N: fuse (14-38)

page 146

54. 滴々金   Dīdījīn   N: "Drops of Gold" (type of
fireworks, somewhat like a
sparkler; 5-42)

55. 地老鼠   Dìlaǒshǔ   N: "Ground Mice" (type of fire-
works, moves around quickly
on the ground like mice)

56. 神書帯（帶）箭   Shénshūdàijiàn   N: "Letter to the Spirits car-
ried by an Arrow" (type of
fireworks)

57. 辞（辭）岁（歲）   císuì   VO: "dismiss the year," pay one's
year's end respects to rela-
tives and friends on New
Year's Eve (11-94)

58. 安放   ānfàng   FV: put away, place (=放 fàng)

59. 素裙   sùqún   PH: plain skirt (M: 條 tiáo; 5-75)

*60. 打扮   dǎbàn   FV: put on make-up (7-40)

61. 花枝招展   huāzhīzhaōzhǎn   EX: "flower branch beckoning
and opening," attracting
people's attention like a
flowering branch (of beau-
tifully dressed women)

*62. 冲［沖］   chōng   FV: dash against, rush at

*63. 屋頂   wūdǐng   N: roof of a house

page 147

64. 太师（師）椅   taìshīyǐ   N: wooden armchair, lounge
chair (named after the 太師
or Grand Tutor of old China)

65. 起立   qǐlì   FV: stand up

66. 鉄（鐵）皮   tiěpí   N: sheet metal

67. 染   rǎn   FV: be infected with, "catch"
(a bad habit or a contagious
disease; 10-103)

68. 鴉片烟[煙]癮　yāpiàn yānyǐn　PH: opium addiction

69. 警察局　jǐngchájú　N: police station

70. 流浪　liúlàng　FV: wander, roam about

71. 文　wén　M: cash (for money in old China)

72. 襤褸　lánlǚ　SV: tattered (of clothes), in rags

73. 同事　tóngshì　VO/N: work together/co-worker, colleague

74. 央告　yānggaò　FV: beg, beseech (5-60)

75. 禀报[報]　bǐngbaò　FV: report to a superior

76. 久而久之　jiǔ'érjiǔzhī　EX: after a while, in the course of time

77. 旧(舊)例　jiùlì　PH: established custom

page 148

78. 破烂(爛)　pòlàn　SV: in rags, tattered

*79. 縮　suō　FV: shrink, draw back (1-8)

*80. 唯[惟]恐　weíkǒng　PH: to fear only (P-29, 9-125)

81. 夹(夾)衫　jiáshān　N: lined inner garment (M:件 jiàn)

82. 余(餘)烬(燼)　yújìn　N: ashes, embers

83. 杂(雜)货店　záhuòdiàn　N: department store, grocery

84. 寡妇(婦)　guǎfu　N: widow (7-90)

85. 男丁　nándīng　N: male human being, man

86. 老家人　laǒjiārén　N: servant who has served many years in the same household (9-132)

page 149

87. 年初二　nián chū'èr　PH: second day of the new year

88. 万(萬)想不到　wànxiǎngbudaò　PH: would never have thought of (some fact; 5-54)

89. 玄青   xuánqīng   ADJ: black

90. 背心   bèixīn   N: vest, waistcoat (M: 件 jiàn)

91. 無可奈何   wúkě'naihé   EX: "without being able to do
                                                 about it what," having no
                                                 alternative, helpless

*92. 凄[淒]哀   qī'aī   SV: sad, mournful

page 150

93. 傅粉   fùfěn   VO: apply or rub in powder
                                                 (= 擦粉 cāfěn)

94. 伤(傷)感   shānggǎn   SV: sad, depressed

95. 無端地   wúduānde   A: without cause or reason

96. 没有两(兩)样(樣)   meíyou liǎngyàng PH: "there are not two (dif-
                                                 ferent) ways," exactly the
                                                 same (6-19)

97. 生性   shēngxìng   N: inborn nature, natural dis-
                                                 position

98. 多愁善感   duōchoúshàn'gǎn   EX: "much grief, easily affected,"
                                                 sad and sensitive, sentimental

*99. 尽(儘)管   jǐnguǎn   A: (here) just, only

100. 并(並)肩   bìngjiān   A: with shoulders together or
                                                 next to each other, shoulder
                                                 to shoulder (1-90)

*101. 别   bié   FV: part with, leave

*102. 凄[淒]楚   qīchǔ   SV: sad and sorrowful, heart-
                                                 rending

page 151

103. 拖累   tuōleǐ   FV: involve someone else, cause
                                                 someone else to suffer

104. 悲观(觀)   bēiguān   SV: pessimistic

105. 丧(喪)气(氣)话   sàngqihuà   N: gloomy or despondent talk
                                                 (distinguish 喪, 衣 yī,
                                                 3-163 袁 yuán, 6-73 哀 aī,
                                                 and 15-47 滾 gǔn)

106. 籠罩〔罩〕 lǒngzhaò FV: cover completely, permeate (15-46)

107. 境遇 jìngyù N: condition, circumstances

108. 摆(擺)布(佈) baǐbù FV: manage, control, arrange

*109. 作主 zuòzhǔ VO: have control over oneself, come to a decision

page 152

110. 何尝(嘗) hécháng A: why, how

111. 惊(驚)惧(懼) jìngjù SV: scared, frightened

112. 心境 xīnjìng N: mood

113. 动(動)辄〔輒〕 dòngzhé A: frequently, easily

114. 生悲 shēngbeī FV: become sad

115. 变(變)更 biàngēng FV/N: change (1-123, 10-105)

116. 好比 haǒbǐ A: like, as if (= 好像 haǒxiàng)

*117. 噩梦(夢) èmèng N: nightmare (also written 惡夢; M: 4-115 场 chǎng)

*118. 乐(樂)观(觀) lèguān SV: optimistic (opposite of 15-104 悲觀 beīguān)

119. 可为(為) kěweí PH: be able to do

120. 下嘴唇〔脣〕皮 xiàzuǐchúnpí N: lower lip (7-57)

page 153

*121. 挽回 wǎnhuí FV: save (from a dangerous situation)

122. 封面 fēngmiàn N: cover (of a book or magazine)

123. 叠(疊) diē FV/M: pile up, accumulate/pile (1-50)

124. 条(條)桌〔棹〕 tiaózhuō N: long and narrow table (M: 張 zhāng)

125. 乞丐 qǐgaì N: beggar

*126. 掩   yǎn   FV: cover up, shut (1-52)

127. 失眠   shīmián   VO: suffer from insomnia

*128. 爱(愛)惜   aìxī   FV: be careful with, love and cherish

*129. 偎   weī   FV: hug, embrace

page 154

130. 月缺   yuè quē   PH: the moon is "lacking something"--i.e., is not full

131. 梧桐树(樹)   wútóngshù   N: Chinese plane tree (Sterculia platanifolia)

132. 芽   yá   BF: bud, sprout (FF: 芽子 yázi, 芽兒 yár)

133. 绿叶(葉)成荫   lùyèchéngyīn   EX: "green leaves create shade," very luxuriant foliage (绿, usually pronounced lǜ, is here given the literary reading lù)

134. 相像   xiāngxiàng   SV: similar

135. 翻来(來)复(覆)去   fānlaífānqù   PH: toss and turn, roll about

*136. ...个(個)不停   ...ge bùtíng   PT: (the pattern FV 個不停 means 'FV an endless one' or 'FV incessantly'; thus, 響個不停 xiǎngge bùtíng means 'emit sound endlessly';other common examples are 説個不停 shuōge bùtíng 'talk on forever', 打個不停 dǎge bùtíng 'fight on endlessly', and 罵個不停 màge bùtíng 'scold for a very long time')

137. 往事依稀浑似梦(夢)

Wǎng shì yīxī hún sì mèng

The past is indistinct--confused like a dream

都 随（隨）風 雨 到 心 头（頭）。

Dū suí fēng yǔ .daò   xīntoú

It is recalled by the wind and the rain to my heart

<u>page 155</u>

138. 門縫	ménfèng	N:	crevice or crack in a door (10-61)
139. 張 一眼	zhāng yìyǎn	PH:	take one look at (3-26)
140. 年节（節）	niánjié	N:	New Year's and other holidays (14-8)
141. 特地	tèdì	A:	on purpose, specially
142. 散心	sànxīn	VO:	relax by a change of surroundings, cheer up
143. 爽快	shuǎngkuai	SV:	in good spirits, relaxed, happy
144. 絮々地	xùxùde	A:	continuously, without cease (1-3)
145. 詢問	xúnwèn	FV:	inquire, ask about

CHAPTER SIXTEEN

page 156

*1. 交談　　　　jiāotán　　　FV: converse, talk, discuss

2. 無可如何　　wúkěrúhé　　EX: cannot but, have no other
　　　　　　　　　　　　　　　　　choice than

*3. 未免　　　　weimiǎn　　　A: "it must be admitted that,"
　　　　　　　　　　　　　　　　　"can't say that it isn't"

page 157

4. 零落　　　　língluò　　　SV: desolate, bare

5. 門房　　　　ménfáng　　　N: room by the entrance to a
　　　　　　　　　　　　　　　　　house where the porter or
　　　　　　　　　　　　　　　　　doorman stays

6. 吆喝　　　　yāohe　　　　FV: shout, cry

7. 骰子　　　　shaǐzi　　　N: playing die, dice (M: 顆 kē)

8. 悠閑〔閒〕　youxián　　　SV: leisurely, unhurried

*9. 撞击〔擊〕　zhuàngjí　　FV: strike, hit

10. 滚动〔動〕　gǔndòng　　　FV: roll around (15-47)

11. 調和　　　　tiaóhé　　　FV: mix, blend, harmonize

12. 賭博　　　　dǔbó　　　　FV: gamble

page 158

13. 拉了一个(個)角来(来) lāle yíge　PH: "brought a player over"
　　　　　　　　　　　jiaǒ laí　　　(7-39)

14. 攪乱〔亂〕　jiaǒluàn　　FV: disturb, ruffle (10-114)

15. 賭气〔氣〕　dǔqì　　　　A/VO: spitefully, out of rage/
　　　　　　　　　　　　　　　　　do something out of spite
　　　　　　　　　　　　　　　　　(16-12)

16. 次第　　　　cìdì　　　　A: one by one, in sequence

page 159

17. 背馬也   beìchí   FV: "gallop" or travel in
                                        opposite directions

18. 鎮靜   zhènjìng   FV: calm down, compose (oneself)

19. 紛乱 (亂)   fēnluàn   ADJ: confused, chaotic (10-47)

*20. 阻拦 (攔)   zǔlán   N/FV: hindrance, obstruction/
                                        hinder, obstruct (=5-22
                                        攔阻 lánzǔ)

21. 紫藤 [籐]   zǐténg   N: wisteria (a climbing vine;
                                        3-92, 10-24)

22. 花架   huājià   N: flower frame, trellis (15-9)

23. 靠背椅   kaòbeìyǐ   N: chair with a high and straight
                                        back (M: 把 bǎ)

24. 挑   tiaō   FV: choose, select (6-64)

25. 秀气 (氣)   xiùqi   SV: elegant, graceful (3-8)

26. 屏住呼吸   bǐngzhù hūxī   PH: hold one's breath (8-9, 12-25)

27. 不消説   bùxiaōshuō   PH: it's not necessary to say,
                                        needless to say (possibly
                                        a contraction of 不需要
                                        説 bùxūyaò shuō)

page 160

28. 道喜   daòxǐ   VO: offer congratulations (10-3)

*29. 小老婆   xiaǒlaǒpo   N: concubine (6-111)

30. 挂 [掛] 鐘   guàzhōng   N: wall clock

*31. 宁 (寧、寧)...也不 níng...yě bù PT: rather ... than

page 161

32. 早迟 (遲)   zaǒchí   N: "earliness-lateness," time
                                        (6-197)

33. 粗鲁   cūlǔ   SV: rude, impolite, rough (also
                                        written 粗鹵)

34. 委婉   weǐwǎn   SV: soft-spoken, unobtrusive

35. 寻(尋)根究底   xúngēnjiùdǐ   EX: "search out the root, examine the foundation," make
a thorough investigation,
get to the bottom of something

36. 嘘一口气(氣)   xū yìkǒu qì   PH: release a mouthful of breath,
breathe a sigh of relief

37. 呸   peī   I: bah (snort of contempt)

38. 認賬   rènzhàng   VO: recognize, admit (a fact)

39. 賴別人   laì biéren   PH: accuse another falsely (11-42)

page 162

40. 好心   haǒxīn   A/N: with good intentions,
meaning well/good intentions

41. 豈有此理   qǐyǒucǐlǐ   EX: "how is there this princi-
ple?" how unreasonable (7-129)

*42. 吵架   chaǒjià   VO: quarrel, fight

43. 求饒   qiúraó   VO: seek pardon, beg forgiveness

44. 庇护(護)   bìhù   FV/N: protect, shelter/shelter

45. 忘我   wàngwǒ   ADJ: forgetting the "ego",
oblivious to one's personal
condition

46. 耳語   ěryǔ   N/FV: whisper

47. 窺   kuī   FV: peer through, peep

48. 托   tuō   FV: carry, prop up, support (on
the palm)

49. 小指   xiaǒzhǐ   N: little finger

50. 銜   xián   FV: hold in the mouth

51. 灯(燈)盘(盤)   dēngpán   N: base of a lamp

52. 长(長)生果   chángshēngguǒ   N: peanut (花生 huāshēng is
more common)

page 163

*53. 手指   shoǔzhǐ   N: finger (手指頭 shoǔzhítou
is more common)

*54. 帳子   zhàngzi   N: bed canopy (10-8)

*55. 跟前   gēnqián   PW: in front of (something)

56. 花卉   huāhuì   N: flowers

*57. 淌   tǎng   FV: flow down, drip (e.g., tears and drops of sweat)

page 164

58. 把心一橫   bǎ xīn yìhéng   PH: "stiffen up the heart," with great determination (14-102)

59. 賭咒   dǔzhoù   FV: make an oath, swear (11-6, 16-12)

60. 固执(執)   gùzhí   SV: obstinate, stubborn

*61. 馮   Féng   N: （人名）

*62. 討   tǎo   FV: marry (of a man marrying a woman)

63. 任憑   rènpíng   A: no matter how, no matter what

CHAPTER SEVENTEEN

page 165

1. 輸   shū   FV: lose (money in gambling, or a game, etc.)

2. 嗯、   ňg   I: (indicates assent; 11-77)

3. 沮丧（喪）   jǔsàng   SV: discouraged and disappointed, crestfallen

4. 懊恼（惱）   aònaǒ   SV: irritated, vexed

5. 笔（筆）   bǐ   M: (for sums of money)

page 166

6. 拉...上場   lā...shàngchǎng   PH: pull...onto the scene

7. 郑（鄭）重   zhèngzhòng   SV: careful, solemn

8. 抽屉   chōuti   N: drawer (of a desk or dresser)

*9. 鎖   suǒ   FV/N: lock (M: 把 bǎ)

10. 破例   pòlì   VO: break a custom, make an exception to a rule

11. 旺   wàng   SV: fierce, bright

12. 烤火   kaǒhuǒ   VO: warm (one's hands, feet, etc.) by a fire

13. 撇下   piēxià   RC: leave behind (9-23)

14. 吉利   jílì   SV: auspicious, lucky (15-40)

15. 童言無忌、大吉大利   tóng yán wú jì, dà jí dà lì   EX: "Children's words have no taboos (i.e., they say what they like), (may there be) much good fortune and great prosperity"

16. 門柱   ménzhù   N: door post (at the side of doors; 1-112)

17. 串   chuàn   M: string, rope (for items strung together, such as pearls, cash, and firecrackers)

page 167

18. 晨光   chénguāng   N: morning light

19. 拜年   bàinián   VO: call on another and offer New Year's greetings

20. 嬉笑   xīxiào   FV: laugh merrily

21. 喜神方   xǐshénfāng   N: "Place of the God of Good Luck" (according to the dates given in the Imperial Almanac, different places within cities were considered auspicious each year, and it was customary for people to walk in those directions on New Year's)

22. 出行   chūxíng   FV: "go outside" (the custom of allowing women, shortly after New Year's, to go outside their homes for one day)

23. 抛头(頭)露面   pāotóulùmiàn   EX: "throw out the head and expose the face," go out and be seen in public (of women at New Year's in old China)

24. 静僻   jìngpì   SV: quiet or out of the way, secluded (=1-24 僻静 pìjìng)

25. 饱看   bǎokàn   PH: look until satisfied, take a good look at

26. 留恋(戀)不舍(捨)   liúliànbùshě   EX: "keep a fondness and not give it up," be unwilling to part with (something; 4-116)

27. 撞見   zhuàngjian   RC: run into, bump into, meet (16-9)

28. 日程   rìchéng   N: daily schedule or program, itinerary

*29. 正月   zhèngyuè   N: January (= 一月 yíyuè)

page 168

30. 气〔氣〕氛	qìfen	N:	atmosphere, mood
31. 筹〔籌〕码	chóumǎ	N:	gambling chip
32. 狮子筹〔籌〕	shīzichóu	N:	(type of game)
33. 安置	ānzhi	FV:	set up, arrange
34. 炉灶〔竈〕	lúzaò	N:	cooking stove (15-28)
35. 杂〔雜〕事	záshì	N:	varied things, miscellania
36. 清雅	qīngyǎ	SV:	clean and neat, graceful
37. 席	xí	N:	feast, celebration (M:桌 zhuō)
38. 举〔舉〕止大方	jǔzhǐdàfang	EX:	"deportment very elegant," have a dignified air (11-74)
39. 洒〔灑〕脱	sǎtuo	SV:	free and easy, graceful
40. 派头〔頭〕	pàitou	N:	manner, air
41. 同盟会〔會〕	Tóngménghuì	N:	revolutionary party founded in 1905 which advocated the overthrow of the Manchus and the establishment of a republican form of government; it was organized by Sun Yat-sen and was the forerunner of the Guómíndǎng
42. 会〔會〕员	huìyuán	N:	member of an organization
43. 仇〔讎〕满	chóumǎn	ADJ:	"hating the Manchus," anti-Manchu (14-111)
44. 现刻	xiànkè	A:	at the moment, now
45. 交涉署	Jiaōshèshǔ	N:	Bureau for Foreign Affairs (8-52, 8-76)
46. 开〔開〕通	kaītōng	SV:	open-minded, enlightened, progressive
47. 续娶	xùqǔ	FV:	remarry (of men; 6-17)
48. 独〔獨〕养〔養〕女	dúyǎngnǚ	N:	only daughter
49. 自幼	zì yoù	PH:	since childhood (1-84)

page <u>169</u>

50. 烟〔煙〕火   yānhuo   N: fireworks

51. 拗不过（過）   aòbuguò   RC: cannot be so stubborn as to resist (doing something)

52. 扭 燃、   niǔrán   FV: turn on (a light; 1-21, 6-167)

53. 綠 繐、紅罩〔罩〕   lǜsuìhóngzhaò   EX: "green silk tassles, red lampshade"

54. 辨 認、   biànrèn   FV: identify, recognize, distinguish

55. 斑点（點、点）   bāndiǎn   N: spot, dot

56. 爽快   shuǎngkuai   SV: straightforward (15-143)

*57. 答复（覆）   dáfu   FV/N: answer, reply

page <u>170</u>

58. 楼（樓）房   loúfáng   N: building of two or more stories (M: 所 suǒ, 座 zuò)

59. 濃密   nóngmì   SV: dense, thick

60. 金絲   jīnsī   N: gold thread (1-30)

61. 笔（筆）直   bǐzhí   ADJ: "as straight as a writing brush," very straight

62. 陰綠色   yīnlǜsè   N: dark green color

63. 哈ㄆ   hāhā   ON: (sound of hearty laughter)

*64. 盘（盤）旋   pánxuán   FV: circle, hover around

65. 巨大   jùdà   SV: very great, huge

66. 霎时（時）間   shàshíjiān   A: in a very short while (= 一會兒 yīhuěr)

67. 領悟   lǐngwù   FV: realize, comprehend

page <u>171</u>

*68. 动（動）静   dòngjing   N: signs of action being taken, movement

*69. 頸項   jǐngxiàng   N: neck (四川; 14-32)

70. 撒布（佈）   sǎbù   FV: scatter, sprinkle (10-101)

*71. 观（觀）众（眾）   guānzhòng   N: audience, spectators

72. 灿（燦）烂（爛）   cànlàn   ADJ: resplendent, brilliant (15-52)

73. 笛   dí   BF: flute (FF: 笛子 ; M: 管 guǎn)

74. 飘扬   piāoyáng   FV: blow about in the wind, flutter, drift (1-4, 12-107)

75. 梅花三弄   Méihuāsānlòng   N: "Plum Blossom Ditty" (title of a piece of music)

76. 胡琴   húqin   N: two-stringed violin (common Chinese musical instrument, used especially in Beǐjing opera; M: 把 bǎ)

77. 和   hè   FV: harmonize, match (13-57)

78. 神话国（國）土   shénhuà guótǔ   PH: "mythical lands," fairyland

*79. 渺茫   miǎománg   SV: endlessly vast, misty, vague (1-9)

80. 繁琐   fánsuǒ   SV: minute and complicated, petty

81. 梦（夢）景   mèngjǐng   N: dreams, visions

82. 飘荡   piāodàng   FV: drift or float freely (3-111, 12-55)

83. 曲   qǔ   N: song, piece of music (M: 支 zhī)

page 172

84. 拍掌   pāizhǎng   VO: clap one's hands, applaud

*85. 浮   fú   FV: float (3-76)

86. 稀薄   xībó   SV: thin, diluted (e.g., air, liquids, sounds)

87. 悠扬   yōuyáng   SV: gently flowing, mellow (16-8)

88. 响（響）彻   xiǎngchè   FV: penetrate with sound, pervade

89. 驱散   qūsàn   FV: drive off, disperse

90. 流行   liúxíng   SV: "going around," popular

91. 混杂（雜）　　　hùnzá　　　　　FV: mix, blend

92. 各个（個）　　　gègè　　　　　　PN: everyone

93. 溶化　　　　　　rónghuà　　　　FV/N: dissolve/solution (cf. 1-48
　　　　　　　　　　　　　　　　　　　融化 rónghuà: these two
　　　　　　　　　　　　　　　　　　words are sometimes confused
　　　　　　　　　　　　　　　　　　although, strictly speaking,
　　　　　　　　　　　　　　　　　　溶化 is used for the dis-
　　　　　　　　　　　　　　　　　　solving of solids in liquids
　　　　　　　　　　　　　　　　　　and 融化 for the melting
　　　　　　　　　　　　　　　　　　of solids into liquid form)

94. 哄然　　　　　　hōngrán　　　　ADJ: very loud and roaring

*95. 碎　　　　　　　suì　　　　　　FV: break up into little pieces,
　　　　　　　　　　　　　　　　　　shatter (P-21, 10-62, 12-64)

page 173

96. 缓々地　　　　　huǎnhuǎnde　　A: slowly, gradually (15-34)

97. 驶　　　　　　　shǐ　　　　　　FV: sail, run (of ships and
　　　　　　　　　　　　　　　　　　vehicles)

*98. 出乎意料之外　chūhūyìliàozhīwài　PH: contrary to expectations,
　　　　　　　　　　　　　　　　　　unexpectedly (6-88)

99. 泊　　　　　　　bó　　　　　　　FV: moor, anchor (a boat)

100. 龙（龍）灯（燈）lóngdēng　　　　N: dragon lantern dance

101. 年长（長）　　niánzhǎng　　　ADJ: old, aged

102. 陈（陳）迹[蹟跡]chénjī　　　　N: trace, vestige (1-71, 5-17)

CHAPTER EIGHTEEN

1. 馬房   mǎfáng   N: horse compound, stable (includes living quarters for the grooms)

2. 砍   kǎn   FV: chop, cut down (e.g., trees)

3. 鋸   jù   FV: saw

4. 竹筒   zhútǒng   N: bamboo tube

5. 削   xiaō   FV: sharpen, slice

6. 舂   chōng   FV: pound out, beat (6-35)

7. 火藥[約]   huǒyaò   N: gunpowder

8. 賞鑒[鑑]   shǎngjiàn   FV: enjoy, appreciate (also 鑒賞 jiànshǎng)

9. 长(長)板凳[櫈]   chángbǎndèng   N: long-planked bench (M:條 tiaó; 5-48)

10. 俘虜(虜)   fúlǔ   N: captive, prisoner

*11. 期待   qǐdaì   N/FV: waiting/await, expect

12. 迎接   yíngjiē   FV: welcome, greet, receive

13. 看台[臺]   kàntaí   N: observation platform

14. 封   fēng   FV/M: seal/(for letters and telegrams)

15. 妥当(當)   tuǒdàng   SV: proper, satisfactory

16. 帖子   tiězi   N: card, note (M:張 zhāng)

17. 有把握   yǒu bǎwò   PH: have a grasp of something, have something under control, have confidence in something

18. 乏味　　　　　fáweì　　　SV: "lacking flavor," mono-
　　　　　　　　　　　　　　　　　tonous, dull

19. 惦記　　　　　diànji　　　FV: be concerned about, think
　　　　　　　　　　　　　　　　　of

20. 告辞（辭）　　gaòcí　　　VO: say good-bye, take one's
　　　　　　　　　　　　　　　　　leave

21. 破口罵[罵]道　pòkoǔmà daò　PH: say while scolding loudly
　　　　　　　　　　　　　　　　　or abusing freely (4-31)

22. 混賬　　　　　hùnzhàng　　ADJ: good-for-nothing, rotten
　　　　　　　　　　　　　　　　　(originally--and often
　　　　　　　　　　　　　　　　　still--written 混帳, i.e.,
　　　　　　　　　　　　　　　　　'mix curtains'- 'be in the
　　　　　　　　　　　　　　　　　wrong bed'-'immoral')

page 176

23. 小的　　　　　xiaǒde　　　N: "the little one," I, me
　　　　　　　　　　　　　　　　　(used in self reference by
　　　　　　　　　　　　　　　　　servants when speaking to
　　　　　　　　　　　　　　　　　their masters)

24. 头（頭）脑（腦）toúnao　　N: head, leader (四川)

25. 头（頭）焦額烂(爛) toújiaō'élàn　EX: "head scorched, forehead
　　　　　　　　　　　　　　　　　pulped" (3-127, 14-100)

26. 光　　　　　　guāng　　FV/SV/A: be all used up, be naked/
　　　　　　　　　　　　　　　　　smooth/only (8-36)

27. 养（養）息　　yǎngxí　　　FV: rest and care for oneself,
　　　　　　　　　　　　　　　　　recuperate

*28. 气（氣）恼（惱）qì'naǒ　　SV: angry (10-12)

29. 不中用　　　　bùzhōngyòng　SV: not useful, useless

30. 滾　　　　　　gǔn　　　　IE: "Scram," "Beat it," "Get
　　　　　　　　　　　　　　　　　out" (usual meaning, as on
　　　　　　　　　　　　　　　　　next page of 家, 1. 14,
　　　　　　　　　　　　　　　　　is 'to roll')

31. 脾味　　　　　píweì　　　N: temper, disposition

32. 頂撞　　　　　dǐngzhuàng　FV: offend by rude words, dis-
　　　　　　　　　　　　　　　　　pute, argue (16-9)

*33. 斷（斷）續地　duànxùde　　A: "off and on," intermittently

34. 表功   biǎogōng   VO: announce or show off one's
                                            achievements

page 177

35. 夸(誇)奖(奬)   kuājiǎng   FV/N: praise

36. 閑〔閒〕人   xiánrén   N: idler, person with nothing
                                            to do (3-136)

37. 混进(進)   hùnjìn   PH: enter randomly or at will

38. 从(從)头(頭)到尾   cóngtoúdaòweǐ   EX: "from head to tail"

39. 节〔節〕   jié   M: section, link (of something
                                            long)

40. 編扎(紮)   biānzā   FV: weave together, fasten

41. 鱗甲   línjiǎ   N: hard scales (like those
                                            of crocodiles and dragons)

42. 竹竿   zhúgān   N: bamboo pole (M: 根 gēn)

43. 宝(寶、寳)珠   baǒzhū   N: large and ornamented ball
                                            of colorful paper streamers
                                            at the head of the dragon
                                            in a dragon dance

44. 牠   tā   PN: it (third person singular
                                            animate but nonhuman pronoun)

45. 摆(擺)尾   baǐweǐ   VO: wag the tail

46. 就地   jiùdì   PH: on the ground

47. 活像   huóxiàng   PH: look completely like, be
                                            the spitting image of

48. 助长〔長〕   zhùzhǎng   FV: encourage, increase (a ten-
                                            dency)

49. 威势(勢)   weīshì   N: awesomeness, power

50. 發怒   fānù   VO: become angry (3-108)

51. 躲閃   duǒshǎn   FV: dodge away from (something;
                                            7-127)

52. 受惊(驚)   shoùjīng   VO: be frightened (3-40)

53. 呼嘯   hūxiaò   FV/N: howl, roar (of beasts)

54. 縛	fú	FV: bind, tie (3-32)
55. 梯子	tīzi	N: ladder (M: 張 zhāng; 14-66)

page 178

56. 光赤	guāngchì	ADJ: naked, bare (5-11, 18-26)
57. 發狂	fākuáng	VO: become mad, go crazy
58. 大…特…	dà…tè…	PT: to…very greatly (thus, 大響特響 dàxiǎngtèxiǎng means 'to sound very greatly or loudly'; similarly, 大吃特吃 dàchītèchī 'to eat very greatly or much')
59. 文雅	wényǎ	SV: refined, graceful
60. 赤裸〔躶〕	chìluǒ	FV: be naked (18-56)
61. 手杖	shǒuzhàng	N: cane, walking stick (M: 根 gēn)
62. 結实(實)	jiēshi	SV: sturdy, solid, strong
63. 腕力	wànlì	N: strength of the wrist (6-199)
*64. 任	rèn	FV: let, allow (16-63)
65. 防御(禦)	fángyù	FV: defend, guard
66. 狂呼	kuánghū	PH: shout or cry madly (18-57)
67. 剧(劇)烈	jùliè	SV: intense, strenuous, fierce
68. 威武	wēiwǔ	SV: awe-inspiring
69. 支解	zhījiě	FV: dismember
70. 四处(處)奔逃	sìchùbēntaó	EX: "four places run and escape," run away in all directions (P-26)
71. 不相呼应(應)	bùxiāng hūyìng	PH: not cooperate mutually, not be in coordination with each other

page 179

72. 扛	káng	FV: carry on one's shoulders, lift up

73. 硬着头(頭)皮   yìngzhe toúpí   PH: "harden the scalp," bear up, brace oneself, put up a stiff upper lip

74. 听(聽)从(從)   tīngcóng   FV: listen and follow (another's advice), obey (12-129)

75. 平坦   píngtǎn   SV: smooth, level

76. 堆满   duīmǎn   FV: pile up, accumulate (1-47)

77. 密々麻々   mìmimámá   PH: very dense

78. 小伙〔影〕子   xiǎohuǒzi   N: young man, fellow, guy

*79. 猛   měng   SV: fierce, violent

80. 抵御(禦)   dǐyù   FV: resist, ward off

81. 完好   wánhǎo   SV: perfect, flawless

*82. 一瞬間   yíshùnjiān   A: in the twinkling of an eye, in an instant

83. 精光   jīngguāng   A: bare, with nothing left on (18-26)

84. 伴   bàn   FV: accompany (6-91, 8-23)

85. 一拐一拐   yìguǎiyìguǎi   PH: swaying back and forth, limping

page 180

*86. 陆(陸)續   lùxù   A: continuously, one after another

87. 拆除   chaīchú   FV: dismantle, pull down, tear down

88. 低級   dījí   SV: "low class," vulgar

89. 見解   jiànjiě   N: idea, opinion, point of view

90. 真不愧   zhēn búkuì   PH: really be worthy of, really deserve (to be called something)

91. 千金小姐   qiānjīn xiaójie   N: "one thousand gold piece miss," young lady from a wealthy family

92. 建筑（築）   jiànzhú   FV/N: build, construct/buildings,
                                                      construction

page 181

*93. 脾气（氣）   píqi   N: temper, disposition (3-54,
                                                      18-31)

CHAPTER NINETEEN

page 182

1. 元宵节（節）   Yuánxiaōjié   N: Lantern Festival (falls on the fifteenth day of the first full moon in the new year, marks the end of New Year's festivities)

2. 玉盘（盤）   yùpán   N: jade plate or tray (often a symbol for the moon)

3. 天幕   tiānmù   N: "heavenly curtain," sky

4. 清辉[輝、暉]   qīnghuī   N: brightness, light

5. 惜别   xībié   PH: reluctant to part company (15-101)

6. 游[遊]玩   yóuwán   FV: have fun, recreate (8-45)

7. 划船   huáchuán   VO: row a boat

8. 吵   chǎo   FV: be noisy, quarrel (16-42)

9. 藤[籐]篮   ténglán   N: wicker basket (3-92)

10. 一行八个（個）人   yìxíng báge rén   PH: in a group of eight people traveling together

11. 鱼贯地   yúguànde   A: "like fish passing through," in a column, proceeding one by one

page 183

12. 一纵   yízòng   A: in one perpendicular or vertical movement

13. 回应[應]   huíyìng   N: echo, repercussion (8-79)

14. 猫[貓]   maō   N: cat (M: 隻 zhī)

15. 哂笑   shěnxiaò   A: smiling mockingly

*16. 害羞   haìxiū   SV: ashamed, bashful

17. 乖   guāi   SV: good, well-behaved (of children; distinguish 乖, 3-165 乘 chéng (chèng), and 4-10 剩 shèng)

page 184

18. 姜太公在此，諸神迴[迴]避   Jiāng Tàigōng zài cǐ, zhū shén huíbì   EX: "Old Master Jiāng is here, let all the spirits withdraw" (姜太公 was a sage of early China who helped 武王 Wǔ Wáng found the 周 Zhōu Dynasty; he was very talented and famous especially as an exorciser of ghosts)

19. 竹梢   zhúshāo   N: bamboo branch tips

20. 閃   shǎn   FV: slip aside, dodge (1-91, 18-51)

21. 竹丛(叢)   zhúcōng   N: bamboo grove or thicket (8-88)

22. 观(觀)音竹   Guānyīnzhú   N: "Goddess of Mercy" bamboo (type of bamboo)

23. 点(點、點)   diǎn   FV: touch, tap (9-72)

24. 道   dào   FV: think, believe (here, = 以為 yǐwei; 1-59, 7-60)

25. 着迷   zhāomí   VO: become bewitched by, go crazy about

26. 反唇[脣]   fǎnchún   A: rebutting, rebuking

*27. 洒[灑]   sǎ   FV: sprinkle, splash

28. 分辨   fēnbiàn   FV: distinguish (distinguish 3-158 分辯 fēnbiàn 'make excuses')

29. 摸索   mōsuǒ   FV: feel and grope (3-126)

30. 探路   tànlù   VO: feel out a road, test a road

page 185

31. 思議   sīyì   FV: think, imagine

32. 松濤   sōngtāo   N: rustling of the wind in pine trees (14-43)

33. 浮沉〔沈〕   fúchén   FV: float and sink, rise and fall

34. 水波   shuǐbō   N: wave (of water; 14-51)

35. 橢(橢)圓形   tuǒyuánxíng   N/ADJ: oval shape

36. 唼喋   shàdié   ON: (sound of fish or ducks feeding)

37. 以至于(於)無   yǐzhìyúwú   PH: to the point of nothingness

38. 拴   shuān   FV: tie up, fasten

*39. 仰头(頭)   yǎngtóu   VO: raise one's head

40. 苏(蘇)东(東)坡   Sū Dōngpō   N: the 號 haò or literary name of 蘇軾 Sū Shì [1036-1101], famous Chinese poet and essayist; dismissed from office in 1072 to 黄州 Huángzhōu for lampooning several censors in verse, he built himself a hut there on the 東坡 dōngpō 'eastern slope' of a hill, whence his name

41. 水調歌头(頭)   Shuǐdiaò Gētóu   N: (name of a melody by which 詞 cí style poems are mentioned)

42. 明月几(幾)时(時)有

Míng yuè jǐshí yoǔ

When will there be a bright (i.e., full) moon?

把酒問青天

Bǎ jiǔ wèn qīng tiān

I hold my wine and ask blue heaven

不知天上空闕

Bùzhī tiānshàng kōngquè

I do not know, in the celestial palaces,

今夕是何年

Jīn xì shì hé nián

Which year tonight is (note: 空 kōng is here a misprint for 宮 gōng, which occurs in most editions of the poem)

| 43. 管 | guǎn | M: (for flutes and pens; 6-205) |
| 44. 洞簫 | dòngxiāo | N: bamboo flageolet (type of small flute; 10-116) |

page 186

45. 幽美	yōuměi	SV: serene and beautiful
*46. 爆發	bàofā	FV: flare up, erupt (13-111)
47. 纜	lǎn	N: cable, hawser
48. 桨 (槳)	jiǎng	N: oar
49. 滷菜	lǔcài	N: snacks such as beef, chicken, and eggs cooked in soy sauce
50. 花生米	huāshēngmǐ	N: peanut kernels (peanuts which have been shelled)
51. 玫瑰	méigui	N: rose (M: 朵 duǒ)
52. 木塞	mùsāi	N: a cork
53. 遮拦 (攔)	zhēlán	N: obstruction (4-90)
54. 飲	yǐn	BF: imbibe, drink (13-120)
55. 沐	mù	FV: wash, bathe

page 187

56. 紗	shā	N: gauze, sheer cloth
57. 桥 (橋) 畔	qiáopàn	PW: at the side of a bridge (14-50)
58. 峻峭	jùnqiào	SV: high and steep, precipitous
*59. 水閣	shuǐgé	N: water pavilion
*60. 腹	fù	BF: stomach, abdomen
61. 京戏 (戲、戲)	jīngxì	N: Beǐjing opera
62. 矮	ǎi	SV: short, low
63. 搖	yáo	FV: row (a boat)
64. 宽敞	kuānchǎng	SV: spacious, roomy (4-112)

65. 嚼   jiaó   FV: chew

66. 平稳、(穩、)   píngwěn   SV: smooth and steady

67. 石級   shíjí   N: stone steps (=1-127石階 shíjiē)

page 188

68. 嗔怪地   chēnguàide   A: rebukingly, scoldingly (14-126)

69. 險些兒   xiǎnxiēr   A: almost, nearly

70. 服气(氣)   fúqì   FV: yield, submit

71. 掩飾   yǎnshì   FV: hide, conceal, cover

72. 口直心快   kǒuzhíxīnkuài   EX: "mouth straightforward, mind quick," quick-witted, sharp (in speech)

page 189

73. 一个(個)不小心   yíge bùxiaǒxīn PH: "as soon as he didn't pay attention" (=一不小心 yí bùxiaǒxīn)

74. 稳(穩)住   wěnzhù   RC: steady, make firm (19-66)

*75. 外婆   waìpó   N: maternal grandmother (= 外祖母 waìzǔmǔ; 3-135)

76. 蕙、   Huì   N: (人名)

77. 芸   Yún   N: (人名)

*78. 去世   qùshì   FV: pass away, die (14-12)

*79. 光陰   guāngyin   N: "light and shade," time

80. 怀(懷)念、   huaínià   FV/N: think of longingly, remember with nostalgia/memory

81. 感、慨   gǎnkaǐ   SV: deeply touched

82. 筵席   yánxí   N: feast, banquet (17-37)

*83. 依然、   yīrán   A: as before, as usual, still (1-126)

84. 树(樹)倒猢狲散   shù daǒ húsūn sàn EX: "when the tree topples over the monkeys disperse"

85. 怨气（氣）　　　yuànqi　　　N: displeasure, malcontent (2-29)

86. 套　　　　　　　tào　　　　FV/M: cover, envelop/set (of cups, clothing, etc.)

<u>page 190</u>

87. 疑惧（懼）　　　yíjù　　　　N: doubt and fear, anxiety

88. 蕩桨（槳）　　　dàngjiǎng　VO: paddle with oars (3-111, 19-48)

89. 沉〔沈〕寂　　　chénjí　　　N: stillness, quiet (1-111)

90. 开（開）朗　　　kāilǎng　　FV: clear up (e.g., the sky; 10-20)

91. 浩大　　　　　　hàodà　　　SV: great, vast, expansive

92. 显（顯）明　　　xiǎnmíng　SV: clear, apparent

93. 謝　　　　　　　xiè　　　　FV: wither, die, fall off (of flowers)

94. 余（餘）香　　　yúxiāng　　PH: lingering fragrance (5-4)

95. 斜坡　　　　　　xiépō　　　N: slope (5-32, 19-40)

96. 堤　　　　　　　tí　　　　　N: dike, embankment

97. 池　　　　　　　chí　　　　N: pool, pond

98. 桥（橋）洞　　　qiáodòng　N: arch under a bridge

99. 景致〔緻〕　　　jǐngzhì　　N: scenery

<u>page 191</u>

100. 姑少爷（爺）　gūshàoyé　N: (here) husband

101. 噘〔撅〕嘴　　juēzuǐ　　　VO: protrude one's lips, pout

102. 酸痛　　　　　suāntòng　N: dull ache, soreness

103. 天足　　　　　tiānzú　　　N: natural feet (as opposed to 纏足 chánzú or 5-69 纏脚 chǎnjiǎo 'bound feet')

104. 新房　　　　　xīnfáng　　N: bridal chamber

105. 板子　　　　　bǎnzi　　　N: wooden plank (here, for spanking), paddle

106. 眠　　　　　　　　mián　　　　　BF: to sleep (15-127)

107. 夸(誇)光耀[火耀]　kuāyaò　　　FV: flaunt, show off

page 192

108. 預[豫]許　　　　　yùxǔ　　　　FV: promise beforehand, predict

109. 殘廢　　　　　　　cánfeì　　　FV: be crippled

110. 出气(氣)　　　　　chūqì　　　　VO: vent one's anger

111. 空洞　　　　　　　kōngdòng　　SV: empty, hollow

112. 發育　　　　　　　fāyù　　　　FV: grow, develop (physically)

113. 劝(勸)慰　　　　　quànweì　　FV: comfort (someone who is upset), console

114. 泣訴　　　　　　　qìsù　　　　FV: tell one's sorrows or grievances in tears (4-3)

115. 凝聚　　　　　　　níngjù　　　FV: gather together, concentrate

page 193

116. 漫　　　　　　　　màn　　　　BF: overflowing, boundless, vast

*117. 惊(驚)恐　　　　jīngkǒng　　SV: fearful, afraid

118. 波紋　　　　　　　bōwén　　　N: "wave pattern," ripple (14-51, 19-34)

119. 光滑　　　　　　　guānghuá　SV: glossy and smooth, polished

120. 風波　　　　　　　fēngbō　　　N: disturbance, incident (14-51)

121. 俯瞰　　　　　　　fǔkàng　　　FV: gaze downward, overlook (6-200)

122. 垣墙(牆)　　　　　yuánqiáng　N: wall (M: 道 daò, 堵 dǔ)

page 194

123. 許可　　　　　　　xǔkě　　　　N/FV: permission, consent/permit

124. 龙(龍)　　　　　　Lóng　　　　N: (人名)

125. 聖賢之書　　　　　shèngxiánzhīshū　EX: classics by sages and virtuous men

126. 肉麻　　　　　　roùmá　　　　　N/SV: "one's flesh goosebumpy," disgust, revolt/disgusting, revolting, coarse

127. 明如白日　　　　míngrúbáirì　　　EX: "bright as daylight," clear as day, very obvious

128. 側面　　　　　　cèmian　　　　　PW: side, flank (3-44)

129. 別　　　　　　　bié　　　　　　A: additionally, another (here, = 另外 lìngwaì)

130. 情趣　　　　　　qíngqù　　　　　N: emotion, feeling, sentiment

131. 湯圓兒　　　　　tāngyuár　　　　N: sweet glutinous rice balls, dumplings

page 195

*132. 几（幾）时（時）　jǐshí　　　　　A: what time, when (14-95)

133. 号（號）外　　　haòwaì　　　　　N: extra, special edition (of a newspaper; M: 張 zhāng)

134. 莫名其妙　　　　mòmíngqímiaò　　EX: "no name its strangeness," be baffled, be puzzled (also written 莫明其妙; 1-74)

135. 国（國）民公报(報)　Guómín Gōngbaò　N: National Day (name of a newspaper)

136. 討伐　　　　　　taǒfá　　　　　FV: make war against so as to vindicate one's authority, punish militarily

*137. 軍长（長）　　　jūnzhǎng　　　　N: army commander

138. 前綫［線］　　　qiánxiàn　　　　N: front line (of a war)

CHAPTER TWENTY

page 196

1. 打败仗	dǎ baìzhàng	PH:	be defeated in war
2. 巷战(戰)	xiàngzhàn	N:	alley warfare, fighting in the streets
*3. 放弃(棄)	fàngqì	FV:	let go of, relinquish, abandon (12-76)
4. 地盘(盤)	dìpán	N:	region under one's sphere of influence, territory
5. 心上心下	xīnshàngxīnxià	EX:	"heart up, heart down," very excited
6. 徬徨無主	pánghuángwúzhǔ	EX:	anxious and not knowing what to do

page 197

7. 慌張	huāngzhāng	SV:	nervous and excited, panicky (1-40)
8. 接二連三	jiē'èrliánsān	EX:	"connected two, joined three," one after the other, continuously
9. 鮮血淋々	xiānxuèlínlín	EX:	"fresh blood drip-drip," drenched with fresh blood, all bloody
10. 烂(火闌)	làn	FV:	pulp, mangle (18-25)
11. 太陽穴	taìyángxuè	N:	temple (of the head)
12. 可怖	kěbù	SV:	frightening, terrifying
13. 但願	dànyuàn	PH:	"only hope," hope very much

page 198

*14. 索性	suǒxìng	A:	might as well
15. 全武行	quánwǔháng	N:	brawl, free-for-all (originally a type of fighting scene in a play)

16. 一道	yídaò	A:	together
17. 杠［槓］子	gàngzi	N:	crossbar, door bolt
18. 优（優）劣	yōuliè	N:	good and bad (of something)

page 199

19. 怦々	pēngpēng	ON:	(sound of the heart beating excitedly)
20. 消夜	xiaōyè	N:	snack eaten at night, midnight snack (also written 宵夜)
21. 地窖	dìjiaò	N:	cellar, underground vault
22. 挨	aí	FV:	wait out (1-102)
23. 傳述	chuánshù	FV:	spread orally, make known
24. 惊（驚）天动（動）地	jīngtiāndòngdì	EX:	"frighten heaven, move the earth," world-shaking, earth-shattering, tremendous
25. 突（災）禍	zaīhuò	N:	calamity, disaster, misery
26. 伤（傷）口	shāngkoǔ	N:	wound
27. 搐动（動）	choūdòng	FV:	shake involuntarily, have a spasm or convulsion, quiver
28. 滩（灘）	tān	M:	pool (of water, blood, etc.)
*29. 蒼白	cāngbaí	SV:	pale, pallid

page 200

30. 失神	shīshén	VO:	"lose spirit," not pay attention, be absent-minded
31. 悄然	qiaōrán	A:	quietly (9-90)
32. 若干	ruògān	ADJ:	a certain amount of, several
33. 槍子	qiāngzǐ	N:	gun bullets (usually pronounced 槍子兒 qiāngzǐr)
34. 嗤々	chīchī	ON:	"whoosh," "hiss" (sound of bullets singing through the air; 10-53)

*35. 完了   wánle   IE: "it's all over," "we're
                                             finished" (i.e., there
                                             is no hope left)

36. 嘩啦   huālā   ON: (sound of thunderous noise)

37. 粒   lì   M: kernel (for beads, grains
                                             of rice, etc.)

38. 鉄（鐵）沙   tiěshā   N: shrapnel

39. 坍   tān   FV: collapse, cave in

40. 我們死定了   wǒmen sǐdìngle   PH: "We'll die for sure"
                                             (＝我們一定要死了
                                             wǒmen yídìng yào sǐle; the
                                             verbal suffix 定 dìng
                                             indicates the certainty of
                                             the action of the verb; 3-55)

*41. 挨   aī   FV: suffer (something; 1-102,
                                             20-22)

42. 跺[跥]脚[脚]   duòjiǎo   VO: stamp one's feet

page 201

*43. 悲惨（慘）   beīcǎn   SV: tragic, pathetic (4-1, 6-73)

44. 呼号（號）   hūhaó   FV/N: cry, wail

45. 絞痛   jiaǒtòng   FV: afflict with a "twisting"
                                             or gripping pain (2-66)

*46. 脆弱   cuìruò   SV: weak, fragile, delicate (3-161)

47. 喊杀（殺）声（聲）   hǎnshāshēng   N: "shout 'kill!' voices," voices
                                             of soldiers shouting "kill,
                                             kill" in close-range combat

48. 惊（驚）号（號）   jīnghaó   N: cry of alarm (20-44)

49. 冲（衝）锋   chōngfēng   FV: charge (in an attack; 15-62)

50. 閃耀[燿]   shǎnyaò   FV: flash, sparkle (1-91)

51. 跳躍   tiaòyuè   FV: jump, leap, hop

52. 腥   xīng   SV: rank, smelling like stale
                                             meat or fish

*53. 瘋狂   fēngkuáng   SV: mad, crazy (3-90, 9-53)

54. 渴血	kěxuè	PH: thirst for blood, be bloodthirsty
55. 猛兽（獸）	měngshòu	N: ferocious beast (18-79)
56. 田坎	tiánkǎn	N: small path in the fields
57. 拿…作儿戏（戲戲）	ná…zuò érxì	PH: "take…as child's play," treat lightly
58. 激斗（鬪、鬥）	jīdòu	FV: struggle very excitedly

page 202

59. 镇住	zhènzhù	RC: calm down, compose one-self (16-18)
60. 火柴	huǒchái	N: match (for lighting fires; = 洋火 yánghuo; M: 根 gēn)
61. 豆大	dòudà	ADJ: as big as a bean, bean-size
62. 摇晃	yáohuàng	FV: shake violently
63. 震撼	zhènhàn	FV: shake violently
64. 轧々	yàyà	ON: (sound of creaking)

page 203

65. 天际（際）	tiānjì	N: horizon
66. 無恙	wúyàng	PH: without disease or injury, unharmed
67. 屋脊	wūjǐ	N: "backbone" or ridge of a house roof
68. 绝迹 [跡、蹟]	juéjī	VO: disappear without a trace, vanish (P-17, 1-71)
69. 大清早	dà qīngzǎo	A: early in the morning
70. 蓬松（鬆）	péngsōng	ADJ: disheveled, tangled (hair)
71. 倦容	juànróng	N: tired look or countenance (1-117)
72. 打中	dǎzhòng	RC: hit (of a bullet, arrow, etc.; 6-61)
73. 奔	bēn	FV: flee, run (P-26)

*74. 千万（萬）   qiānwàn   A: "by a thousand ten thou-
                                        sands",by all means, be
                                        sure to

75. 提防   tífáng   FV: take precautions, be on
                                         the alert

76. 頓挫   dùncuò   N: rising and falling (of
                                        the voice or of music)

page 204

77. 稳（穩）重   wěnzhòng   SV: steady and calm, digni-
                                         fied (19-66, 19-74)

78. 通行無阻   tōngxíng wúzǔ   PH: "through movement, no
                                         obstruction," unobstructed
                                         travel everywhere

79. 惊（驚）慌   jīnghuāng   SV: frightened and confused,
                                         in a panic (1-40)

80. 兵工厂（廠）   bīnggōngchǎng   N: arsenal

81. 省方   shěngfāng   N: the provincial side, the
                                        authorities

82. 領事   lǐngshì   N: consul

83. 調停   tiáotíng   FV: settle a dispute, mediate

84. 下野   xiàyě   VO: "descend to the commoners,"
                                         quit, resign (of an offi-
                                         cial from an official post)

85. 虛惊（驚）   xūjīng   N: "empty fear," false alarm,
                                        needless scare

86. 家常衣服   jiācháng yīfu   N: ordinary plain clothes
                                        (such as those worn commonly
                                        around the house)

page 205

87. 張惶   zhānghuáng   SV: in a panic, alarmed (also
                                         written 張皇 ; 6-115, 20-7)

88. 非常   fēicháng   ADJ: (here) "not ordinary,"
                                          extraordinary, unusual (this
                                          is the original meaning of
                                          the word; now, it is usually
                                          an adverb and means 'very',

as in 非常好 fēicháng hǎo, literally 'not the ordinary good but a special kind of good--extremely good')

89. 起身	qǐshēn	VO:	get up
90. 霹靂	pīlì	N:	thunderclap, sudden great noise (as of thunder and explosions)
91. 驟雨	zòuyǔ	N:	sudden rainstorm, shower (4-94)
92. 机(機)关(關)槍	jīguānqiāng	N:	machine gun (M: 架 jià)
93. 步槍	bùqiāng	N:	rifle (M: 桿 gǎn)
94. 尊	zūn	M:	(for cannons and Buddhist statues)
95. 板壁	bǎnbì	N:	wall made of wooden boards that partitions a house or room
96. 边(邊)沿	biānyán	N:	border, edge
97. 哀号(號)	aīhaó	N/FV:	sad lament, wail of grief/ cry out sadly (6-73, 20-44)
98. 勃發	bófā	FV:	break out, begin suddenly

page 206

99. 惨(慘)白	cǎnbaí	SV:	pale with grief, dreadfully pale (4-1)
100. 臉無人色	liǎnwúrénsè	EX:	"face does not have human color," very pale-faced
101. 炮[砲、礮]子	paòzǐ	N:	cannon shell (usually pronounced 炮子兒 paòzǐr; 20-33)
102. 打穿	dǎchuān	RC:	hit through from one side to the other (the RE 穿 chuān means 'through'; 5-72)

page 207

103. 步哨	bùshaò	N:	sentry, guard

104. 生机（機）	shēngjī	N:	vitality, life
105. 黄昏	huánghūn	N:	dusk
106. 面紗	miànshā	N:	face veil (for women)
107. 神秘	shénmì	SV:	mysterious, mystical
108. 紅霞	hóngxiá	PH:	red clouds (as in the evening at sunset)
109. 薔薇	qiángweí	N:	rambler rose (type of climbing rose)
110. 暮靄	mù'aǐ	N:	evening mist
111. 傍	bàng	FV:	go by the side of, go near (1-20)
112. 丛（叢）	cōng	BF:	grove, bush, thicket (8-88, 19-21)
113. 复（覆）盖（蓋）	fùgaì	FV:	cover

page 208

114. 由 … 而 … 而	yóu...ér...ér	PT:	from...to...to (here 由密而稀而暫時停止了 yóu mì ér xī ér zhànshí tǐngzhǐle means 'from being dense became scattered, and then temporarily stopped'; for 稀 xī cf. 11-92)
115. 凉［涼］意	liángyì	N:	feeling of coldness, chilliness (7-109, 13-36)
116. 簪立	sǒnglì	FV:	rise up, tower (5-6, 8-102)
117. 白灿（燦）々	baícàncàn	PH:	white and bright, resplendent (17-72)
118. 桃树（樹）	taóshù	N:	peach tree (M: 棵 kē)
119. 困居	kùnjū	PH:	live under great hardships (often because of war)
120. 分心	fēnxīn	VO:	distract
*121. 倚	yǐ	FV:	lean against
122. 眺望	tiaòwàng	FV:	look at from far away, stare at

123. 恰似人　　qiàsì　　　PH: just like, just as if
　　　　　　　　　　　　　　　(9-144, 13-23)

124. 匹　　　　pǐ　　　　　M: (for waves and mountains;
　　　　　　　　　　　　　　　四川 ; used in Standard
　　　　　　　　　　　　　　　Mandarin for horses)

125. 浪　　　　làng　　　　N: (ocean) wave

126. 垂柳　　　chuíliǔ　　　N: weeping willow (2-14)

127. 綰住　　　wǎnzhù　　　RC: bind up, knot together

page 209

128. 心如死灰　xīnrúsǐhuī　EX: "heart like dead ashes,"
　　　　　　　　　　　　　　　feel that no hope is left

129. 私房話　　sīfánghuà　　N: private or personal talk

130. 庄(莊)重　zhuāngzhòng　SV: dignified, solemn

page 210

131. 抿嘴　　　mǐnzuǐ　　　A: pursing and spreading
　　　　　　　　　　　　　　　one's lips slightly

132. 表孃[娘]々　biǎoniángniáng　N: maternal aunt (= 阿姨 āyí;
　　　　　　　　　　　　　　　2-40)

133. 年头(頭)　niántou　　　N: year (here, of age; reck-
　　　　　　　　　　　　　　　oned by counting both the
　　　　　　　　　　　　　　　year of a person's birth
　　　　　　　　　　　　　　　and the year at hand; thus,
　　　　　　　　　　　　　　　if 海臣 Hǎichén had, for
　　　　　　　　　　　　　　　example, been born in No-
　　　　　　　　　　　　　　　vember, 1917, and it were
　　　　　　　　　　　　　　　now January, 1921, he would
　　　　　　　　　　　　　　　have five 年頭 niántou
　　　　　　　　　　　　　　　but not yet--not until No-
　　　　　　　　　　　　　　　vember, 1921--four 歲 suì;
　　　　　　　　　　　　　　　4-44)

134. 岔开(開)　chàkai　　　FV: divert attention

CHAPTER TWENTY-ONE[1]

<u>page 211</u>

1. 損害	sǔnhài	N/FV:	damage
2. 开(開)花炮彈	kaīhuāpaòdàn	N:	fragmentation bomb
3. 只(隻)身	zhīshēn	ADJ:	alone, all by oneself
*4. 允許	yǔnxǔ	N/FV:	permission/permit (7-109)
*5. 挑	tiaō	FV:	carry on one's shoulder with a pole (16-24)
*6. 全副	quánfù	ADJ:	complete, entire (as of a person's skill, energy, etc.)
*7. 本領	běnlǐng	N:	ability, skill
8. 可口	kěkoǔ	SV:	"can mouth," palatable, edible, delectable (cf. the Chinese translation of the soft drink Coca-cola: 可口可樂 Kěkoǔkělè, literally 'palatable and enjoyable')
9. 胃口	weìkoǔ	N:	appetite

<u>page 212</u>

10. 不期地	bùqǐde	A:	unexpectedly (12-120)
*11. 抑或	yìhuò	A:	or
12. 飯量	fànliàng	N:	capacity for eating, appetite
13. 非有...不	feī yoǔ...bù	PT:	if there isn't...not, must have

---

[1]Note: starting with the notes to this chapter, the asterisk (*) no longer indicates only items that reoccur three times or more but all items that reoccur at least once in the remainder of the book (see <u>Abbreviations and Conventions Employed</u>, p.xvi.)

14. 下咽〔嚥〕   xiàyàn   FV: get down one's throat, swallow (3-103)

15. 豆腐   dòufu   N: bean curd (14-100)

16. 豆花   dòuhuā   N: type of very watery bean curd of custard-like consistency, eaten as a dessert or snack

17. 断（斷）絕   duànjué   FV: break off, sever (6-67)

*18. 触（觸）   chù   FV: butt, knock against (15-15)

19. 示意   shìyì   VO: indicate one's wish or intention (usually by facial expression or gestures), signal

20. 岔嘴   chàzuǐ   VO: interrupt, butt in (a conversation; 2-68, 20-134)

*21. 努嘴   nǔzuǐ   VO: protrude one's lips, pout

22. 东（東）張西望   dōngzhāngxīwàng   EX: "(to the) east look, (to the) west gaze," look in all directions (3-26)

23. 时（時）事   shíshì   N: current events

24. 三岔路口   sānchàlùkoǔ   N: junction where three roads meet (20-134, 21-20)

25. 栅子   zhàzi   N: series of upright posts across a street, barricade (12-72)

page 213

*26. 謙遜   qiānxùn   SV: humble, modest (7-142)

27. 德不足以服人，才不足以济（濟）变（變）   dé bùzú yǐ fú rén, caí bùzú yǐ jì biàn   PH: "virtue not sufficient to make men obey, talent not sufficient to alleviate distress"

28. 醸   niàng   FV: "brew, ferment," lead slowly to, form gradually

29. 苦我将（將）士，劳（勞）我人民   kǔ wǒ jiàngshì, laó wǒ rénmín   PH: "distress my generals and men, trouble my people"

30. 决﹝決﹞意、   juéyì   FV: make up one's mind, decide

31. 糜烂（火闌）   mílàn   FV: devastate, lay waste to

32. 兵临（臨）城下   bīnglínchéngxià   EX: "soldiers approach beneath
                                            city wall," soldiers have
                                            arrived just outside the
                                            city

*33. 扯   chě   FV: tug, pull (1-2)

34. 不要命   búyaò mìng   PH: "not want (your) life,"
                                            want to die

*35. 庙（廟）宇   miaòyǔ   N: temple (M: 所 suǒ; 12-37)

36. 逆军   nìjūn   N: rebellious troops

37. 师﹝師﹞长﹝長﹞   shīzhǎng   N: division commander (in
                                            the military)

38. 痛陈（陳）   tòngchén   PH: state severely, denunciate

*39. 礼﹝禮﹞教   lǐjiaò   N: traditional ethical teach-
                                            ings (3-4)

40. 帅﹝帥﹞   shuaì   BF: military commander (FF: 統
                                            帥 tǒngshuaì; distinguish
                                            帥 and 21-37 師 shī)

41. 吁（籲）請   yùqǐng   FV: request, beseech

42. 领衔   lǐngxián   FV: be the first to sign on a
                                            list of signatures (16-50)

page 214

43. 抄过（過）去   chaōguoqu   RC: cut across, take a short cut

44. 走哪兒去   zoǔ naǔ qù   PH: "Where are you going?" (= 到
                                            哪兒去 daò naǔ qù; 四川)

*45. 恶（惡）狠々   èhěnhěn   A: savagely, meanly (12-102)

*46. 禁不住   jīnbuzhù   RC: unable to withstand, cannot
                                            help but (3-13)

47. 剛々   gānggāng   A: (here) just, exactly

*48. 心腸   xīncháng   N: mood, state of mind (14-35)

page 215

49. 缺陷　　　　　　quēxiàn　　　　N: defect, inadequacy

50. 一片新綠　　　　yípiàn xīnlù　　PH: "an expanse of fresh
　　　　　　　　　　　　　　　　　　　　greenery" (15-133)

*51. 画〔畫〕眉　　　huàméi　　　　　N: thrush (bird; M: 隻 zhī)

52. 指头〔頭〕　　　zhítou　　　　　N: finger (16-53)

53. 袷〔裌〕衫　　　jiáshān　　　　 N: shirt-like garment with
　　　　　　　　　　　　　　　　　　　　a lining (M: 件 jiàn;
　　　　　　　　　　　　　　　　　　　　=15-81 夾衫 jiáshān)

54. 問个〔個〕明白　wèn'ge míngbai　PH: "ask an understanding one,"
　　　　　　　　　　　　　　　　　　　　ask something so that one
　　　　　　　　　　　　　　　　　　　　can understand (15-136)

55. 草坪　　　　　　caǒpíng　　　　 N: grassy and level piece of
　　　　　　　　　　　　　　　　　　　　ground, lawn (M:塊 kuaì)

page 216

56. 稀落地　　　　　xīluòde　　　　 A: sparsely scattered (11-92,
　　　　　　　　　　　　　　　　　　　　14-46)

57. 撫弄　　　　　　fǔnòng　　　　　FV: handle, stroke (10-79)

58. 扇动〔動〕　　　shāndòng　　　　FV: move back and forth, flutter
　　　　　　　　　　　　　　　　　　　　(1-140)

*59. 垂死　　　　　　chuísǐ　　　　 ADJ: near death, dying (2-14)

60. 蝴蝶　　　　　　húdié　　　　　 N: butterfly (M: 隻 zhī)

*61. 饒恕　　　　　　raóshù　　　　　FV: forgive, pardon (14-86)

*62. 苦涩〔澀〕　　　kǔsè　　　　　 SV: bitter, harsh (12-36)

63. 亏〔虧〕負　　　kuīfu　　　　　 FV: be deficient in friendship,
　　　　　　　　　　　　　　　　　　　　wrong someone

*64. 爱〔愛〕撫　　　aìfǔ　　　　　　FV: caress lovingly (10-79)

*65. 好容易　　　　　haǒ róngyi　　 PH: very difficult (= 好不容易
　　　　　　　　　　　　　　　　　　　　haǒ bùróngyi, but even more
　　　　　　　　　　　　　　　　　　　　emphatic; depending on con-
　　　　　　　　　　　　　　　　　　　　text, a 不 bù occurring
　　　　　　　　　　　　　　　　　　　　after 好 haǒ 'very' some-
　　　　　　　　　　　　　　　　　　　　times--perhaps by irony--
　　　　　　　　　　　　　　　　　　　　does not negate it)

page 217

*66. 怜（憐）惜   liánxī   FV: pity, feel tender regard for (someone)

67. 双（雙）关（關）   shuāngguān   ADJ: ambiguous, interpretable in two ways

*68. 扎   zā   FV: bind, fasten (14-24, 18-40)

69. 洋头（頭）绳   yángtoúshéng   N: (piece of) woolen yarn imported from abroad (M: 根 gēn)

*70. 告别   gaòbié   VO: part, say farewell (18-20)

*71. 掏出   taōchū   RC: draw out, pull out

page 218

72. 心乱（亂）如麻   xīnluànrúmá   EX: "heart tangled like flax," extremely confused and disturbed (2-93, 14-87)

73. 拊心   fǔxīn   VO: touch one's hand lightly to one's chest (an expression of distress)

74. 追悔   zhuīhuǐ   FV: regret (10-74)

75. 嫌疑   xiányí   N: suspicion

*76. 为（爲）…着想   weì…zhaóxiǎng   PH: look after the interests of, think of (someone)

*77. 何等   héděng   A: how, to what degree (= 多麽 duōma)

78. 失悔   shīhuǐ   FV: regret, be sorry

page 219

79. 忖度   cǔnduò   FV: consider, try to gauge what is on another's mind

80. 打青草滚   dǎ qīngcaǒgǔn   PH: roll around on green grass

81. 吮   shǔn   FV: suck, lick

82. 采（採）   caǐ   FV: pick, collect (flowers, mulberry leaves, etc.)

83. 指甲花   zhǐjiahuā   N: balsam flowers (so called because 指甲 'fingernail' polish is made from them)

84. 月食虫   yuèshí   N: lunar eclipse

85. 追忆（憶）   zhuīyì   FV: think back to, recall

86. 年光   niánguāng   N: years, time (19-79)

*87. 保重   baǒzhòng   FV: take good care of (one-self; often said when parting with someone)

*88. 哭肿（腫）   kūzhǒng   RC: cry so much as to make (the eyes) swollen (4-82)

page 220

89. 分别   fēnbié   FV/N/A: (here) be separated from, part with (usually: 'differentiate')/difference/ separately

90. 相对（對）而泣   xiāngduì'érqì   EX: "mutually facing to cry," cry in front of one another (4-3)

91. 宽心   kuānxīn   VO: set one's mind at rest, free oneself from anxiety

*92. 扶   fú   FV: hold up, support

*93. 要好   yaòhaǒ   SV: have a close relationship, get along well with (of friends and lovers)

CHAPTER TWENTY-TWO

*1. 馬主扎（紮）   zhùzhā   FV: camp at, be stationed at (of troops; 21-68)

2. 新委任   xīn wěirèn   PH: newly appointed or commissioned (12-109)

3. 三五成群〔羣〕   sānwǔchéngqún   EX: "in threes and fives forming groups," in groups of several people each

4. 狼狽   lángbeì   SV: helpless, desperate (according to tradition, the 狽, a type of wolf with short forelegs, often rode with its paws on the back of the 狼, a wolf with short hindlegs; describes helpless dependence and desperation)

5. 裹腿   guǒtuǐ   N: gaiter, legging (distinguish 裹 and 裏 lǐ)

6. 番号（號）   fānhaò   N: numerical designation of a military unit

*7. 掮   qián   FV: carry on one's shoulder

8. 找人寻（尋）事   zhaǒrénxúnshì   EX: "look for people, search for incidents," look for trouble, try to incite something (6-146)

9. 故技   gùjì   N: old trick

*10. 排   paí   N: platoon (of soldiers)

11. 开（開）拔   kaībá   FV: break up, move, depart (of troops; 14-129)

12. 打發   dǎfā   FV: dispatch, send off

page 222

*13. 承　　　　　　　chéng　　　　　FV: receive (14-73)

*14. 厚待　　　　　　hòudài　　　　　N/FV: generous treatment/treat
　　　　　　　　　　　　　　　　　　　　generously

*15. 过（過）意不去　guòyibúqù　　　SV: sorry, uncomfortable (often
　　　　　　　　　　　　　　　　　　　　because of someone else's
　　　　　　　　　　　　　　　　　　　　favors)

*16. 缓　　　　　　　huǎn　　　　　　FV: delay, postpone (15-34)

17. 过（過）府　　　guòfǔ　　　　　PH: drop by (someone's house;
　　　　　　　　　　　　　　　　　　　　= 到府上去 dào fǔshang qù)

18. 傳諭　　　　　　chuányù　　　　FV: relay information, give
　　　　　　　　　　　　　　　　　　　　instructions through another
　　　　　　　　　　　　　　　　　　　　(=20-23 傳述 chuánshù)

19. 掛（掛）念　　　guàniàn　　　　FV: worry, be anxious

20. 即刻　　　　　　jíkè　　　　　　A: immediately (17-44)

*21. 挽留　　　　　　wǎnliú　　　　　FV: detain, hold back (10-49)

22. 安閑（閒）　　　ānxián　　　　　SV: leisurely, serene

23. 不知不覺（覺）地 bùzhībùjuéde　　EX: "not know, not feelingly,"
　　　　　　　　　　　　　　　　　　　　unaware, unconsciously (3-153)

24. 降临（臨）　　　jiànglín　　　　FV: descend, approach

*25. 謠言　　　　　　yáoyán　　　　　N: rumor (8-42)

26. 搶劫　　　　　　qiǎngjié　　　　FV: rob, take by force (7-83,
　　　　　　　　　　　　　　　　　　　　12-54)

*27. 首富　　　　　　shǒufù　　　　　N: richest household (of an area)

28. 首当（當）其冲（衝）shǒudāngqíchōng EX: "first to face its upheaval,"
　　　　　　　　　　　　　　　　　　　　first to bear the brunt of
　　　　　　　　　　　　　　　　　　　　(15-62)

page 223

*29. 不好　　　　　　bùhǎo　　　　　AV: feel embarrassed or ill at
　　　　　　　　　　　　　　　　　　　　ease (to do something; here
　　　　　　　　　　　　　　　　　　　　= 不好意思 bùhǎoyìsi)

30. 老丈人　　　　　lǎozhàngren　　N: father-in-law (of a man)

31. 大难(難)临(臨)头(頭)　dà'nànlíntoú　EX: "great calamity approaches head," disaster is almost at hand (6-198)

32. 好人得恶(惡)报(報)　haǒ rén dé èbaò　PH: a good person receives evil retribution

33. 遭禍事　zaō huòshì　PH: suffer calamity, meet with disaster (8-97)

34. 浴　yù　FV: bathe, take a bath in

page 224

*35. 知觉(覺)　zhǐjué　N: consciousness

36. 禱祝　daǒzhù　FV: pray (6-58, 6-62)

37. 时(時)刻　shíkè　N: times

38. 待决〔決〕　daìjué　PH: await execution (a criminal)

39. 死刑囚　sǐxíngqiú　N: prisoner who has been sentenced to death (6-117, 10-1)

40. 避难(難)　bì'nàn　VO: avoid trouble, escape calamity

41. 顫栗〔慄〕　zhànlì　FV: tremble with fear (also written 戰栗 ; 3-41)

*42. 嬉戏〔戲、虛〕　xīxì　FV: play merrily (17-20)

43. 思潮　sīchaó　N: prevailing way of thinking, popular ideas (11-4)

44. 爱(愛)倫·凯　Aìlún Kaǐ　N: Ellen Key (1849-1926), Swedish essayist and educator who advocated freedom of speech and women's liberation (P-9)

45. 与(與)謝野晶子　Yǔxièyě Jīngzǐ　N: Akiko Yosano (1878-1941), Japanese romantic poet who was popular in China during the 1920's (10-68)

46. 奇耻大辱　qíchǐdàrù　EX: "extraordinary shame, great insult," outrage and humiliation (11-46)

page 225

*47. 躺椅　　　　　　tǎngyǐ　　　　　N: reclining chair (M: 把 bǎ)

*48. 悲伤（傷）　　　bēishāng　　　　FV: be sad or sorrowful about

49. 惨（慘）淡（澹）地 cǎndànde　　　A: laboriously, ardently (4-15)

page 226

*50. 宰割　　　　　　zǎigē　　　　　　FV: butcher, slaughter

51. 凝固　　　　　　nínggù　　　　　　FV: congeal (19-115)

52. 失火　　　　　　shīhuǒ　　　　　　VO: catch fire

53. 蚕（蠶）食　　　cánshí　　　　　　FV: eat away at (like a silkworm on a mulberry leaf), encroach steadily on (11-91)

54. 小半　　　　　　xiǎobàn　　　　　ADJ/N: smaller half

*55. 当（當）铺　　　dàngpu　　　　　　N: pawnshop

page 227

56. 改装（裝）　　　gǎizhuāng　　　　VO: change into different clothes, disguise oneself

57. 照管　　　　　　zhàoguǎn　　　　　FV: take care of, manage

58. 一把火　　　　　yìbǎ huǒ　　　　　PH: "with a handful of fire"

*59. 嘶声（聲）　　　sīshēng　　　　　A: with a hoarse voice

60. 未必　　　　　　wèibì　　　　　　A: not necessarily (=不一定 bùyídìng)

61. 变（變）兵　　　biànbīng　　　　　N: mutinous troops

62. 一死　　　　　　yìsǐ　　　　　　　PH: "a dying"

63. 留一个（個）种（種）liú yíge zhǒng　PH: "keep a seed," leave someone to continue the family line

64. 悲愤　　　　　　bēifèn　　　　　　N: grief and resentment (6-73, 12-84)

*65. 保护（護）　　　bǎohù　　　　　　FV/N: guard, protect/protection

page 228

66. 衣襟〔衿〕 yījīn   N: lapel or lower corner of a garment

*67. 恳（懇）求 kěnqiú   FV: earnestly entreat, beseech

*68. 看在···面上 kànzai...miànshang   PH: consider (someone's) interests, do for (someone's) sake

page 229

69. 异（異）乎 yìhū   PH: different from (here, 乎 hū is a CV of place like 在 zai and 於 yú; 17-98)

70. 神奇 shénqí   SV: mysterious, wondrous

71. 滋味 zīwei   N: taste, experience

*72. 柔和 róuhé   SV: soft, gentle, tender (6-87)

73. 警醒 jǐngxǐng   FV/SV: be alert, be quick to awake (4-120)

*74. 噴 pēn   FV: puff out, blow out (6-204)

page 230

1. 疑虑（慮） yílǜ N: apprehension, misgiving

2. 包袱 baōfu N: bundle in a cloth wrapper, burden

3. 頂 dǐng M: (for hats and sedan chairs)

4. 杆（桿） gǎn M: (for rifles, pistols, and spears)

5. 开（開）往 kaīwǎng FV: move to, leave for

6. 光顧 guānggù N: "honorable patronage," presence, visit (polite; here used sarcastically)

7. 筹（籌）划（劃） choúhuà FV: plan (7-35, 17-31)

page 231

*8. 侄［姪］兒 zhír N: nephew

9. 馬弁 mǎbiàn N: low grade military officer who serves as orderly for men of higher rank

10. 汉（漢）子 hànzi N: guy, type (of man)

*11. 傲慢 aòmàn SV/N: haughty, overbearing/haughtiness, arrogance (12-82)

*12. 牙齿（齒） yáchǐ N: tooth

13. 来（來）意 laíyì N: reason for coming, intention

14. 連长（長） liánzhǎng N: company commander (8-32)

*15. 岁（歲）月 suìyuè N: "years and months," years

16. 名誉（譽） míngyù ADJ/N: honorary/reputation, honor

17. 衣冠不整 yīguānbùzhěng EX: "clothes and hat not neat," poorly dressed

18. 敬意、   jìngyì   N: respect, regard (13-36, 20-115)

19. 忌憚   jìdàn   N/FV: fear (the kind that keeps a person from doing wrong), scruples/have scruples about

20. 财产(產)权(權)   cáichǎnquán   N: property right

21. 盒子炮[砲、駁]   hézipaò   N: Mauser pistol (type of hand gun)

22. 士大夫   shìdàfū   N: intelligentsia, literati, gentry

*23. 謹慎   jǐnshèn   N/SV: prudent caution, prudence/careful

24. 明哲保身   míngzhébaǒshēn   EX: "a bright and wise (man) protects (his own) body," a wise man avoids trouble so as to safeguard his personal security

25. 古訓   gǔxùn   N: ancient teaching

26. 努眼睛   nǔ yǎnjing   PH: scowl, glower (21-21)

page 232

*27. 尖   jiān   SV: sharp, pointed (11-84)

28. 沫   mò   N: saliva, spittle

29. 胭脂   yānzhi   N: rouge (type of cosmetic; 9-103)

30. 腰身   yāoshēn   N: waistline (of a garment; 10-83)

31. 瞟一眼   piǎo yìyǎn   PH: give (someone) a quick glance from the side

32. 土娼   tǔchāng   N: local and low class prostitute

33. 不成体(體)統   bùchéng tǐtǒng   PH: improper (of a person's conduct or behavior)

34. 达(達)官貴人   dáguānguìrén   EX: "those who have advanced to the rank of officials, and nobles," prominent and honorable people

35. 消遣   xiaōqiǎn   FV: engage in recreation or diversion, pass away the time

*36. 聚談　　　　　　　jùtán　　　　FV: gather together to converse, speak together

37. 臥[臥]室　　　　　wòshì　　　　N: bedroom (M: 間 jiān; = 臥房 wòfáng; 12-26)

38. 腔調　　　　　　　qiāngdiào　　N: tone of voice

39. 居住权[權]　　　jūzhùquán　　N: right of residence (23-20)

<u>page 233</u>

40. 維护[護]　　　　weíhù　　　　FV: safeguard, preserve, protect

41. 淫乱[亂]　　　　yínluàn　　　SV/N: debauched, depraved/debauchery (11-30)

42. 毒气[氣]　　　　dúqì　　　　N: poison gas

43. 家風　　　　　　　jiāfēng　　　N: family reputation

44. 护[護]法　　　　hùfǎ　　　　VO: uphold the law

45. 厉[厲]声[聲]　　lìshēng　　　A: with a harsh and angry voice

46. 世家　　　　　　　shìjiā　　　N: family that has held official ranks for many generations

47. 声[聲]誉[譽]　　shēngyù　　　N: fame, reputation (23-16)

48. 計較　　　　　　　jìjiào　　　FV: mind, care

49. 捏[捏]一把汗　　niē yìbǎ hàn　PH: "knead one fistful of sweat," be seized with fear or deep concern (1-45)

50. 西充县[縣]　　　Xīchōng Xiàn　PW: (name of a district in Sì-chuan province)

51. 丢　　　　　　　　diū　　　　FV: (here) give up

52. 印　　　　　　　　yìn　　　　N/FV: seal, chop (M: 顆 kē)/print

53. 輕佻　　　　　　　qīngtiaó　　SV: flippant, flirtatious

*54. 辰[脣]　　　　　chún　　　　BF: lip (FF: 7-57 嘴脣 zuǐchún)

55. 丰(豐)腴　　　　fēngyú　　　SV: plump, buxom and fair

56. 媚人　　　　　　　meìrén　　　PH: "please people," attractive (1-19)

page 234

57. 亭亭玉立   tíngtíngyùlì   EX: "pavilion-like stand like jade," tall, slim and graceful (describes the standing figure of a beautiful woman)

*58. 白晳[晰]   báixī   ADJ: white (skin; cf. 3-59, where 晰, an alternate form of 晳, occurs)

59. 瞪眼睛   dèng yǎnjing   PH: stare, look straight ahead at (often in anger)

60. 老子   laōzi   N: "daddy" (here indicates the speaker himself; by calling himself the father of 克明 Kèmíng, the orderly shows great contempt for him, since a father is much superior to his son)

*61. 处(處)置   chǔzhì   FV: manage, settle

62. 非常之糟   feīchángzhīzaō   EX: very much messed up

page 235

*63. 妨   fáng   FV: hinder, obstruct, interfere with (8-27)

64. 护(護)身符   hùshēnfú   N: amulet or charm for self-protection

65. 此風是不可长(長)的   cǐ fēng shi bùkěchángde   PH: "this trend cannot become longer," this sort of thing cannot be allowed to continue

*66. 八字鬍   bázìhú   N: mustache shaped like the character 八 (=6-109 八字鬚 bázìxū)

67. 見扣(機)行事   jiànjīxíngshì   EX: "see opportunity, do things," act as the circumstances dictate

*68. 重复(復)   chóngfù   FV: repeat

69. 操之过(過)激   caōzhīguòjī   EX: "grasp it, surpass overflowing," act too rashly (急 jí is often used here instead of 激 jī)

| 70. 司令部 | sīlìngbù | N: commander's headquarters (8-31) |
| 71. 索取 | suǒqǔ | FV: ask for, obtain |

page 236

72. 师（師）	shī	N: division (military; 21-37)
73. 旅	lǚ	N: brigade (military)
74. 团（團）	tuán	N: regiment (military)
75. 营（營）	yíng	N: battalion (military)
76. 駐此	zhù cǐ	PH: "is stationed here" (文言; 22-1)
77. 字样（樣）	zìyàng	N: characters, words (this expression is used after the characters or words mentioned)

78. 軍长（長）張令：此系民房，禁止駐兵

Jūnzhǎng Zhāng lìng: cǐ xì mínfáng, jìnzhǐ zhù bīng

By order of Commander Zhāng: this is civilian housing, stationing of soldiers forbidden (19-137)

*79. 揮	huī	FV: shake off, wave away (3-29)
*80. 現	xiàn	FV: become manifest, appear (現 is here a verb and not the first syllable of 現在 xiànzài 'now')
81. 可耻	kěchǐ	SV: shameful (11-46)
*82. 嘴巴	zuǐba	N: mouth (cf. 3-58 on the use of the suffix 巴 ba)
83. 厭恶（惡）	yànwu	FV: loath, dislike

page 237

1. 善忘   shànwàng   SV: forgetful, weak of memory (=14-131 健忘、jiànwàng; 11-34)

2. 来（來）訪   laífǎng   PH: coming to visit, visit

*3. 指点（點）   zhǐdiǎn   FV: point out (mistakes or pitfalls), give guidance, advise

page 238

4. 軟[軟]綿[綿]々   ruǎnmiánmián   A: "soft and downy," soft, weak, delicate (1-57, 14-25)

*5. 四肢   sìzhǐ   PH: four limbs, extremities

6. 惊（驚）詫   jīngchà   SV: surprised, startled

*7. 瞞   mán   FV: hide the truth from, deceive

*8. 迸   bèng   FV: burst, gush forth, blurt out

page 239

*9. 伏   fú   FV: bend down

*10. 枕   zhěn   BF: pillow (FF: 枕頭 zhěntou)

11. 起伏   qǐfú   FV: rise up and fall down, undulate, quiver (24-9)

*12. 陷   xiàn   FV: fall or sink into (12-117)

13. 啜泣   chuòqì   FV: sob (10-78)

14. 緣分   yuánfèn   N: fated or predestined relationship between two people

15. 今生   jīnshēng   N: present life (as distinct from past and future lives)

16. 酸辛   suānxīn   N: difficulties, hardships

17. 結果〔菓〕   jiēguǒ   VO: bear fruit (this is the original meaning of 結果 jiēguǒ 'result, outcome'; 18-62)

18. 哀莫大于〔於〕心死   aī mò dà yú xīn sǐ   EX: "of griefs there is none greater than that the heart dies" (from 莊子 Zhuāngzǐ, 田子方篇 Tiánzǐfāng Piān)

page 240

19. 苦楚   kǔchǔ   N: pain, suffering (15-102)

*20. 傾訴   qīngsù   FV: pour out (complaints), get something off one's chest (10-91, 19-114)

21. 杜詩   Dù shī   PH: "a poem by Dù Fǔ" (杜甫 Dù Fǔ [712-770] is one of China's two most famous poets--the other is 李白 Lǐ Baí)

22. 眼枯即見骨

     Yǎn kū jí jiàn gǔ

When the eyes are dry (from weeping) then one sees the bones--

天地終無情

     Tiān dì zhōng wú qíng

But neither in heaven nor on earth is there any compassion at all

(from the poem 新安史 Xīn'ānshǐ by 杜甫 Dù Fǔ)

page 241

23. 心肝   xīn'gān   N: "heart and liver," conscience

*24. 敏感   mǐn'gǎn   SV: sensitive

*25. 花   huā   SV: blurred, smudged

*26. 頑皮   wánpí   N/SV: mischievousness/mischievous, naughty (usually of children)

27. 嫌弃（棄）　　xiánqì　　　FV: throw away in disdain, reject, refuse (12-76, 21-75)

28. 認　　　　　rèn　　　　　FV: recognize (someone as an honorary relative)

*29. 原諒　　　　yuánliàng　　FV: forgive, pardon

page 242

*30. 胸口　　　　xiōngkoǔ　　　N: chest, breast (4-113)

31. 医（醫）治　　yīzhì　　　　FV: cure medically (a disease)

32. 医（醫）迷（斷）根 yīduàngēn　RC: "heal to the point of cutting off the root (of an illness)," cure completely

33. 見效（交力）　jiànxiaò　　FV: be efficacious, have value (見 jiàn here indicates passive)

34. 丸藥（药）　　wányaò　　　N: pill of medicine (M: 丸 wán)

35. 补（補）藥（药）bǔyaò　　　N: "medicine that makes up deficiencies (in the body)," tonic

36. 鏡匣　　　　jìngxiá　　　N: vanity case

page 243

1. 将(將)領　　　jiànglǐng　　　N: high-ranking military officers

2. 从(從)而　　　cóngér　　　A: thereupon, as a result, then

*3. 創刊　　　chuàngkān　　　FV: put out the first issue (of a periodical; 6-165)

*4. 黎明周[週]报(報)　Límíng Zhoūbaò　N: <u>Dawn Weekly</u> (name of a newspaper)

5. 論点(點、点)　　lùndiǎn　　　N: point of discussion, issue

6. 贊助　　　zànzhù　　　FV/N: assist, support/assistance

page 244

7. 中坚(堅)　　　zhōngjiān　　　ADJ: main, most important

8. 高他一班　　　gaō tā yìbān　　　PH: "one class higher than him" (=比他高一班 bǐ tā gaō yìbān; 8-56)

*9. 空幻　　　kōnghuàn　　　SV: illusory, unreal (3-157)

10. 崇高　　　chónggaō　　　SV: lofty, exalted

11. 課余(餘)的时(時)間　kèyúde shíjiān　PH: time left over after classes

*12. 傳播　　　chuánbō　　　FV: spread, disseminate

13. 茶棚　　　chápéng　　　N: tea booth

14. 社友　　　shèyoǔ　　　N: "friends of a society," members of an organization (17-42)

page 245

15. 播种(種)者　　bōzhǒngzhě　　N: sower of seed (25-12)

16. 感染　　　gǎnrǎn　　　FV: become infected or imbued with (10-103, 15-67)

17. 夸（誇）大   kuādà   SV: overconfident, exaggerated

18. 校样（樣）   jiàoyàng   N: galley proof (in printing;
                                              9-55)

*19. 朴（樸）实（實）   pǔshí   SV: simple, plain, honest

20. 园（園）地   yuándì   N: environment, circumstances

21. 摆（擺）出…面孔   bǎichū…miànkǒng PH: display…(kind of) facial
                                              expression (4-50, 4-83)

*22. 狡猾   jiǎohuá   SV: crafty, cunning

*23. 肚皮   dùpí   N: abdomen, belly

24. 子侄[姪]辈   zǐzhíbeì   PH: "generation of the sons
                                              and nephews," younger
                                              generation of children in
                                              a family (23-8)

page 246

*25. 欲望   yùwàng   N: longing, desire

*26. 激情   jīqíng   N: extreme emotion

*27. 献（獻）身   xiànshēn   FV: offer or dedicate oneself
                                              (to some cause)

*28. 渺小   miǎoxiǎo   SV: minute, tiny (17-79)

29. 奋（奮）斗（鬬、鬥）Fèndoù   N: Struggle (name of a magazine
                                              published in 1923 by Chinese
                                              students in France)

30. 半月刊   bànyuèkān   N: semimonthly (publication;
                                              6-165)

*31. 横溢   héngyì   FV: overflow with, be brimming
                                              over with (14-102)

32. 奢侈品   shēchǐpǐn   N: luxury article (12-77)

*33. 恋（戀）爱（愛） liàn'ai   N/FV: romantic love/love roman-
                                              tically (12-32)

34. 輕惹情絲   qīngrěqíngsī   EX: "lightly rouse the silken
                                              ties of love," fall in
                                              love with casually

35. 立誓   lìshì   VO: vow, swear

page 247

*36. 污泥   wūní   N: mud

37. 忠順   zhōngshùn   SV: loyal and obedient (6-43)

*38. 莫大   mòdà   ADJ: "none greater than,"
                                  greatest (1-74, 8-66)

39. 付印   fùyìn   FV: hand over for printing,
                                  send to press for publication

40. 刃鳴   Rènmíng   N: (覺慧 Juéhuì's pen name;
                                  the name seems strange to
                                  琴 Qín because 刃 means
                                  'slaughter with the blade
                                  of a sword' and 鳴 may
                                  refer to 鳴鳳 Míngfèng)

page 248

41. 偏   piān   A: against expectations,
                                  perversely, contrarily
                                  (=14-84 偏々 piānpiān)

42. 口气（氣）   kǒuqi   N: way of speaking, tone of
                                  voice

43. 南犬（獻）丑（醜） xiànchǒu   VO: "offer up one's ugliness,"
                                  show one's poor skill or
                                  talent (polite expression)

44. 鼓吹   gǔchuī   FV: advocate, promote

45. 先鋒   xiānfēng   N: trail-blazer, vanguard

*46. 逼   bī   FV: press, pressure, force (10-26)

47. 常态（態）   chángtai   N: normal way or appearance

page 249

48. 节（節）省   jiéshěng   FV/SV: save (i.e., not waste)/
                                  thrifty, economical

49. 歧視   qíshì   FV/N: "look upon in a different
                                  way," discriminate against/
                                  discrimination

*50. 冤[寃]枉   yuānwang   SV: not worthwhile, in vain

51. 西装（裝）   xǐzhuāng   N: suit, Western clothes
                                  (M: 套 tào)

52. 合身　　　　　　　héshēn　　　　　　SV: well-fitting (of clothes)

*53. 豈但...便是　　　qǐdàn...biànshi　PT: not only...even (7-129)

page 250

*54. 透露　　　　　　　toùlù　　　　　　FV: reveal, disclose (7-28)

55. 迫切　　　　　　　pòqiè　　　　　　SV: urgent

56. 开 (開) 端　　　　kaīduān　　　　　VO/N: begin something, set a
　　　　　　　　　　　　　　　　　　　　　precedent/beginning (10-31)

57. 学 (學) 力　　　　xuélì　　　　　　N: strength or depth of knowl-
　　　　　　　　　　　　　　　　　　　　edge, scholastic ability

58. 深究　　　　　　　shēnjiū　　　　　FV: delve deeply into something,
　　　　　　　　　　　　　　　　　　　　deliberate, study

*59. 障碍 (礙)　　　　zhàng'aì　　　　　N: impediment, obstruction
　　　　　　　　　　　　　　　　　　　　(8-27)

60. 潔白　　　　　　　jiébaí　　　　　　SV: white (3-24)

61. 娟秀　　　　　　　juānxiù　　　　　SV: good-looking, pretty, graceful

62. 字迹 [跡、蹟] zìjī　　　　　　　N: "character traces," hand-
　　　　　　　　　　　　　　　　　　　　writing, characters (5-17)

page 251

63. 按語　　　　　　　ànyǔ　　　　　　N: comments and notes by the
　　　　　　　　　　　　　　　　　　　　editor of a piece of writing

64. 轟动 (動)　　　　hōngdòng　　　　　FV: excite, cause an uproar (9-131)

65. 以身作則　　　　　yǐshēnzuòzé　　　EX: "take one's body, make pattern
　　　　　　　　　　　　　　　　　　　　(for others to follow)," set
　　　　　　　　　　　　　　　　　　　　an example for others

66. 后 (後) 頸　　　　houjǐng　　　　　N: nape, back of the neck (17-69)

67. 截齐 (齊)　　　　jiéqí　　　　　　FV: cut even (hair)

68. 衣領　　　　　　　yīlǐng　　　　　　N: collar (of a piece of clothing)

69. 高談闊 [濶] 論 gaōtánkuòlùn　　EX: "highly speak, broadly dis-
　　　　　　　　　　　　　　　　　　　　cuss," talk in a free, all-
　　　　　　　　　　　　　　　　　　　　embracing, and lively manner

70. 飄逸　　　　　　　piaōyì　　　　　　ADJ: graceful

71. 委瑣　　　　　wěisuǒ　　　　　FV: be petty or insignificant

*72. 清朗　　　　　qīnglǎng　　　　SV: clear and loud (of a person's voice; 19-90)

page 252

73. 嬌小　　　　　jiāoxiǎo　　　　ADJ: delicate, slight (11-75)

74. 贊許　　　　　zànxǔ　　　　　N/FV: approval/approve

*75. 老密斯　　　　lǎomìsī　　　　N: "old miss," old maid (密斯 is a transliteration of English 'miss')

*76. 朗朗地　　　　lǎnglǎngde　　　A: bright and clear, in a resonant voice, loudly (25-72)

page 253

77. 諸如此类(類)　zhūrúcǐlèi　　　EX: "all like this kind," such matters as this

*78. 花样(樣)　　　huāyàng　　　　N: style, fashion

79. 制止　　　　　zhìzhǐ　　　　　FV: control, stop

80. 流氓　　　　　liúmáng　　　　N: hoodlum, villain, rogue

81. 觯身　　　　　tuǒshén　　　　N: flirt, rascal

82. 尼姑　　　　　nígū　　　　　N: Buddhist nun (the comparison is made because nuns had their heads shaved; 5-61)

*83. 屁股　　　　　pìgu　　　　　N: buttocks, rump

84. 不堪入耳　　　bùkānrù'ěr　　　EX: "cannot bear to enter the ears," painful for the ears, offensive (8-106)

85. 指手划(畫)脚(腳)　zhǐshǒuhuàjiǎo　EX: "point with hands, draw with feet," gesticulate profusely

86. 糾纏(纏)不清　jiūchánbùqīng　　EX: become entangled or involved in something impure (10-50)

87. 拿...没有办(辦)法　ná...méiyou bànfa　PH: have no way of dealing with someone, be unable to do something to or about someone

88. 色鬼　　　　　sèguǐ　　　　　N: "lust devil," sex maniac, "wolf"

*89. 經得起   jīngdeqǐ   RC: be able to pass through
                                          an experience, tolerate

page 254

90. 啦   la   P: (fusion of 了 le and 阿 a)

91. 干（乾）哥ㄟ   gān'gēge   N: adopted older brother (not
                                          formally adopted but in a
                                          relationship somewhat like
                                          that of a godchild)

92. 蓉   Róng   N: （人名）

93. 老光眼鏡   laǒguāngyǎnjìng   N: presbyopic glasses (for old
                                          people who have become far-
                                          sighted; M: 副 fù)

94. 韓愈、   Hán Yù   N: Hán Yù (768-824), famous
                                          Chinese poet and essay writer

95. 师（師）説   Shīshuō   N: "On Teachers" (title of a
                                          well-known essay by Hán Yù)

96. 咬耳朵[呆]   yaǒ ěrduo   PH: "bite (someone's) ear,"
                                          whisper into another's ear

97. 練習簿   liànxíbù   N: exercise notebook (7-86)

98. 鉛笔（筆）   qiānbǐ   N: pencil (M: 枝 zhī)

*99. 無心   wúxīn   PH: "not have heart," uninten-
                                          tional, not on purpose

page 255

100. 独（獨）断（斷）   dúduàndúxíng   EX: "alone decide, alone act,"
     独行   act on one's own, act ar-
                                          bitrarily (also 獨行獨斷,
                                          cf. 家 p. 259, 1. 12)

101. 养（養）育   yǎngyù   FV: raise and educate, rear

page 256

102. 狂草   kuángcaǒ   ADJ: wildly scribbled (9-53)

103. 理智   lǐzhì   N: intellect, reason

*104. 与（與）其…不如   yǔqí...bùrú...   PT: rather than...it's better
                                          to..., instead of...rather...

105. 踏实（實）   tàshí   SV: "treading on reality,"
                                          realistic, practical

106. 由衷之言　　　yóuzhōngzhīyán　　EX: "words from the inner heart," words from the depths of one's heart, sincere words

107. 試問　　　　shìwèn　　　　　　FV: pose a question, ask

108. 目不識丁　　　mùbùshídīng　　　EX: "eyes do not recognize (even a very simple character like 丁," completely illiterate, ignorant

109. 官僚　　　　　guānliáo　　　　　N: official, bureaucrat

110. 紈袴子弟　　　wánkùzǐdì　　　　N: "silk pajama sons and younger brothers," young man from a wealthy family, playboy (9-106)

*111. 逃避　　　　　táobì　　　　　　FV: evade, run away from

*112. 提亲(親)　　　tíqīn　　　　　　VO: bring up the subject of marriage, propose marriage (6-33)

113. 女婿〔壻〕　　nǚxu　　　　　　N: son-in-law

page 257

*114. 顧念　　　　　gùniàn　　　　　FV: consider, take into account

115. 播弄　　　　　bōnòng　　　　　FV: dally with, play with

116. 問号(號)　　　wènhaò　　　　　N: question mark

117. 拥(擁)抱　　　yǒngbaò　　　　FV: hug, embrace

118. 酬报(報)　　　choúbaò　　　　N: reward, recompense (also 報酬)

119. 落伍　　　　　luòwǔ　　　　FV/SV: fall out of ranks, be behind the times or backward/out of date

*120. 抱恨終身　　　baòhènzhōngshēn　EX: "harbor resentment one's whole life," feel remorse for the rest of one's life

page 258

*121. 两(兩)点(點)鐘　liǎngdiǎnzhōng　PH: two hours (=兩個鐘頭 liǎngge zhōngtoú; here, not '2:00'; 15-33)

122. 恶(惡)魔　　　èmó　　　　　　N: evil spirit, demon, devil

123. 寢(寢)室	qǐnshì	N:	bedroom (M: 閒 jiān)
124. 修头(頭)髮	xiū tóufa	PH:	trim one's hair
125. 細心考究	xìxīnkǎojiū	EX:	"make small the heart, examine and investigate," be very careful and fussy (7-148)
126. 叩声(聲)	kòushēng	N:	sound of knocking (15-26)
127. 舍监(監)	shèjiān	N:	dormitory superintendent
128. 暗号(號)	ànhaò	N:	secret sign or signal, password
129. 暴露	baòlù	FV:	expose, be exposed (25-54)
*130. 輕視	qīngshì	N/FV:	derision/deride, look down upon

page 259

131. 胆(膽)壯(壮)	dǎnzhuàng	PH:	be courageous or fearless
*132. 借此	jiècǐ	PH:	"borrow this," make us of something (in order to do something else), by means of this
133. 辯才	biàncaí	N:	skill in argumentation, oratorical eloquence (3-62, 7-155)
134. 黃金时(時)代	huángjīnshídaì	N:	"yellow gold period," the Golden Age (period in Chinese history when everything was perfect), the good old days
*135. 祈求	qíqiú	FV:	entreat, beseech
136. 欲語又止	yùyǔyòuzhǐ	EX:	"wish to speak, again stop," want to speak but, on second thought, decide not to

page 260

137. 吃(喫)著不尽(盡)	chīzhuóbújìn	EX:	"eat and wear not exhaust," eat and dress without financial considerations, have enough money to live on for life

138. 謝絕   xièjué   FV: decline (an offer or request)

*139. 名声(聲)   míngshēng   N: reputation, fame (23-16)

140. 鐐銬   liaókaò   N: manacle, fetter

141. 灌溉   guàn'gaì   FV: irrigate (farm land with water)

142. 野兽(獸)   yěshoù   N: wild animal, beast (20-55)

page 261

*143. 咽[嚥]   yàn   FV: swallow, gulp down

144. 遙远(遠)   yaóyuǎn   SV: far, remote, distant

145. 嘔心血   oǔ xīnxuè   PH: "vomit heart-blood," think so hard on or be affected by a subject as to make one's heart bleed

146. 迷斤(鏃斤)腸   duàncháng   FV: "break apart the bowels," be heartbroken (21-48)

147. 渴欲   kěyù   AV: yearn, desire (4-43, 25-25)

148. 訴諸正义(義) sùzhūzhèngyì   EX: "appeal to justice" (諸 zhū 'to' is a so-called fusion or allegro form, being a contraction of 之 zhī plus 於 yú)

*149. 掙脱   zhēngtuō   FV: break away from, shake off

page <u>262</u>

1.	生	shēng	FV: grow, develop (here, 長 zhǎng)
2.	浮肿（腫）	fúzhǒng	SV: bloated, swollen (3-76, 21-88)
3.	摇蕩〔盪〕	yáodàng	FV: swing, wobble (3-111)
4.	慢騰々地	mànténgténgde	A: very slowly (of the voice)

page <u>263</u>

5.	使性子	shǐ xìngzi	PH: let one's temper flare, become stubborn and upset (9-136)
6.	安分守己	ānfènshǒujǐ	EX: "be content with one's lot and guard oneself (from doing wrong)," satisfied and law-abiding
7.	裁缝	cáifeng	N: tailor
*8.	首飾	shǒushi	N: jewelry
*9.	打岔	dǎchà	FV: interrupt (20-134)
10.	防衛	fángwei	FV: defend, guard
*11.	賴	lài	FV: rely or depend on (11-42, 16-39)
12.	蹂躪	róulìn	FV: trample
13.	术（術）語	shùyǔ	N: technical terminology, special jargon (e.g., of linguistics, sociology, etc.)
14.	苦役	kǔyì	N: difficult labor, hard work
15.	报（報）酬	bàochóu	N: reward, recompense (11-98, 25-118)

*16. 摧殘   cuīcán   FV: destroy, ruin

*17. 和善   héshàn   SV: affable, kind, gentle

page 264

18. 幻象   huànxiàng   N: mental image, illusion,
                                    vision

19. 强〔強〕似人   qiángsì   PH: be better than

20. 顧不周到   gùbuzhoūdaò   RC: not be able to consider
                                    thoroughly, not take into
                                    careful consideration

*21. 情願   qíngyuàn   AV: be willing (to do something)

page 265

22. 發慈悲   fā cíbeī   PH: show mercy or pity

*23. 潮月   chaó   N: tide (6-172)

24. 喉   hoú   BF: throat (FF: 30-29 喉嚨
                                    hoúlong)

25. 塞住   saīzhù   RC: stop or plug up (3-102, 19-52)

*26. 摩撫   mófǔ   FV: pass one's hand over, stroke
                                    (=10-79 撫摩)

27. 好心的人   haǒxīnde rén   EX: "people with good hearts
    終有好报（報）的 zhōng yoǔ haǒ baòde eventually get their just
                                    rewards" (22-32)

page 266

*28. 衫子   shānzi   N: woman's garment (M: 件 jiàn)

29. 底襟角   dǐjīnjiaǒ   N: lower corner of a garment

30. 摸熟   mōshoú   RC: figure out, be clear about
                                    (3-126)

page 267

*31. 引誘   yǐnyoù   FV: entice, lure, attract

32. 細孔   xìkǒng   PH: small opening (4-50)

33. 花紋   huāwén   N: pattern, design

34. 軒昂   xuānáng   SV: lofty, proud, dignified (3-87, 7-77)

35. 朝夕   zhaōxì   A: "morning and evening," always

*36. 拥（擁）挤（擠） yǒngjǐ   FV: crowd, squeeze in (13-30)

*37. 窗台〔臺〕 chuāngtaí   N: window sill

page 268

*38. 分离（離） fēnlí   N/FV: separation, division/ separate, divide

39. 死别 sǐbié   PH: parting by death (15-101)

*40. 威胁（脅、脅） weīxié   FV/N: threaten, intimidate/threat

page 269

41. 傳聞 chuánwén   N: hearsay, rumor

*42. 哭訴 kūsù   PH: tell (one's misfortunes, etc., to someone) in a grieving manner (= 哭着説 kūzhe shuō; 19-114)

43. 陰影 yǐnyǐng   N: shade, shadow

page 270

44. 字眼 zìyǎn   N: word (usually pronounced 字眼兒 zìyǎr)

45. 标（標）致〔緻〕 biaōzhì   SV: good-looking, attractive (of women)

46. 鄙夷 bǐyí   FV: disdain, scorn (8-94)

47. 死老头（頭）子 sǐ laǒtoúzi   N: old man who is more dead than alive (4-84)

*48. 嘲罵〔罵〕 chaómà   FV/N: ridicule and abuse (3-17)

49. 借故 jiègù   VO: find a pretext (for doing something; = 找理由 zhaǒ lǐyoú; 25-132)

page 271

*50. 絶早 juézaǒ   A: very early

51. 难(難)得   nándé   A/SV: not easily, with difficulty/ "difficult to obtain (a chance to do something)"

*52. 疏远(遠)   shūyuǎn   SV: distant (of relationships between people)

53. 厮[廝]守   sīshǒu   FV: serve and take care of one another

page 272

54. 甘心   gānxīn   AV/SV: be willing (12-122)

55. 徘徊   páihuái   FV: walk to and fro, hesitate

56. 错过(過) 机[機]会(會)   cuòguo jīhui   PH: miss an opportunity, lose a chance

*57. 专(專)心   zhuānxīn   A: with one mind, concentratedly

page 273

*58. 稿件   gǎojiàn   N: manuscript

59. 原稿纸   yuángǎozhǐ   N: manuscript paper (26-58)

60. 螞蟻   mǎyǐ   N: ant (M: 隻 zhī)

61. 只消   zhǐ xiāo   PH: need only (16-27)

page 275

*62. 孔教会(會)   Kǒngjiàohuì   N: Confucian Ethics Society

*63. 討老婆   tǎo laǒpo   PH: seek a wife, get married (6-111, 12-75, 16-29)

64. 薛月秋   Xuē Yuèqiū   N: (人名)

65. 方鑑舜   Fāng Jìshùn   N: (人名)

66. 学(學)生潮   Xuésheng Chaó   N: Student's Tide (name of a magazine published in Sìchuan during the May Fourth period; 26-23)

67. 名流   míngliú   N: socially prominent person

68. 哦   ó   I: (indicates surprise or doubt)

page 276

*69. 遵守   zūnshǒu   FV: observe, keep (a promise, law, etc.)

*70. 遣   qiǎn   FV: send, dispatch (someone somewhere; contrast 遣 and 1-42 遺 yí)

71. 怀(懷)抱   huáibaò   N/FV: bosom and arms, embrace/ carry at one's breast (13-29)

72. 虎口   hǔkoǔ   N: tiger's mouth

73. 贖罪   shúzuì   VO: atone for a sin

74. 走了好一陣   zoǔle haǒ yízhèn   PH: "walked for quite a long while"

page 277

75. 終局   zhōngjú   N: end, conclusion (11-50)

76. 苦刑   kǔxíng   N: bitter punishment, torture

77. 目的地   mùdìdì   N: destination

78. 一幕一幕地   yímùyímùde   A: one act at a time, act by act

79. 重現   chóngxiàn   FV: reappear (23-68, 23-80)

*80. 辨物   biànwù   VO: distinguish things (19-28)

*81. 显(顯)露   xiǎnlù   FV: appear, become manifest

82. 身殉   shēnxùn   FV: sacrifice oneself (for something)

*83. 树(樹)梢   shùshaō   N: tree twig (19-19)

page 278

84. 面々   miànmiàn   A: from all sides

85. 墮落   duòluò   FV: fall, sink

86. 伸展   shēnzhǎn   FV: stretch, spread out

*87. 不禁   bùjīn   AV: be unable to avoid (doing something), cannot help but (21-46)

*88. 痛惜   tòngxī   FV: regret deeply

89. 寄身   jìshēn   VO: deliver or entrust one's
                                    body (to some place or
                                    someone)

90. 接吻   jiēwěn   N/VO: kiss (6-201)

page 279

91. 乐（樂）园（園） lèyuán   N: paradise

*92. 迷糊   míhu   FV: blur, dim

page 280

93. 縱身   zòngshēn   VO: straighten up one's body,
                                    jump up (19-12)

page <u>281</u>

*1. 發問　　　　　fāwèn　　　　N/FV: questions which are asked/
　　　　　　　　　　　　　　　　　　ask questions

2. 自尊心　　　　　zìzūnxīn　　　N: sense of self-esteem,
　　　　　　　　　　　　　　　　　　self-respect

3. 圍攻　　　　　　wéigōng　　　　N/FV: attack from all sides

4. 押送　　　　　　yāsòng　　　　FV: send to another place
　　　　　　　　　　　　　　　　　under escort

page <u>282</u>

*5. 老混蛋　　　　　laǒ hùndàn　　N: "old scoundrel," "bastard"
　　　　　　　　　　　　　　　　　　(18-22)

6. 复（復）原　　　fùyuán　　　　FV: recover (from an illness;
　　　　　　　　　　　　　　　　　also written 復元)

7. 心胸　　　　　　xīnxiōng　　　N: mind, heart (4-113)

page <u>283</u>

8. 怨憤　　　　　　yuànfèn　　　　SV/N: bitter/bitterness (emotional;
　　　　　　　　　　　　　　　　　　also written 怨忿 ; 3-137,
　　　　　　　　　　　　　　　　　　14-81)

9. 自尽（盡）　　　zìjìn　　　　　FV: commit suicide (= 自殺
　　　　　　　　　　　　　　　　　zìshā)

*10. 尸[屍]首　　　shīshoǔ　　　　N: corpse (M: 具 jù; =13-108
　　　　　　　　　　　　　　　　　屍骨豊 shītǐ)

11. 烈性　　　　　　lièxìng　　　　ADJ: of ardent disposition, strong
　　　　　　　　　　　　　　　　　in character (12-79)

12. 倒楣　　　　　　daǒmeí　　　　SV: out of luck, unfortunate
　　　　　　　　　　　　　　　　　(written variant of 8-62
　　　　　　　　　　　　　　　　　倒霉)

page <u>284</u>

13. 狠心　　　　　　hěnxīn　　　　SV: heartless, cruel (contrast
　　　　　　　　　　　　　　　　　狠 and 22-4 狼 láng 'wolf';
　　　　　　　　　　　　　　　　　12-102)

14. 撈   laō   FV: pull out, drag up (usually from water), fish up

15. 眈々地   dāndānde   A: paying close attention to

16. 粗暴   cūbaò   SV: rough, coarse (of people and their actions)

page 285

17. 無能   wúnéng   SV: incompetent, without talent (4-38)

18. 受之非分[份]   shoùzhīfeīfèn   EX: "receive it, it is not one's lot," receive something without deserving it (26-6)

19. 践踏   jiàntà   N/FV: trampling/trample, tread (1-53)

page 286

*20. 停頓   tǐngdùn   FV: pause, stop

21. 支(枝)开(開)   zhīkai   FV: "branch off," change direction of

22. 季   jì   BF: season (of the year; FF: 季節 jìjié; distinguish from 香 xiāng and 李 lǐ)

23. 坟(墳)   fén   N: grave (=12-127 墳墓 fénmù)

page 287

24. 非分[份]   feīfèn   ADJ: "not one's lot," not fated to happen to one (27-18)

*25. 心跳   xīntiaò   N: heartbeat

26. 吐露   tǔlù   FV: "spit forth," confess, disclose (3-155)

27. 高潔   gaōjié   SV: noble and pure, exalted and immaculate (3-24)

28. 埋怨   mányuàn   FV: harbor resentment toward, blame (someone; notice that 埋 has two pronunciations: mán, as in 埋怨, and maí, as in 12-125 埋葬 maízàng 'bury')

29. 一举(舉,擧)   yìjǔyídòng   PH: every movement (6-114)
一动(動)
*30. 身世   shēnshì   N: background, experiences of
                                            one's life

page 288

31. 卑不足道   bēibùzúdaò   EX: "so base as to be insuffic-
                                            ient to talk about," too
                                            inferior to be worth men-
                                            tioning (8-94)

32. 遗弃(棄)   yíqì   FV: cast away, abandon, desert
                                            (6-155, 12-76)

33. 自量   zìliàng   FV: assess one's own abilities,
                                            know one's limits

*34. 缩短   suōduǎn   FV: shorten (15-79)

*35. 切   qiè   A: strongly, urgently

page 289

36. 病体(體)   bìngtǐ   N: diseased body

37. 問候   wènhou   FV: greet, give one's regards to

38. 近況   jìnkuàng   N: recent condition or situation
                                            (a common formula in letters
                                            is 近況如何 jìnkuàng rúhé
                                            'How have you been lately?')

39. 署名   shǔmíng   N: signed name, signature (8-52,
                                            17-45)

40. 要来(來)   yaòlai   RC: ask for (something)

*41. 过(過)虑(慮)   guòlǜ   N: overanxiousness, excessive
                                            worry (5-24)

42. 琐碎   suǒsuì   SV: petty and varied (17-95,
                                            25-71)

*43. 妒[妬]忌[嫉]   dùjì   SV: jealous (more frequently 忌
                                            妒)

*44. 万(萬)一   wànyi   A: "one chance in 10,000," in
                                            case, if by some chance

page 290

*45. 瘦削	shòuxuē	ADJ: slim, gaunt (1-32)
*46. 喜悦	xǐyuè	SV: happy, joyous
47. 絕大	juédà	ADJ: very great

CHAPTER TWENTY-EIGHT

15. 湿（濕、溼）淋々 shīlínlín   PH: damp and dripping (20-9)

16. 解除   jiěchú   FV: remove

page 295

*17. 言行不符   yánxíngbùfú   EX: "words and deeds do not tally," act differently from the way one speaks, not practice what one preaches

18. 探問   tànwèn   FV: inquire

19. 厭倦   yànjuàn   FV/SV: be disgusted with, be sick and tired of (1-117, 23-83)

20. 不配   búpeì   PH: not fit, unqualified (to do something)

*21. 加重語气（氣）   jiāzhòng yǔqì   PH: emphasize

*22. 忄不（懷）疑   huaíyí   FV/SV: harbor doubts about, suspect/doubtful, suspicious (2-79, 13-29)

page 296

23. 凉〔涼〕爽   liángshuǎng   SV: cool and comfortable (15-143)

24. 底   dǐ   BF: background or foundation (FF: 1-136 底子 dǐzi)

25. 正楷   zhèngkaǐ   N: regular square style of characters in Chinese calligraphy (1-137)

*26. 我鳥卵石   éluǎnshí   N: "goose egg stones," pebbles (7-63)

*27. 槐树（樹）   huaíshù   N: locust tree, acacia (M: 棵 kē)

28. 石榴树（樹）   shíliúshù   N: pomegranate tree (M: 棵 kē)

29. 鮮艳（豐色、豔）   xiānyàn   SV: bright-colored, resplendent (14-60)

30. 綠叶（葉）丛（叢）生 lùyècōngshēng   EX: "green leaves grow in clumps," very luxuriant foliage (15-133, 20-112)

*31. 独（獨）院 dúyuàn   N: house that only one family lives in

page 297

32. 天色   tiānsè   N: coloring or meteorological condition of the sky

*33. 嘘   xū   I: "Shhh..." (symbolic command for silence; 16-36)

*34. 砰   pēng   ON: "bang" (sound of crashing, falling, etc.; 20-19)

35. 鬼々祟々 guǐguǐsuìsuì PH: sly and stealthy (distinguish 祟 from 25-10 崇 chóng)

*36. 嶄新   zhǎnxīn ADJ: brand new

*37. 金陵高寓 Jīnlíng Gāo Yù PH: "Residence of the Gāo family of Nánjīng" (金陵 is the old name for 南京)

38. 吐舌头（頭） tǔ shétou PH: stick out one's tongue (3-155, 7-139)

39. 不止   bùzhǐ   A: "does not stop at," not only

page 298

*40. 輕蔑   qīngmiè FV/N: despise, disdain/contempt

*41. 崩潰   bēngkuì FV: cave in, collapse, break down

*42. 夸（誇）張 kuāzhāng FV: exaggerate (18-35, 25-17)

43. 开（開）步 kāibù   A: starting to move one's feet

44. 洋布长（長）衫 yángbù chángshān N: long gown made from cloth imported from abroad (M: 件 jiàn; 26-28)

45. 打臉水   dǎ liǎnshuǐ PH: bring water for washing one's face

page 299

46. 冒雨   màoyǔ   VO: brave the rain (4-80)

47. 前头（頭）太々 qiántou taìtai N: "the earlier ma'am" (i.e., 覺民 Juémín and 覺慧 Juéhuì's real and first mother)

48. 尺（盡）心   jìnxīn   VO: "exhaust one's heart,"
                                              devote one's entire energy
                                              (to something)

page 300

49. 为（為）人子者
Weí   rén   zǐ   zhě
Those who are the sons of people (i.e., children)

居 不 主 奥
Jū   bù   zhǔ'aò
Do not live in the best section of the house

坐 不 中 席
Zuò   bù   zhōngxí
Do not sit in the central seat

行 不 中 道
Xíng   bù   zhōngdaò
Do not walk in the middle of the road

立 不 中 門
Lì   bù   zhōngmén
And do not stand in the middle of the door   (from the 禮記 Lǐ Jì
or Records of Ritual)

50. 五 刑 之 屬 三 千
Wǔxíng   zhǐ   shǔ   sānqiān
To the Five Punishments belong three thousand (crimes)

而 罪 莫 大 于 不 孝
Eŕ   zuì   mò   dà   yú   búxiaò
And there is no crime greater than being unfilial

要 君 者 無 上
Yaōjūnzhě   wú   shàng
He who intimidates his ruler has no respect for his superiors

非聖人者無, 法

Fēishèngrénzhě   wú fǎ

He who denounces the sages has no respect for the law

非孝者無, 亲（親）

Fēixiàozhě   wú qīn

He who denounces filial piety has no respect for his parents (from
the 孝經 Xiào Jīng or <u>Classic</u> <u>of</u> <u>Filial</u> <u>Piety</u>)

51. 行莫回头（頭）

Xíng mò huí toú

In walking do not turn turn your head back

語莫掀唇

Yǔ mò xiān chún

In talking do not open your lips (in an unbecoming manner)

坐莫动（動）膝

Zuò mò dòng xī

In sitting do not move your knees

行莫搖裙

Xíng mò yaó qún

In walking do not sway your skirt (from the 女四書   Nǚ Sì Shū or
<u>Women's</u> <u>Four</u> <u>Books</u>)

*52. 人迹〔跡、蹟〕rénjī   N: human trace (5-17)

*53. 熟習   shúxi   FV/SV: be thoroughly familiar
                                          with (14-118)

54. 眼珠   yǎnzhū   N: pupil of the eye

55. 抛擲   paōzhì   FV: toss, throw away (11-11,
                                          14-52)

<u>page 301</u>

56. 沙沙   shāshā   ADJ: crisp, rasping (of sounds;
                                          3-164)

57. 敗叶(葉)	bàiyè	N:	shriveled fallen leaves
*58. 定眼	dìngyǎn	VO:	fix one's eyes upon something (=9-28 定睛 dìngjīng)
59. 迷失	míshī	FV:	lose
60. 惶惑	huánghuò	SV:	nervous, uneasy
61. 舒适(適)	shūshì	SV:	comfortable, cosy
62. 仰臥[卧]	yǎngwò	FV:	lie on one's back (12-26, 19-39, 23-37)
63. 閑[閒]适(適)	xiánshì	SV:	quiet and comfortable
64. 岩[巖]石	yánshí	N:	rock, crag

page 302

65. 訪寻(尋)	fǎngxún	FV:	inquire about, look for, search (6-146)
66. 洋楼(樓)	yánglóu	N:	Western style house (M: 所 suǒ)

page 303

67. 官吏	guānlì	N:	government official (distinguish 吏 , 12-96 史 shǐ, and 1-123 更 gèng[gēng])
68. 貪圖	tāntú	FV:	desire, long for
69. 聘金	pìnjīn	N:	money paid to the parents of a bride at a betrothal (3-1)
70. 一官半职(職)	yìguānbànzhí	EX:	"one official, half an office," official post
*71. 打消	dǎxiāo	FV:	destroy, cancel

page 304

72. 失而复(復)得	shī'érfùdé	PH:	"lost but again obtained," regained
73. 破涕为[爲]笑	pòtìwéixiào	EX:	"break one's snivel to make a smile," break into laughter while still crying
74. 小徑[俓]	xiǎojìng	N:	small path (14-35)

*75. 凹入　　　　　　　aōrù　　　　　FV: indent inward (凹 and 4-103 凸 tú are good examples of ideographic characters)

*76. 生路　　　　　　　shēnglù　　　　N: life route, way to survive (M: 條 tiáo)

77. 顛簸　　　　　　　diānbǒ　　　　　FV: shake, joggle

78. 頂上　　　　　　　dǐngshàng　　　PW: on top

79. 浪花　　　　　　　lànghuā　　　　N: spray of breaking waves (20-125)

80. 上身　　　　　　　shàngshēn　　　N: upper part of one's body, part of one's body above the waist

page 305

81. 汽艇　　　　　　　qìtǐng　　　　　N: motorboat (M: 隻 zhī)

82. 开〔開〕足馬力　　kāizú mǎlì　　PH: turn on sufficient horse-power, increase horsepower

83. 死々地〚　　　　　sǐsǐde　　　　　A: "for dear life," with the utmost of one's ability

84. 水痕　　　　　　　shuǐhén　　　　N: mark in water (here, the line of foam in front of the approaching motorboat; 5-17)

*85. 挾　　　　　　　　xié　　　　　　FV: clasp, carry (13-47)

*86. 吵鬧〔鬧〕　　　chǎonaò　　　　SV/FV: very noisy/quarrel (19-8)

page 306

*87. 狼藉　　　　　　　lángjí　　　　　SV: disorderly, in total dis-array (also written 狼籍)

*88. 泪〔淚〕花　　　　leǐhuā　　　　　N: teardrop

*89. 連累　　　　　　　liánleǐ　　　　FV: involve (someone else in something; 15-103)

*90. 躊躇　　　　　　　chóuchú　　　　FV: hesitate, waver

*91. 倉卒間　　　　　　cāngcùjiān　　A: in a hurry (also written 倉促間)

92. 木片   mùpiàn   N: wooden board (M: 塊 kuài)

93. 飄風浮   piāofú   FV: float (1-4, 17-85)

page 307

*94. 卷（捲）   juǎn   FV/SV/M: roll/curly/roll, reel (of film)

95. 凉〔涼〕蓆   liángxí   N: sleeping mat (usually of straw or bamboo, used in the summer; M: 張 zhāng)

96. 麻布   mábù   N: hemp fabric (14-87)

97. 死气（氣）沉々   sǐqìchénchén   EX: "death air very heavy," hopeless and gloomy, lifeless

98. 蚊子   wénzi   N: mosquito (M: 隻 zhī)

page 308

99. 酣睡   hānshuì   FV: sleep very soundly (as if intoxicated)

CHAPTER TWENTY-NINE

1. 綺霞　　　　Qǐxiá　　　　　N: （人名；20-108）

*2. 翠环（環）　Cuìhuán　　　　N: （人名）

3. 寄飯的丫头（頭）　jìfànde yātou　N: servant girl that works in someone else's home for room and board for a set period of time after which she may return to her own home(10-27)

4. 治　　　　　zhì　　　　　　FV: heal, cure (24-31)

5. 悲悼　　　　bēidào　　　　FV: mourn

6. 流傳　　　　liúchuán　　　FV: circulate, spread (as of rumors)

7. 官厅（廳）　guāntīng　　　N: government office

8. 封禁　　　　fēngjìn　　　FV: close down and prohibit

9. 部下　　　　bùxià　　　　N: those under the command of someone, subordinates

10. 訂户　　　　dìnghù　　　　N: subscriber (= 訂閱者 dìngyuèzhě; 7-20)

11. 社址　　　　shèzhǐ　　　　N: address of an organization

12. 营（營）業　yíngyè　　　　N/FV: business operations/do business

13. 孤单（單）　gūdān　　　　SV: solitary, alone (P-16)

*14. 鋪板　　　　pùbǎn　　　　N: shutter in front of a shop (M: 張 zhāng)

*15. 卸　　　　　xiè　　　　　FV: take down, remove

16. 顧忌　　　　gùjì　　　　　N/FV: scruples/have scruples about (23-19)

*17. 暢談   chàngtán   PH: talk freely and enjoyably
                                         (11-24)

18. 俱乐(樂)部   jùlèbù   N: club, association (translit-
                                        eration of English <u>club</u>; note
                                        that here, as with most for-
                                        eign words that have been
                                        borrowed into Chinese, a new
                                        meaning has been superimposed
                                        on the transliteration: the
                                        "all happy section")

19. 發稿期   fāgǎoqí   N: date for sending out a manu-
                                        script for publication (26-58)

*20. 朗讀   lǎngdú   FV: read aloud (19-90, 25-76)

21. 警察厅(廳)   jǐngchátīng   N: police station (15-69)

*22. 起稿   qǐgǎo   VO: prepare a draft, write up
                                        (26-58, 29-19)

23. 淺陋   qiǎnloù   SV: shallow and crude, vulgar

page 311

24. 通順   tōngshùn   SV: fluent, smooth (of writings)

25. 牢騷   laósao   N: complaint (cf. 發牢騷
                                        fā laósao 'complain')

26. 銷路   xiāolù   N: market, demand, (here) cir-
                                        culation

27. 代派处(處)   daìpaìchù   N: branch outlet, agent

page 312

*28. 月捐   yuèjuān   N: monthly contribution
                                        (M: 17-5 筆 bǐ)

*29. 繳   jiǎo   FV: hand in, pay (here,= 交 jiāo)

30. 神經病   shénjīngbìng   N: mental illness, insanity

31. 把我没有   bǎ wǒ meíyou   PH: "could do nothing about me"
     办(辦)法   bànfa   (25-87)

*32. 要命   yaòmìng   A: "wants one's life," "some-
                                        thing terrible," extremely,
                                        desperately (21-34)

*33. 寄放   jìfàng   FV: place or leave something in another's custody

34. 佩服   pèifu   FV: admire and respect

page 313

*35. 鬍鬚   húxū   N: whiskers, beard (6-109, 23-66)

36. 銅元   tóngyuán   N: copper coin

*37. 奉命令   fèng mìnglìng   PH: receive orders (from a superior), act on orders

38. 上头（頭）   shàngtou   N: person on top, the authorities

*39. 束   shù   M/FV: bundle/tie on, bind (3-32)

40. 沒收   mòshōu   FV: confiscate

41. 質問   zhìwèn   FV: interrogate, question

42. 安分〔份〕   ānfèn   SV: content with one's lot, peaceful (26-6)

43. 管閑〔閒〕事   guǎn xiánshì   PH: concern oneself with matters not one's own, meddle in other people's affairs (3-136)

page 314

44. 公函   gōnghán   N: official letter (M: 封 fēng; 11-88)

45. 当（當）众（眾） dāngzhòng   A: in the presence of all (3-141)

*46. 过（過）于（於） guòyú   A: excessive, too much (here, = 太 tài)

47. 偏激   piānjī   SV: tending toward agitation, radical

*48. 安宁（寧）   ānníng   N/SV: peace, tranquility/peaceful, tranquil

49. 即   jí   A: immediately (文言; 22-20)

50. 發行   fāxíng   FV: circulate, publish (periodicals)

51. 措辞（辭）   cuòcí   N: wording, style (of a letter, essay, etc.)

52. 别开(開)生面	biékāishēngmiàn	EX:	"additionally open a new side," do something in an unusual way, introduce a novelty (19-129)
53. 割断(斷)	gēduàn	RC:	cut off
54. 初生兒	chūshēng'ér	N:	first-born child, newly born child
55. 益	yì	BF:	benefit, advantage
56. 友誼	yǒuyì	N:	friendship
57. 根深蒂固	gēnshēndìgù	EX:	"root deep, stem firm," deep-rooted, firmly established
*58. 搔	sāo	FV:	scratch
59. 顧問	gùwèn	N:	adviser (in government, not at a university; 'academic adviser' is 指導教授 zhǐdǎojiàoshòu)

page 315

60. 演説辞(辭)	yǎnshuōcí	N:	words of a speech (M: 篇 piān)
61. 拟(擬)稿子	nǐ gǎozi	PH:	prepare the draft of a manuscript; 26-58, 29-22)
62. 欢(歡)迎弄得不成其为(為)欢(歡)迎	Huānyíng nòngde bùchéng qí wéi huānyíng	PH:	"The welcome was turned into something not like a welcome"
63. 热(熱)烘々	rèhōnghōng	A:	hot and blazing
64. 通告	tōnggào	N:	public notice, announcement
*65. 筹(籌)备(備)	chóubei	FV:	prepare and plan (23-7)
66. 議决[決]	yìjué	FV:	decide, resolve (often at a meeting)
*67. 閲报(報)处(處)	yuèbàochù	N:	place for reading newspapers, magazines, etc. (6-187)
68. 陈(陳)列	chénliè	FV:	display
69. 閲覽	yuèlǎn	FV:	read (=6-187 閲讀 yuèdú)

page 316

*70. 利群〔羣〕   Lì Qún Yuèbàochù   N: "Benefit the Masses" Reading
     閲报〔報〕处〔處〕   Room (29-67)

71. 發刊   fākān   FV: bring out the first issue,
                                     launch (a newspaper or maga-
                                     zine; 6-165, 25-3)

72. 开〔開〕幕   kāimù   N/VO: "raise the curtain," opening,
                                     beginning/open (26-78)

73. 血統   xuètǒng   N: blood relationship, lineage

74. 赤誠   chìchéng   SV: sincere, loyal, upright
                                     (5-11, 7-154)

75. 利害关〔關〕   lìhài guānxi   PH: relations of profit and loss,
    系〔係〕   considerations of interest
                                     (distinguish 利害 lìhài
                                     'benefit and injury' from 厲
                                     害 lìhai 'fierce, severe';
                                     although 利害 is some-
                                     times used for 厲害 , the
                                     two expressions are best
                                     kept apart)

76. 就緒   jiùxù   FV: be near completion, take
                                     shape

77. 茶点〔點、點〕   chádiǎn   N: tea and pastry, refreshments

78. 尽〔盡〕情地   jìnqíngde   A: to one's heart's content

79. 分享   fēnxiǎng   FV: share

80. 欢〔歡〕聚   huānjù   PH: gather together happily
                                     (15-39)

81. 惨〔慘〕痛   cǎntòng   SV: painful, agonizing (4-1)

page 317

82. 同桌〔棹〕者   tóngzhuōzhě   N: tablemate, person at the
                                     same table as oneself (often
                                     simply 同桌 ; 15-73)

83. 鍍   dù   FV: plate (metals)

*84. 知了   zhīliǎo   N: cicada (M: 隻 zhī)

*85. 啼   tí   FV: cry, wail, call (of animals)

page 318

86. 枒〔椏〕枝　　　　yāzhī　　　　N: branch of a tree (M: 根 gēn)

87. 烏鴉巢　　　　　　wūyāchaó　　N: crow's nest (distinguish 烏 from 鳥 niǎo and 巢 from 菓 guǒ; 9-142)

88. 小鴉　　　　　　　xiaǒyā　　　N: little crow (M: 隻 zhī)

89. 呀ㄠ　　　　　　　yāyā　　　　ON: (sound of birds and doors squeaking)

90. 扑〔撲〕翅　　　　pūchì　　　　VO: beat wings (of a bird; 10-19, 11-54)

*91. 慈愛（愛）　　　　cí'aì　　　　SV: loving, kind (of a superior to an inferior, e.g., parents to children)

92. 和諧　　　　　　　héxié　　　　SV: harmonious

93. 相思　　　　　　　xiāngsī　　　ADJ: pining for one another (of lovers)

*94. 寄托〔託〕　　　　jìtuō　　　　FV: consign, commit

95. 哀婉　　　　　　　aīwǎn　　　　SV: sad and tender (10-111)

page 319

96. 卖（賣）唱　　　　maìchàng　　FV: "sell singing," earn one's living by singing

*97. 瞎子　　　　　　　xiāzi　　　　N: blind person

98. 假嗓　　　　　　　jiǎsǎng　　　N: falsetto voice

99. 鄙俗　　　　　　　bǐsú　　　　SV: vulgar, coarse (8-94, 26-46)

100. 警覺（覺）　　　　jǐngjué　　　SV: watchful, alert

*101. 旦角　　　　　　　dànjiaǒ　　　N: actor who plays female role in Beǐjing opera (7-39, 9-61)

*102. 張碧秀　　　　　　Zhāng Bìxiù　N: (人名)

103. 摆（擺）架子　　　baǐ jiàzi　　PH: pretend to be, pose (as something one is not)

page 320

*104. 苦衷   kǔzhōng   N: difficulties or problems
                                     not easily understood by
                                     others

105. 急躁   jízào   SV: rash and impatient (8-98)

106. 烦   fán   SV: bored, fed up

107. 蟋蟀   xīshuài   N: cricket (the insect; M: 隻
                                     zhǐ)

108. 凄〔凄〕切   qīqiè   SV: sorrowful, mournful (4-1)

109. 网（網）   wǎng   N: net

110. 任是   rènshi   A: even

*111. 隐（隱）藏   yǐncáng   FV: hide, conceal (1-78, 6-106)

112. 細致〔緻〕   xìzhìzhīdiǎn N: point of elegance
     之点（點、点、）
page 321

113. 吸引   xīyǐn   FV: attract (8-9, 14-114)

114. 欣賞   xīnshǎng   FV: enjoy, admire (18-8)

*115. 游〔遊〕伴   yóubàn   N: person with whom one takes
                                     part in some sort of rec-
                                     reation, companion (8-23,
                                     19-6)

116. 壮（壯）胆（膽）   zhuàngdǎn   VO: pluck up one's courage,
                                     become courageous (25-131)

*117. 燒紙錢   shāo zhǐqián PH: burn paper money (paper
                                     money was believed to be
                                     the currency of the spirit
                                     world; it was burned as an
                                     offering to the spirits, so
                                     they would be kind to the
                                     souls of the deceased)

118. 惊（驚）怪   jīngguài   SV: startled, puzzled

page 322

119. 头（頭）七   tóuqī   N: first seventh day (after
                                     someone has died)

*120. 不枉   bùwǎng   PH: not in vain or useless (25-50)

121. 生前跟她   shēngqián gēn tā PH: "before, when she was still
      好一場[塲]   haǒ yìchǎng   alive, was a good friend of
                                          hers for a while"

122. 陰間   yīnjian   N: Hades, place of the dead

123. 眨眼睛   zhǎ yǎnjing   PH: wink or blink one's eyes

124. 忍痛   rěntòng   VO: hold back one's grief

page 323

125. 踉蹌地   liàngqiàngde   A: walking unsteadily

126. 昏迷   hūnmí   SV: in a coma, delerious (3-22,
                                      20-105)

127. 邓(鄧)孟德、   Dèngmèngdé   N: (人名)

128. 講堂   jiǎngtáng   N: lecture hall

CHAPTER THIRTY

1. 誕辰　　　　　dànchén　　　　N: birthday (11-17)

2. 公賬　　　　　gōngzhàng　　　N: (here) family account (6-96)

3. 款〔欵〕子　　kuǎnzi　　　　　N: fund, sum of money (M: 17-5 筆 bǐ)

4. 强調　　　　　qiángdiaò　　　FV: emphasize, stress

5. 担（擔）　　　dàn　　　　　　M: picul (measure of weight equal to 100 catties or about 133 lbs.)

6. 租谷（穀）　　zūgǔ　　　　　　N: grain taken in as rent for land

7. 管事　　　　　guǎnshì　　　　N/VO: administrator, caretaker/ take care of things

8. 参（參）照、　cānzhaò　　　　CV: according to

9. 拟（擬）　　　nǐ　　　　　　　FV: prepare, draft (29-61)

10. 办（辦）事处（處）bànshìchù　N: office (of an organization; 6-101, 7-3)

11. 賀礼（禮）　　hèlǐ　　　　　　N: congratulatory present (6-76)

12. 散發　　　　　sànfā　　　　　FV: distribute, give out

13. 請帖　　　　　qǐngtiě　　　　N: invitation card (M: 張 zhāng; 18-16)

14. 張灯（燈）結彩　zhāngdēngjiécaǐ　EX: "hang up lanterns, tie on colored hangings," decorated with lanterns and colored ornaments

15. 富丽（麗）堂皇　fùlìtánghuáng　EX: splendid and dignified, majestic

16. 精致〔緻〕　　jīngzhì　　　　SV: fine, exquisite (29-112)

17. 班   bān   M: troupe or company (of actors)

18. 名角   míngjiǎo   N: famous opera actor (29-101)

19. 川戏（戲、戲）   Chuānxì   N: Sìchuan opera (as opposed to other styles like 京戲 jīngxì 'Beǐjing opera')

20. 布帷   bùweí   N: cloth screen or curtain (7-30)

21. 戏（戲、戲）目   xìmù   N: drama program or schedule

22. 卓越   zhuōyuè   SV: outstanding, remarkable

23. 便宜   piányi   FV/SV: let (someone) off easy/ inexpensive, cheap

24. 現身   xiànshēn   VO: "make manifest the body," appear (23-80)

25. 集团（團）   jítuán   N: group

26. 洋琴   yángqín   N: Chinese musical instrument like a zither or small harp that is played with two bamboo rods

27. 大賀寿（壽）   Dà Hè Shoù   N: "Greatly Congratulating Someone On His Birthday" (title of a birthday melody)

28. 淫蕩   yíndàng   SV: lewd, lascivious (3-111, 23-41)

*29. 喉嚨   hoúlong   N: voice, throat (26-24)

30. 口技   koǔjì   N: mimicry

31. 調情   tiaóqíng   VO: flirt

32. 开（開）鑼   kaīluó   VO: "start hitting the gong," begin (3-166)

33. 出（齣）   chū   M: (for plays and operas)

34. 应（應）景   yìngjǐng   ADJ: appropriate to the occasion (because of 高老太爺 Gaō Laǒtaìye's birthday, a few special birthday plays were performed)

*35. 权（權）威   quánweī   N: authority (in some field of knowledge), prestige

page 326

36. 細致〔緻〕   xìzhì   SV: fine, elegant (29-112)

37. 打餅調叔   Dǎ Bǐng Tiáo Shū   N: "Making Cakes to Seduce
                                      One's Brother-in-law"
                                      (title of a Sìchuan play)

38. 桂花亭   Guìhuā Tíng   N: "Cassia Tower" (title of
                                      a Sìchuan play)

39. 翠屏山   Cuìpíng Shān   N: "Cuìpíng Mountain" (title
                                      of a Beǐjing play)

40. 战〔戰〕宛城   Zhàn Wǎnchéng   N: "Making War on Wǎn City"
                                      (title of a Beǐjing play)

41. 听〔聽〕差   tīngchāi   N: servant, errand man

*42. 宏亮   hóngliàng   SV: loud and clear, sonorous
                                      (of a voice)

43. 口齿〔齒〕   kǒuchǐ   N: "mouth and teeth," voice,
                                      pronunciation

44. 賞   shǎng   FV: bestow upon, give a reward
                                      to (of a superior to an
                                      inferior; 12-10)

45. 賞封   shǎngfēng   N: envelope containing money
                                      presented to one

46. 飞〔飛〕眼風   fēi yǎnfēng   PH: "fly the eye breeze," flirt
                                      with one's eyes, look at
                                      (someone) seductively

47. 陪酒   peǐjiǔ   FV: accompany a patron in drink-
                                      ing (of a courtesan, bar
                                      girl, etc.)

48. 岳丈   yuèzhàng   N: father-in-law (wife's father)

49. 小惠芳   Xiǎo Huìfāng   N: (人名)

50. 灌酒   guànjiǔ   VO: force a person to drink wine
                                      (25-141)

51. 部   bù   M: (for mustaches, sets of books,
                                      and vehicles)

*52. 鬍子   húzi   N: mustache, beard (23-66, 29-35)

53. 張小桃　　　　Zhāng Xiǎotaó　　N: (人名)

54. 敬酒　　　　　jìngjiǔ　　　　　VO: propose a toast, toast

55. 丑(醜)态(態)　choǔtaì　　　　　N: scandalous behavior, un-
　　　　　　　　　　　　　　　　　　seemly conduct (25-43, 25-47)

56. 交头(頭)接耳　jiaōtoújiē'ěr　　EX: "join heads, connect ears,"
　　　　　　　　　　　　　　　　　　whisper into each other's
　　　　　　　　　　　　　　　　　　ears

57. 寿(壽)星　　　shoùxīng　　　　　N: "star" of a birthday cele-
　　　　　　　　　　　　　　　　　　bration, person whose birth-
　　　　　　　　　　　　　　　　　　day is being celebrated
　　　　　　　　　　　　　　　　　　(usually older people)

58. 珠翠　　　　　zhūcuì　　　　　　PH: pearls and jades, jewelry
　　　　　　　　　　　　　　　　　　(29-2)

59. 踩蹻　　　　　caǐqiaō　　　　　VO: walk on small wooden shoes
　　　　　　　　　　　　　　　　　　tied to one's ankles so
　　　　　　　　　　　　　　　　　　that one sways while walking
　　　　　　　　　　　　　　　　　　(of a female role in Beǐjing
　　　　　　　　　　　　　　　　　　opera)

60. 粉红　　　　　fěnhóng　　　　　SV: pink (14-19)

61. 扭来(來)扭去　niǔlaíniǔqù　　PH: turn and twist back and
　　　　　　　　　　　　　　　　　　forth, wiggle around (9-84)

page 327

*62. 应(應)酬　　　yìngchou　　　　FV/N: entertain, attend to (guests)/
　　　　　　　　　　　　　　　　　　social obligations

63. 酗酒　　　　　xùjiǔ　　　　　　FV: indulge in excessive drinking

64. 从(從)未　　　cóngweì　　　　　A: never before (= 從來沒有
　　　　　　　　　　　　　　　　　　cónglaí meíyou)

65. 凑[湊]数(數)　coùshù　　　　　VO: make up the proper number
　　　　　　　　　　　　　　　　　　(of people to do something)

66. 跑龙(龍)套　　paǒ lóngtaò　　PH: play a very insignificant
　　　　　　　　　　　　　　　　　　role which requires neither
　　　　　　　　　　　　　　　　　　acting nor singing talent
　　　　　　　　　　　　　　　　　　(in Chinese opera)

67. 素色　　　　　sùsè　　　　　　N: plain color (15-59)

68. 接待　　　　　jiēdaì　　　　　FV: receive, attend to (guests)

*69. 差   chāi   FV: send, dispatch (30-41)

page 328

70. 迴〔迴〕光返照、   huíguāngfǎnzhaò EX: "reflected light shines back" (describes the temporary reviving of dying people)

71. 隕落   yǔnluò   FV: fall from a height (like a shooting star)

72. 胸怀（懷）   xiōnghuaí   N: thoughts harbored in one's bosom, one's feelings about things (4-113, 13-29)

73. 来（來）   lai   P: (usually indicates past progressive action; short for 來着 laízhe)

74. 私下   sīxià   A: privately, secretly

page 329

75. 气（氣）色   qìsè   N: complexion, color

page 330

76. 丑角   choǔjiaǒ   N: comedian, clown (in Chinese opera)

77. 长（長）身玉立   chángshēnyùlì   EX: "long body stands like jade," tall and graceful (23-57)

78. 依次地   yīcìde   A: in order or proper sequence

79. 确（確）信   quèxìn   N/FV: firm belief, conviction/ believe firmly (P-30)

80. 信任   xìnren   FV: trust, have faith in

81. 剖   poū   FV: tear open, reveal

82. 在口头（頭）上   zaì koǔtoúshang PH: orally, by word of mouth

page 331

83. 帷幕   weímù   N: cloth screen or partition (7-30, 26-78)

84. 小生   xiaǒshēng   N: young man's role (in Chinese opera)

85. 嬌小玲瓏   jiāoxiǎolínglóng EX: refined and delicate, cute (25-73)

86. 悶   mēn   SV: stuffy (11-38)

page 332

87. 銳利   ruìlì   SV: sharp, pointed (8-69, 11-84)

88. 在兴(興)头(頭)上 zài xìngtoúshang PH: be at the height of happiness

89. 聾   lóng   SV: deaf

90. 光身子   guāng shēnzi   PH: bare one's chest (18-56)

91. 翻觔[筋]斗   fān jǐndǒu   PH: turn a somersault

page 333

92. 打架   dǎjià   FV: have a brawl, fight (16-42)

93. 雀斑   quèbān   N: splotch on one's face, freckle (17-55)

94. 香腸   xiāngcháng   N: sausage (M: 根 gēn; 14-35)

*95. 劊子手   guìzishǒu   N: executioner, hatchetman

page 334

96. 出气(氣)筒   chūqìtǒng   N: duct for venting one's anger (19-110)

97. 眉清目秀   meíqǐngmùxiù   EX: "eyebrows pure and clear, eyes elegant" (8-64, 16-25)

98. 耳墜   ěrzhuì   N: earring (M: 副 fù)

*99. 汪   wāng   N: (for expanses of water; 2-76)

100. 折(摺)扇   zhéshàn   N: folding fan (5-27, 11-97)

*101. 弯(彎)身   wānshēn   VO: bend one's body, bow

page 335

*102. 团(團)扇   tuánshàn   N: circular or moon-shaped fan

103. 污   wū   FV: make dirty; offend (25-36)

104. 賴   laì   FV: delay, procrastinate (11-42, 16-39, 26-11)

*105. 泄〔洩〕漏   xièloù   FV: divulge, disclose, reveal
                                            (9-135)

106. 侄〔姪〕孙〔孫)女 zhísūnnǚ   N: grandniece (23-8)

107. 月份〔分〕   yuèfen   N: month

108. 周正   zhōuzhèng   SV: well-proportioned

page 336

*109. 永别   yǒng bié   PH: part with forever (15-101)

*110. 征〔徵)求   zhēngqiú   FV: solicit, seek

111. 成家   chéngjiā   VO: get married, start a family

page 337

*112. 死命地〕   sǐmìngde   A: with all the strength one
                                            can command (29-32)

113. 看穿   kànchuān   RC: look right through (5-72)

page 338

114. 中世紀〕   Zhōng Shìjì   N: Middle Ages (of Western
                                            civilization)

115. 騎士   qíshì   N: knight

116. 寿(壽)辰   shoùchén   N: birthday (11-17, 30-1)

*117. 应(應.)承   yìngchéng   FV: consent, agree (22-13)

118. 無异〔異)   wúyì   PH: be not different from, be
                                            tantamount to

119. 大錯鑄成   dàcuòzhùchéng   EX: "big mistake is forged to
                                            completion," create a tre-
                                            mendous calamity

120. 請出   qǐng chū   PH: ask someone to come out
                                            (to do something)

121. 算命先生   suànmìng xiānsheng N: fortuneteller

122. 合   hé   FV: put together, combine (re-
                                            fers to the 八字 bázì,
                                            cf. 7-110)

123. 不吉   bùjí   PH: "not auspicious" (17-14)

124. 行賄	xínghuì	VO:	bribe
125. 夫荣(榮)妻貴,大吉大利	Fū róng qī guì, dà jí dà lì	PH:	"The groom will prosper, the bride will amass much honor, there will be much luck and all things will go very smoothly"
126. 批語	pīyǔ	N:	critical comments (11-21)
*127. 胡說	húshuō	N/FV:	nonsense/talk nonsense
128. 字条(條)	zìtiáo	N:	strip of paper with characters written on it (13-18)

page 339

129. 当(當)事人	dāngshìrén	N:	person concerned, the one directly involved
*130. 过(過)問	guòwèn	FV:	ask questions
131. 步驟	bùzòu	N:	procedure, steps (4-94, 20-91)
132. 策略[畧]	cèlüè	N:	strategy, scheme (11-105)
133. 避嫌	bìxián	VO:	avoid suspicion (21-75, 22-40)
134. 指使	zhǐshǐ	N/FV:	behind the scenes instigation or incitement/direct, instigate from behind the scenes
135. 回合	huíhé	N:	encounter, round
136. 揚言	yángyán	VO:	spread the word, pass on information (12-107)

page 340

*137. 手段	shǒuduàn	N:	means, method, scheme
*138. 庚帖	gēngtiě	N:	card containing the horoscopes of a betrothed couple (M: 張 zhāng)
*139. 駁斥	bóchì	FV:	retort angrily, refute (5-58)
*140. 余(餘)地	yúdì	N:	"left over ground," room to maneuver in, leeway (5-4)
*141. 脱离(離)	tuōlí	FV:	separate oneself from, break off from
142. 慢吞吞地	màntūntūnde	A:	very slow (of speech; 3-66)

CHAPTER THIRTY-ONE

page 342

1. 历（歷）書　　　　　lìshū　　　　　N: almanac (11-2, 13-27)

2. 書斋（齋）　　　　　shūzhāi　　　　N: study, private reading room (9-77)

3. 綢　　　　　　　　　chóu　　　　　　N: silk fabric

*4. 沙發　　　　　　　　shāfā　　　　　N: sofa (phonetic loan from English; M: 套 tàò, 把 bǎ)

5. 圓角寬袖　　　　　　yuánjiǎo kuānxiù　PH: round coattails and wide sleeves

*6. 靠手　　　　　　　　kàòshoǔ　　　　N: armrest of a chair

7. 反　　　　　　　　　fǎn　　　　　　FV: rebel, oppose

*8. 沉〔沈〕下臉　　　　chénxia liǎn　　PH: make one's countenance fall, make a long face

9. 加緊（緊）地　　　　jiājǐnde　　　　A: with increased intensity

page 343

10. 定亲（親）　　　　　dìngqīn　　　　VO: arrange a marriage

*11. 責罰　　　　　　　　zéfá　　　　　FV/N: punish/punishment (10-6)

12. 洋学（學）堂　　　　yángxuétáng　　N: Western-style Chinese school (2-53)

13. 造反　　　　　　　　zàofǎn　　　　VO: rebel, revolt (31-7)

14. 响（響）雷　　　　　xiǎngleí　　　　N: thunderclap

15. 戳穿　　　　　　　　chuōchuān　　　RC: pierce or stab through (5-72, 30-113)

*16. 蒼蠅〔虫黽〕　　　　cāngying　　　　N: fly (the insect; M: 隻 zhī)

*17. 釘 → 叮　　　　　　dǐng　　　　　FV: bite (of insects; 釘 is here a misprint for 叮)

18. 割宰　　　　　gēzǎi　　　　FV: butcher, slaughter
　　　　　　　　　　　　　　　　　　　(=22-50 宰割 zǎigē)

*19. 刺耳　　　　　cì'ěr　　　　SV: "stab the ear," unpleasant-
　　　　　　　　　　　　　　　　　　　sounding (1-17, 8-89)

page 344

20. 念及手足之情　niànjí shǒuzúzhī PH: "consider the love between
　　　　　　　　　qíng　　　　　　brothers" (文言；念及 =
　　　　　　　　　　　　　　　　　　　想到 xiǎngdaò; 手足
　　　　　　　　　　　　　　　　　　　'hands and feet' is a lit-
　　　　　　　　　　　　　　　　　　　erary term for 'brothers')

*21. 諒解　　　　　liàngjiě　　　FV/N: forgive and understand/
　　　　　　　　　　　　　　　　　　　forgiveness, understanding
　　　　　　　　　　　　　　　　　　　(24-29)

page 345

22. 私刑　　　　　sīxíng　　　　N: illegal punishment

23. 拷打　　　　　kǎodǎ　　　　FV: beat, torture

*24. 昂然地　　　　ángránde　　　A: in a bold and proud manner,
　　　　　　　　　　　　　　　　　　　haughtily (3-25)

25. 妥协(協)　　　tuǒxié　　　　FV: compromise, reconcile

26. 劝(勸)告　　　quàngaò　　　FV/N: advise, counsel/advice

27. 中听(聽)　　　zhōngtīng　　SV: pleasant to listen to (6-61,
　　　　　　　　　　　　　　　　　　　18-29)

28. 干(乾)着急　　gān zhaōjí　　PH: "become upset all dry,"
　　　　　　　　　　　　　　　　　　　worry about something in
　　　　　　　　　　　　　　　　　　　vain, worry without being
　　　　　　　　　　　　　　　　　　　able to do anything about
　　　　　　　　　　　　　　　　　　　a situation

page 346

29. 拖延　　　　　tuōyán　　　　FV: delay, put off (5-88)

30. 开(開)导(導)　kaīdaǒ　　　FV: explain to someone so as
　　　　　　　　　　　　　　　　　　　to make him understand

31. 雄辩　　　　　xióngbiàn　　FV: argue eloquently and force-
　　　　　　　　　　　　　　　　　　　fully (7-155)

32. 劝(勸)誘　　　quànyoù　　　FV: urge, advise (26-31)

33. 推諉	tuīwěi	FV: make excuses
34. 放任	fàngrèn	FV: leave alone, let someone do as he pleases
35. 承担（擔）	chéngdān	FV: take upon oneself, assume (22-13)
36. 目無尊长（長）	mùwúzūnzhǎng	EX: "in one's eyes are not the elders," disregard one's elders (9-100)
37. 無以对（對）	wú yǐ duì	PH: have no means to treat right
38. 同胞	tóngbāo	ADJ/N: "same womb," born of the same mother/compatriot

page 347

39. 顧全	gùquán	FV: consider, think about
40. 一再	yízài	A: over and over again
41. 幸灾（災）乐（樂）禍	xìngzāilèhuò	EX: "rejoice in someone's calamities, be happy about someone's misfortunes," rejoice in the misfortunes of others
42. 会（會）見	huìjiàn	FV: meet, see
43. 根据（據）地	gēnjùdì	N: base (of operations, in the military, etc.)
44. 大本营（營）	dàběnyíng	N: main camp, headquarters (of an army)
45. 气（氣）冲[沖]冲地	qìchōngchōngde	A: very angrily
46. 拖	tuō	FV: drag on, delay, put off (here, =31-29 拖延 tuōyán)

page 348

| 47. 声（聲）明 | shēngmíng | FV/N: make a statement, announce publicly/announcement, proclamation |
| 48. 在气（氣）头（頭）上 | zài qìtóushang | PH: be at the highest point of a fit of rage (30-88) |

49. 悦来(来)茶园(圓) Yuèláí Cháyuán   N: "'Like to Come' Tea Garden"
                                          (name of a theater; 7-34)

50. 相好   xiānghǎo   N: "mutually on good terms,"
                                          lover, sweetheart

51. 風流韵(音員)事   fēngliúyùnshì   EX: romantic and cultured affairs

52. 私通   sītōng   FV: have illicit sexual inter-
                                          course with

53. 有孕   yǒuyùn   VO: be pregnant

54. 收房   shōufáng   VO: accept (someone) into one's
                                          household as a concubine

page 349

55. 一着   yìzhāo   PH: move, step

56. 抱憾終身   bàohànzhōngshēn   EX: regret or deplore for the
                                          rest of one's life (25-120)

57. 成見   chéngjiàn   N: "formed views," prejudice
                                          (25-49)

page 350

58. 解剖   jiěpoū   FV: dissect, take apart (30-81)

59. 封套   fēngtào   N: envelope (here, = 信封 xìn-
                                          fēng, which is more common)

60. 反复(復、覆)   fǎnfù   A: over and over again,
                                          repeatedly (10-76)

61. 逃獄   taóyù   VO: escape from prison (25-111)

62. 犯人   fànren   N: criminal (6-117)

63. 死囚牢   sǐqiúlaó   N: prison for those sentenced
                                          to death (8-103, 22-39)

page 351

64. 孤兒   gū'ér   N: orphan (P-16)

65. 沉[沈]淪   chénlún   FV: sink and perish (19-33)

66. 絶   jué   FV: break off, stop (21-17)

67. 妄想   wàngxiǎng   N/FV: absurd thoughts, vain
                                              hopes, illusion/have ab-
                                              surd thoughts, dream

68. 情份〔分〕   qíngfèn   N: affection, love

69. 心酸   xīnsuān   SV: heartsick, grief-stricken
                                              (19-102, 24-16)

page 352

70. 逃亡   taówáng   FV: flee, escape (9-54)

71. 影像   yǐngxiàng   N: image

page 353

72. 面談   miàntán   FV: speak face to face with
                                              (someone)

73. 揚々得意   yángyángdéyì   EX: smug and complacent,
                                              self-satisfied (1-85,
                                              12-107)

74. 夏布   xiàbù   N: Chinese linen cloth often
                                              worn in the summer

75. 眼皮   yǎnpí   N: eyelid

76. 信息   xìnxí   N: news, information

page 354

77. 悲喜交集   beīxǐjiaōjí   EX: "grief and happiness inter-
                                              mingled," both sad and happy

page 355

78. 会（會）面   huìmiàn   N/FV: face to face meeting/meet
                                              face to face (31-42)

79. 蔑視   mièshì   FV: disregard, disdain (25-130,
                                              28-40)

80. 牵（牽）手   qiānshoǔ   VO: hold hands

page 356

81. 密圈   mì quān   PH: many circles (Chinese add
                                              small circles to the left
                                              side of characters they con-
                                              sider important, much as we
                                              underline important words
                                              and phrases)

82. 囯（國）民之敌（敵） Guómínzhǐ Dí   N: <u>An Enemy of the People</u>
(title of a drama by Henrik Ibsen, published in 新青年 Xīn Qīngnián from July to October, 1918)

83. 賤   jiàn   BF: mean, lowly (term of deprecation)

<u>page 357</u>

84. 冷落   lěngluò   FV: treat someone coldly, give someone a cold shoulder

85. 説了（個）够[夠]   shuōge goù   PH: "say an enough one," say all one wants to (15-136)

86. 調皮   tiaópí   SV: naughty (24-26)

<u>page 358</u>

87. 墜   zhuì   FV: fall, sink

88. 眼鏡片   yǎnjìngpiàn   N: lens of glasses

<u>page 359</u>

89. 辞（辭）   cí   FV: resign from an office, quit a job (11-94)

90. 病状（狀）   bìngzhuàng   N: condition of someone's illness

<u>page 360</u>

91. 自命   zìmìng   FV: speak of oneself as being something or as having some quality

CHAPTER THIRTY-TWO

page 362

1. 譴責	qiǎnzé	N/FV:	reproach, reprimand
2. 講情	jiǎngqíng	VO:	ask for leniency, intercede on someone else's behalf
3. 自立	zìlì	FV:	"self stand," be financially independent, be self-supporting
4. 草稿	cǎogǎo	N:	rough draft (26-58, 29-61)
*5. 倔强	juéjiàng	SV:	intransigent, stubborn
6. 理性	lǐxìng	N:	rationality, reason (25-103)
7. 媒妁之言	méishuòzhīyán	EX:	"the words of the matchmaker" (6-49)
8. 主婚	zhǔhūn	FV:	arrange a wedding match
9. 惩[懲]罰	chéngfá	N/FV:	punishment/punish (31-11)

page 363

10. 鏜々	tāngtāng	ON:	(sound of gongs gonging)

page 364

*11. 招呼	zhāohu	FV:	(here) let someone know something, tell (2-45)
12. 有喜	yǒuxǐ	VO:	"have joy," be pregnant (31-53)
13. 再三	zàisān	A:	again and again, repeatedly (31-40)
14. 叮囑	dīngzhǔ	FV:	urge or advise repeatedly (7-17)
15. 顧惜	gùxī	FV:	value, be careful with (15-128)

*16. 昏   hūn   SV/FV: feel dizzy/faint (3-22, 5-19)

17. 辣   là   SV: hot (as of spicy food)

18. 喉管   hóuguǎn   N: gullet, throat

19. 發癢 (癢)   fāyǎng   VO: itch, tickle

20. 粘 [黏] 膩   niánnì   SV: sticky

21. 冰窖   bīngjiaò   N: basement for keeping ice
                                    (20-21)

22. 半截   bànjié   N: one half (here, = 一半
                                    yíbàn; 25-67)

23. 拭   shì   FV: wipe, rub (10-65)

24. 蓬头 (頭) 髮   péng tóufa   PH: have one's hair tangled
                                    and disheveled (20-70)

*25. 棺材   guāncaí   N: coffin (M: 具 jù; 6-131)

26. 女流   nǔliú   N: member of the fairer sex,
                                    woman

27. 报 (報) 信   baòxìn   VO: report news, announce
                                    something (31-76)

28. 九泉   jiǔquán   N: "nine springs," Hades,
                                    underworld

29. 飄散   piaōsàn   FV: scatter (as if blown by
                                    the wind; 1-4)

30. 枕畔   zhěnpàn   N: edge of a pillow (14-50,
                                    24-10)

31. 遮掩   zhēyǎn   FV: cover (1-52, 19-53)

32. 趴   pā   FV: lie face down on top of
                                    something, crouch down

33. 永恒 [恆]   yǒnghéng   N/ADJ: Eternity/eternal

34. 后 (後) 事   hoùshì   N: matters such as the funeral
                                    which need to be taken care
                                    of after someone has died

35. 没有主意　　　　meíyou zhúyi　　PH: not know what to do

36. 死而有知　　　　sǐ'éryoǔzhī　　PH: die but still have con-
　　　　　　　　　　　　　　　　　　sciousness

*37. 次数（數）　　　cìshu　　　　　N: number of times (one does
　　　　　　　　　　　　　　　　　　something, etc.)

38. 淨［淨］　　　　jìng　　　　　FV: cleanse, clean

39. 殯殮　　　　　　bìliàn　　　　FV: close a coffin (1-44, 12-89)

page 368

*40. 殮衣　　　　　　liànyī　　　　　N: grave clothes, burial clothes

41. 殮被　　　　　　liànbei　　　　N: burial blanket

42. 憎厭　　　　　　zēngyàn　　　　FV: hate, loathe (8-14, 23-83)

43. 綾　　　　　　　líng　　　　　BF: fine silk cloth (FF: 綾子
　　　　　　　　　　　　　　　　　　língzi)

44. 漆匠　　　　　　qījiang　　　　N: artisan who paints lacquer,
　　　　　　　　　　　　　　　　　　varnisher (the noun suffix
　　　　　　　　　　　　　　　　　　匠 jiàng means 'skilled
　　　　　　　　　　　　　　　　　　worker, craftsman [in some
　　　　　　　　　　　　　　　　　　particular trade]'; cf. 36-26
　　　　　　　　　　　　　　　　　　泥水匠 níshuǐjiàng 'ma-
　　　　　　　　　　　　　　　　　　son', 木匠 mùjiang 'car-
　　　　　　　　　　　　　　　　　　penter', and 鐵匠 tiějiang
　　　　　　　　　　　　　　　　　　'blacksmith'; 1-94)

45. 瞎眼睛　　　　　xiā yǎnjing　　PH: "be blind in the eyes,"
　　　　　　　　　　　　　　　　　　be blind (29-97)

46. 姻緣　　　　　　yīnyuán　　　　N: invisible bond that makes a
　　　　　　　　　　　　　　　　　　man and a woman husband and
　　　　　　　　　　　　　　　　　　wife (24-14)

47. 拆散　　　　　　chaīsàn　　　　RC: break up, split apart (18-87)

*48. 落得...下場［塲］luòdé...xiàchǎng PH: come to (some kind of) a
　　　　　　　　　　　　　　　　　　conclusion, end up (in a
　　　　　　　　　　　　　　　　　　certain way)

*49. 苦命　　　　　　kǔmìng　　　ADJ/N: ill-fated, unlucky/bitter
　　　　　　　　　　　　　　　　　　fate (4-119)

50. 鼻涕　　　　　　bíti　　　　　N: nasal mucus, snot (1-29,
　　　　　　　　　　　　　　　　　　28-73)

51. 木釘   mùdīng   N: small wooden peg (31-17)

*52. 釘牢   dìngláo   RC: nail fast (note how tone distinguishes the noun 釘子 dīngzi 'nail, peg' [32-51] from the verb 釘 dìng 'to nail'; 8-103)

53. 接縫处（處）   jiēfèngchù   N: crack, seam (10-61, 13-14)

54. 漆灰   qīhuī   N: lacquer tree ashes (used as glue; 1-94, 2-1)

*55. 具   jù   M: (for coffins and corpses)

page 369

*56. 灵（靈）柩   língjiù   N: coffin containing a corpse

57. 殡所   bìnsuǒ   N: funeral hall (where caskets are stored prior to burial)

58. 出殡   chūbìn   N/VO: funeral procession (during which a coffin is carried to a grave)/set out on a funeral procession

59. 年久失修   niánjiǔshīxiū   PH: "as the years get long, omit repair," in dilapidated condition

60. 荒凉［涼］   huāngliáng   SV: desolate, deserted (11-70)

61. 殿   diàn   BF: temple, hall

62. 寄殡   jìbìn   FV: deposit (a coffin someplace for later burial; 26-89, 29-33)

*63. 灵（靈）位牌   língweìpaí   N: wooden tablet inscribed with the name of the deceased which is placed before a coffin

64. 没有主   meíyou zhǔ   PH: without owner

65. 兄弟   xiōngdi   N: (here) younger brother (usually: xiōngdì 'older and younger brothers'; 8-110)

page 370

66. 故 胞 姊   gùbāōjiě   N: deceased sister (31-38)

67. 眼帘（簾）   yǎnlián   N: iris (of the eye; 5-20)

*68. 棺盖（蓋）   guān'gaì   N: coffin lid (32-25)

page 371

*69. 灵（靈）   líng   BF: coffin (32-56)

70. 好不寂寞   haǒ bùjímò   PH: very lonely (=好寂寞
                                       haǒ jímò; sometimes, de-
                                       pending on the context,
                                       好不 haǒ bù 'very not'
                                       is equivalent in meaning
                                       to 好 haǒ 'very'; 1-97,
                                       21-65)

71. 語不成声（聲）   yǔbùchéngshēng EX: "words do not become
                                       sound," moan or wail in
                                       a low voice

72. 恨不能   hènbunéng   PH: "hate that one cannot,"
                                       wish very much that one
                                       could (do something diffi-
                                       cult; =1-41 恨不得
                                       hènbudé)

73. 看个（個）明白   kàn'ge míngbai PH: "see a clear one," see
                                       something clearly (15-136,
                                       31-85)

CHAPTER THIRTY-THREE

page 372

1. 再不然、　　　　　zàiburán　　　　A: otherwise

2. 孤立　　　　　　　gūlì　　　　　　SV: isolated, alone (P-16)

page 373

3. 共鳴　　　　　　　gòngmíng　　　　FV/N: have the same feeling or opinion as someone else/ sympathy (10-109)

4. 大意、　　　　　　dàyi　　　　　　SV: careless

5. 差使　　　　　　　chāishǐ　　　　N: job (30-69)

6. 归（歸）　　　　　guī　　　　　　FV: be one's responsibility, belong to

page 374

7. 身后（後）　　　　shēnhòu　　　　PH: after one's death

8. 惨（慘）状（狀）　cǎnzhuàng　　　N: sad or grievous situation (4-1)

9. 窃［竊］听（聽、）　qiètīng　　　FV: eavesdrop

page 375

10. 卖（賣）弄　　　　màinòng　　　　FV: flaunt, show off (25-115)

11. 陪嫁　　　　　　　peíjià　　　　FV: give a dowry to a daughter on her marriage (4-66)

12. 样（樣）子　　　　yàngzi　　　　N: model, sample

13. 一味　　　　　　　yíweì　　　　　A: persistently, invariably

14. 支吾　　　　　　　zhīwu　　　　　FV: make excuses, evade

15. 偶尔（爾）　　　　oǔ'ěr　　　　　A: (here) by chance (5-7)

16. 当（當）卖（賣）　dàngmaì　　　FV: pawn off and sell (22-55)

17. 妓女	jìnǚ	N: prostitute
18. 衰落	shuāiluò	FV: decline and fall, decay (5-16, 9-35)
19. 通	tōng	FV: lead through to, connect with

page 376

20. 罪恶（惡）	zuì'è	N: sin, crime, vice
*21. 摔掉	shuāidiào	RC: throw down
22. 四下	sìxià	PW: all four directions, everywhere
23. 末日	mòrì	N: last day (distinguish 末 and 16-3 未 wèi 'not yet')

page 377

24. 窥探	kuītàn	FV: spy on, peep at (16-47)
25. 羞	xiū	FV: feel ashamed of someone (3-61, 11-46)
26. 牛肚皮	niúdùpí	N: ox belly (the inference is that the knowledge 克定 Kèdìng gained through his studies did not end up in his own stomach but in that of a lowly ox; 25-23)
27. 畜生	chùsheng	N: beast, brute
28. 偏爱（愛）	piānài	N/FV: special or particular love/ love especially, favor (1-12, 29-47)
29. 初犯	chūfàn	N: first offense (31-62)

page 378

| 30. 左右开（開）弓 | zuǒyòukāigōng | EX: "draw a bow from left to right," work both arms back and forth |
| 31. 坐吃山空 | zuòchīshānkōng | EX: "while sitting (idle) eat a mountain (of money) empty," without an income one's savings are quickly exhausted |

32. 养 (養) 活	yǎnghuo	FV:	support (someone so as to keep him alive)
33. 屈辱	qūrǔ	ADJ/N:	humiliating, disgraceful/ humiliation, disgrace (11-108)
34. 結識	jiéshí	FV:	strike up an acquaintance with, associate with (someone)
35. 邪路	xiélù	N:	perverse or wicked road, path of debauchery
36. 私娼	sīchāng	N:	unlawful prostitute (23-32, 31-22)

page 379

37. 隱瞞	yǐnmán	FV:	hide, cover up (the truth; 1-78, 24-7)
38. 債	zhài	N:	loan (M: 17-5 筆 bǐ; 12-1)
39. 欠	qiàn	FV:	owe
40. 打耳光	dǎ ěrguāng	PH:	slap someone on his face
41. 牵 (牽) 連	qiānlián	FV:	involve, implicate (someone else in trouble; here, =28-89 連累 liánlèi; 31-80)
42. 执 (執) 行	zhíxíng	FV:	carry out (an order)
43. 虚 伪 (偽)	xūwěi	SV:	false, hypocritical, insincere (11-26, 13-121)
44. 自豪	zìháo	FV:	be proud of oneself (3-36)

page 380

*45. 棒客	bàngkè	N:	"people with clubs—clubbers," robbers, bandits (四川)
46. 粮 [糧] 税	liángshuì	N:	grain tax
47. 陪奩	péilián	VO:	give a bridal trousseau to one's daughter when she marries
48. 做魁臉	zuò guǐliǎn	PH:	grimace, make a face

page 381

49. 靠背   kàobèi   N: back of a chair (16-23,
                                         31-6)

50. 叛逆   pànnì   N: one who revolts against
                                         his superiors, rebel (21-36)

51. 独〔獨〕断〔斷〕   dúduàn   FV: decide by oneself (3-82,
                                         25-100)

page 382

52. 局面   júmiàn   N: situation, state of affairs

53. 下坡   xiàpō   VO: go down a slope, go downhill
                                         (19-40)

54. 赤手空拳   chìshǒukōngquán EX: "naked hand, empty fist,"
                                         be empty-handed, be unable
                                         to do anything about a sit-
                                         uation (18-56, 28-2)

55. 垮   kuǎ   FV: topple, collapse (distinguish
                                         2-8 跨 kuà 'bestride' and
                                         誇 kuā as in 18-35 誇奬
                                         kuājiǎng 'praise')

56. 败家子   bàijiāzǐ   N: prodigal son who ruins a
                                         family (often pronounced
                                         败家子兒 bàijiāzǐr)

57. 幻灭〔滅〕   huànmiè   N: disillusionment (3-157)

58. 丧〔喪〕失   sàngshī   FV: lose (15-105)

59. 阔〔濶〕   kuò   SV: big, wide (3-31)

60. 相   xiàng   BF: expression (= 樣子 yàngzi)

page 383

61. 颠倒   diāndǎo   FV: turn upside down (28-77)

CHAPTER THIRTY-FOUR

1. 藥[药]引　　　　yàoyǐn　　　N: auxiliary medicine, something given with a medicine to bring out its effects (14-38)

2. 藥[药]罐　　　　yàoguàn　　　N: pottery jar for cooking medicinal preparations

3. 熬、　　　　　　aó　　　　　FV: boil, simmer (14-28)

4. 服藥[药]　　　　fúyào　　　　VO: take or swallow medicine

5. 調笑　　　　　　tiaóxiaò　　　FV: provoke laughter, tease (30-31)

6. 医[醫]藥[药]　　yǐyaò　　　　N: healing drugs, medicine

*7. 求助于(於)　　qiú zhù yú　　PH: seek help from

8. 許愿(願)　　　xǔyuàn　　　　VO: promise offerings to a deity in exchange for divine blessings

9. 奉行　　　　　　fèngxíng　　　FV: perform or carry out something as ordered (29-37)

*10. 道士　　　　　daòshi　　　　N: Taoist priest

11. 作法念、咒　　　zuòfǎniànzhoù　EX: "exercise magical powers and chant incantations" (12-74)

12. 菩薩　　　　　　Púsa　　　　　N: Bodhisattva (Buddhist deity second in importance after Buddha)

13. 点[點、點]　　　diǎn　　　　FV: light (6-167)

*14. 炷　　　　　　zhù　　　　　M: (for sticks of incense)

15. 齐(齊)整　　　qízhěng　　　SV: neat and orderly (=6-78 整齊 zhěngqí)

16. 念ㄅ有詞[辭]   niànniànyǒucí   EX: mumble incantations

17. 見鬼   jiànguǐ   IE: "Nonsense!"

18. 果[菓]品   guǒpǐn   N: items like fruit and pastry

19. 隆重   lóngzhòng   SV: solemn, formal

20. 滑稽   huáji   SV: funny, ridiculous

21. 小时(時)   xiǎoshí   N: hour (= 鐘頭 zhōngtóu)

page 386

22. 誦讀   sòngdú   FV: recite, intone (5-34)

23. 巫师(師)   wūshī   N: sorcerer, wizard

24. 端公   duāngōng   N: sorcerer, wizard (四川)

25. 披头(頭)散髮   pītóusànfǎ   EX: "unroll head, scatter hair,"
                                        with long and uncombed hair
                                        draped over the shoulders

26. 法衣   fǎyī   N: robe or gown worn by priests
                                        (M: 件 jiàn)

27. 粉灰   fěnhuǒ   N: type of powder which is
                                        spread on the gound and
                                        can be ignited

28. 威嚇   weīhè   FV/N: threaten, intimidate/threat,
                                        intimidation (4-97, 26-40)

29. 大扫(掃)除   dà saǒchú   PH: "big sweeping away (of unde-
                                        sirable elements)," large-
                                        scale elimination and puri-
                                        fication (9-96)

page 387

30. 痊愈[痭、癒]   quányù   FV: be cured, recover from
                                        an illness

*31. 滑稽戏(戲、戲)   huájīxì   N: comedy, burlesque, farce
                                        (34-20)

32. 騷扰(擾)   saōraǒ   N/FV: disturbance, harassment/
                                        disturb, harass (8-77)

33. 云动(動)彈   dòngtan   FV: budge, move, stir

*34. 擂   leí   FV: beat, pound (9-70)

page 388

35. 爆炸   baòzhà   FV: explode, blow up (8-41, 13-111)

*36. 事理   shìlǐ   N: facts and principles in-
                               volved in something (11-63)

page 389

37. 把守   bǎshǒu   FV: guard, defend

38. 关(關)口   guānkǒu   N: pass, strategic point
                               (M: 道 daò)

39. 不知所措   bùzhīsuǒcuò   EX: "not know that which should
                               be arranged," not know what
                               to do (29-51)

40. 假借...名义(義) jiǎjiè...míngyì PH: "borrow...name (as opposed
                               to reality or substance),"
                               do something in the name of
                               something else

page 390

41. 嘴巴   zuǐba   N: (here) slap on the face (23-82)

42. 理直气(氣)壮(壯) lǐzhíqìzhuàng EX: "reason straight, spirit
                               strong," speak or act with
                               confidence because one knows
                               one is in the right, be
                               fearless

43. 下贱   xiàjiàn   SV: low, cheap (31-83)

44. 替...着想,   tì...zháoxiǎng PT: look after the interests of,
                               think of (someone; =21-76
                               为...着想, weì...zhaóxiǎng)

45. 悔   huǐ   FV: regret, repent (4-9, 14-88)

46. 仗   zhàng   FV: rely or depend on

page 391

47. 占(佔)便宜   zhàn piányi   PH: take advantage (of someone;
                               30-23)

48. 一哄而散   yīhōngérsàn   EX: "with one loud noise scatter"
                               (describes many people leaving
                               noisily at the same time; 17-94)

49. 捧场[場]   pěngchǎng   VO: render support or assistance
                               by one's presence (7-15)

50. 大获(獲)全胜(勝) dàhuòquánshèng EX: "greatly receive complete vic-
                               tory," win a total victory

CHAPTER THIRTY-FIVE

page 392

1. 口沫　　　　　　　koǔmò　　　　　N: saliva (23-28)

2. 秃頂　　　　　　　tūdǐng　　　　　SV: bald at the crown of one's head, bald-headed (9-25)

3. 威严〔嚴〕　　　　weǐyán　　　　　SV/N: stern, severe/severity, dignity (9-94, 18-49)

4. 磁〔瓷〕杯　　　　cíbeǐ　　　　　　N: porcelain cup (14-56)

page 393

5. 扫〔掃〕兴〔興〕　saǒxìng　　　　SV: disappointed, discouraged

page 394

6. 奇迹〔跡、蹟〕　　qíjī　　　　　　N: miracle

7. 耽〔躭〕误　　　　dānwu　　　　　FV: delay, procrastinate (2-32)

page 395

8. 凯旋　　　　　　　kaǐxuán　　　　FV: return in triumph (as of an army returning from war; 1-43)

9. 預〔豫〕兆　　　　yùzhaò　　　　　N: premonition, omen (4-71, 8-39)

page 396

10. 理会〔會〕　　　　lǐhuì　　　　　FV: pay attention to, take notice of (8-107)

11. 抑制　　　　　　　yìzhì　　　　　FV: restrain, repress (21-11)

12. 膈膜　　　　　　　gémó　　　　　　N: barrier that leads to misunderstanding (5-57)

page 397

13. 筋肉　　　　　　　jīnroù　　　　　N: muscle (3-117)

14. 弛緩　　　　　　chíhuǎn　　　SV: loose and weak (8-86, 22-16)

15. 揚名显(顯)亲(親)　yángmíngxiǎnqīn　EX: "spread (the family) name, make known one's parents," bring honor to one's family (6-20, 12-107)

16. 报(報)丧(喪)　　baòsāng　　VO: announce the news of someone's death (33-58)

page 398

17. 桂堂　　　　　　guìtáng　　　N: special room of a house

18. 两(兩)　　　　　liǎng　　　　M: tael, ounce (of silver)

19. 开(開)路　　　　kāilù　　　VO: "open the road (to the next world)"

20. 法事　　　　　　fǎshì　　　　N: Taoist or Buddhist rituals performed on special occasions (34-11)

21. 小殓　　　　　　xiǎoliàn　　N: ritual of dressing up the dead in preparation for a funeral (12-89)

22. 时(時)辰　　　　shíchen　　　N: time

23. 沐浴　　　　　　mùyù　　　　FV: bathe, cleanse (19-55, 22-34)

24. 空隙[隙]　　　　kòngxì　　　N: empty space, crevice, crack (10-61)

25. 转佛　　　　　　zhuàn Fó　　PH: walk around the coffin of a deceased person and chant incantations (of monks, etc.)

26. 佛号(號)　　　　Fóhaò　　　　N: names of Buddhist deities

27. 兜圈子　　　　　dōu quānzi　PH: walk about in a circle

28. 承重孙(孫)　　　chéngzhòngsūn　N: "inheriting great-grandson," eldest grandson whose deceased father was heir to the grandparents (refers to oneself in the death announcement of one's grandparent; 6-31)

29. 大殓　　　　　　dàliàn　　　　N: ritual of placing the deceased into the coffin and sealing it (35-21)

30. 生肖   shēngxiaò   N: year of the animal in which one was born (in traditional China, each year of a cycle of twelve years was associated with a particular animal: 鼠 shǔ 'rat', 牛 niú 'ox', 虎 hǔ 'tiger', 兔 tù 'rabbit', 龍 lóng 'dragon', 蛇 shé 'snake', 馬 mǎ 'horse', 羊 yáng 'lamb', 猴 hóu 'monkey', 雞 jī 'chicken', 狗 quǎn 'dog', and 猪 zhū 'pig')

page 399

*31. 訣別   juébié   FV: part from, say good-bye to (usually people whom one won't see again; 15-101)

*32. 灵(靈)堂   língtáng   N: funeral parlor (32-69)

33. 彩行   caǐháng   N: store that sells decorations

34. 素彩   sùcaǐ   N: white-colored decorations (in China white is the color of mourning; 30-67)

35. 經堂   jīngtáng   N: prayer hall

*36. 念經   niànjīng   VO: read Buddhist scriptures (5-34)

37. 挽[輓]联(聯、聫)   wǎnlián   N: scroll with matching couplets of characters sent to a funeral in memory of a friend (1-135)

38. 祭幛   jìzhàng   N: silk funeral banner which is hung up on a wall or partition and contains four characters expressing condolences

39. 佛像   Fóxiàng   N: Buddhist idol (M: 20-94 尊 zūn)

40. 閻罗(羅)殿   Yánluódiàn   N: Palace of the God of the Underworld (32-61)

41. 闊[濶]綽   kuòchuò   N/SV: extravagance, affluence/ extravagant, affluent (13-96, 33-59)

42. 成服   chéngfú   VO: put on mourning dress and begin the official period of mourning

43. 紛至   fēnzhì   ADJ: arriving in continuous succession, very numerous (10-47)

44. 吊〔弔〕客   diaòkè   N: visitor at a funeral ceremony, mourner

*45. 灵（靈）帷   língweí   N: curtain surrounding a coffin (32-69)

46. 功用   gōngyòng   N: use, function

47. 吹鼓手   chuīgǔshoǔ   N: bugler and/or drummer, musician (14-113)

48. 叫号（號）   jiaòhaó   FV: shout, cry out loudly (20-44)

49. 嗩呐   suǒnà   N: flute-like instrument of Turkish origin made from wood with a brass mouthpiece

50. 寂然無声（聲）   jí'ránwúshēng   EX: "quiet and without a sound," soundless, still (1-111)

51. 礼（禮）生   lǐshēng   N: master of ceremonies

*52. 暗示   ànshì   N/FV: secret signal (to get someone to do something)/hint, suggest (25-128)

53. 孝子   xiaòzǐ   N: son one of whose parents has died

54. 报（報）单（單）   baòdān   N: announcement of a death sent out to friends and relatives, obituary

55. 泣血稽颡   qìxuèqǐsǎng   EX: "weep blood, knock forehead to the ground" (describes people greatly mourning their parents or grandparents; 34-20)

page 400

56. 答礼（禮）   dálǐ   VO: reciprocate another's greetings, return courtesies (15-43)

57. 草荐   caǒjiàn   N: straw mattress

58. 消极抵抗   xiaōjí dǐkàng   PH: passive resistance

59. 維持場[場]面   weíchí chǎngmiàn   PH: maintain a certain appear-
                                          ance before the public, put
                                          up a front of respectability

60. 磕头（頭）   kètoú   VO: kowtow (=15-26 叩頭 koùtoú)

61. 麻冠   máguān   N: hemp cap (28-96)

62. 孝巾   xiaòjīn   N: "filial streamer" (long
                                          strip of cloth attached to
                                          a hemp cap, part of the tra-
                                          ditional funeral attire)

63. 麻带（帶）   mádaì   N: hemp string

64. 哭丧（喪）棒   kūsāngbàng   N: mourning staff (held by a
                                          son during funeral ceremo-
                                          nies to support himself in
                                          his grief; 33-45)

65. 誦經   sòngjīng   VO: recite Buddhist scriptures
                                          (5-34, 34-22, 35-36)

*66. 烛（燭）花   zhúhuā   N: snuff of a candle (4-17)

67. 烛（燭）油   zhúyoú   N: tallow, melted candle wax

68. 鋏子   jiázi   N: pincers, tongs

page 401

69. 平生   píngshēng   A: throughout one's life, one's
                                          whole life long

70. 搜[蒐]集   soūjí   FV: collect

71. 希罕   xīhan   FV: value, care about

72. 独（獨）吞   dútūn   FV: keep something or pocket a
                                          profit without sharing with
                                          anyone else (3-66)

73. 遺命   yímìng   N: injunctions of a dead per-
                                          son, testamentary orders

74. 遺贈   yízèng   N: testamentary bequest,
                                          legacy

75. 假造   jiǎzaò   FV: falsify, forge

76. 西蜀商業公司   Xīshǔ Shāngyè Gōngsī   N: West Sìchuan Mercantile Corporation (6-98)

77. 股票   gǔpiaò   N: stock certificate (M: 張 zhāng; 6-102)

page 403

1. 生产（產） shēngchǎn FV: give birth

2. 血光之灾（災） xuèguāngzhīzaī EX: "disaster of the blood glow" (the blood of a woman in childbirth was believed to be harmful to the corpse of a deceased elder in the same house)

3. 产（產）妇（婦） chǎnfù N: woman in childbirth

4. 冲〔沖〕犯 chōngfàn FV: attack, invade (15-62)

5. 迁（遷） qiān FV: move, remove

6. 筑（築） zhú FV: build, construct (18-92)

*7. 假坟（墳） jiǎfén N: "false grave," temporary outer covering of bricks for a coffin (27-23)

8. 照办（辦） zhaòbàn FV: handle something according to someone's instructions (30-8)

page 404

9. 利益 lìyi N: interests of someone in a matter, benefit (29-55)

10. 晴天霹雳 qíngtiānpīlì EX: "bolt out of the clear blue sky" (20-90)

11. 待遇 daìyù N: way of treating people (6-107)

12. 宁（寧）可信其有，不可信其无、 níngkě xìn qí yoǔ, bùkě xìn qí wú PH: "Better believe that it exists (i.e., is thus), rather than believe that it doesn't," better play safe (16-31)

13. 担〔擔〕承 dānchéng FV: take upon oneself, assume (=31-35 承擔 chéngdān)

14. 相处（處）   xiāngchǔ   FV: live together, get along
                                           with one another (3-81)

15. 怀（懷）胎   huáitāi   VO: be pregnant (31-53)

page 405

16. 办（辦）妥   bàntuǒ   RC: work something out in a
                                           satisfactory way (18-15)

17. 地板   dìbǎn   N: wooden floor

18. 潮湿（濕、溼）   chaóshī   SV: damp, humid

19. 待合   fúhé   FV: match, correspond to,
                                           agree with

20. 操心   caōxīn   VO: worry (8-54, 23-69)

page 406

21. 提箱   tíxiāng   N: suitcase

*22. 网（網）篮   wǎnglán   N: basket covered with a net
                                           (19-9, 29-109)

23. 出远（遠）门   chū yuǎnmén   PH: travel far away, go on a
                                           long trip

24. 信口   xìnkoǔ   A: said without intending to,
                                           slipped out (of speech;
                                           11-13, 13-103)

25. 竭力   jiélì   AV: use up all one's energy,
                                           try as hard as one can

page 407

26. 泥水匠   níshuǐjiàng   N: mason (32-44)

27. 眼眶   yǎnkuàng   N: eye socket

page 408

28. 証（證）实（實） zhēngshí   FV: confirm, verify

29. 扭手   niǔshoǔ   VO: wring one's hands

30. 景物   jǐngwù   N: scenery, landscape, view

page 409

31. 气（氣）憤不堪   qìfènbùkān   EX: unbearably angry (7-105,
                                                    8-106)

32. 背地   bèidì   PW: behind one's back

33. 承重老爷（爺）   chéngzhònglǎoye   N: "inheriting old master"

page 410

34. 防綫［線］   fángxiàn   N: line of defense (M: 道 dào)

35. 苛刻   kēkè   SV: harsh, merciless, mean

page 411

*36. 拔步   bábù   A: moving forward quickly,
                                                   taking to one's heels
                                                   (14-129, 28-43)

*37. 嘻々   xīxì   ON: (sound of laughter; 17-20)

38. 会（會）   huì   FV: meet, see (31-42, 31-78)

39. 新居   xīnjū   N: new residence (12-117)

page 412

40. 期限   qīxiàn   N: period of time

41. 彈泪（淚）   tánlèi   VO: shed tears

42. 关（關、鬪、関）   guānhuái   FV/N: be concerned about (some-
     怀（懷）   one)/concern (2-49, 13-29)

43. 不胜（勝）依恋（戀） bùshēngyīliàn   EX: "not able to endure longing
                                                   for someone," very unwilling
                                                   to part with a loved one
                                                   (4-116)

44. 破曉   pòxiǎo   N/FV: "daybreak," dawn

45. 經不住   jīngbuzhù   RC: be unable to tolerate
                                                   (25-89)

46. 怪   guài   A: very

page 413

47. 抽空   chōukōng   VO: find time

48. 柔声（聲）　　　róushēng　　　A/N: in a soft and tender tone of voice/soft and tender voice (6-87, 22-72)

49. 去信　　　　　　qùxìn　　　　　VO: send a letter

page 414

*50. 招手　　　　　　zhāoshǒu　　　VO: beckon with one's hand (2-45)

51. 恍惚　　　　　　huǎnghū　　　　SV: confused, dazed (7-118)

52. 胎兒　　　　　　tāi'ér　　　　　N: fetus, unborn baby (36-15)

53. 悲憤交集　　　　bēifènjiāojí　EX: "grief and anger inter-mingled," both sad and happy (22-64, 31-77)

54. 如約　　　　　　rúyuē　　　　　PH: "as agreed" (8-22)

55. 轉啼為笑　　　　zhuǎntíwéixiào　EX: "turn crying to laughing," change from a state of crying to one of laughing (29-85)

56. 监（監）工　　　jiāngōng　　　　VO: supervise work

57. 改口　　　　　　gǎikǒu　　　　　VO: "change one's mouth," say something different from what one has said before

page 415

58. 突出　　　　　　tūchū　　　　　FV: stick or jut out, protrude (4-103)

page 416

59. 难（難）为（為）　nánwei　　　FV: trouble someone to do something, thank someone for his troubles

60. 啰　　　　　　　luo　　　　　　P: (traditional form of the simplified character 4-45 罗)

CHAPTER THIRTY-SEVEN

page 417

1. 帳惘　　chàngwǎng　　SV: depressed, disappointed

page 418

2. 接生婆　　jiēshēngpó　　N: midwife (3-135, 6-111)

3. 包裹　　bāoguǒ　　FV/N: wrap/parcel, package (M: 件 jiàn; 22-5)

4. 襁〔襁〕褓　　qiǎngbǎo　　N: swaddling clothes

page 419

5. 哎哟　　aīyaō　　I: (indicates pain or suffering)

6. 哇　　wā　　ON: (sound of crying)

7. 灶〔竈〕房　　zaòfáng　　N: kitchen (15-28)

page 420

*8. 放　　fàng　　FV: allow, let

page 421

9. 昏厥　　hūnjué　　FV: lose consciousness (32-16)

page 422

10. 加倍　　jiābeì　　A/FV: greatly increased/increase twofold, double

11. 看护〔護〕　　kānhù　　FV/N: take care of, nurse/nurse (看 kān, with the first tone, means to "look" after or take care of)

12. 巨　　jù　　BF: great, large (FF: 17-65 巨 大 jùdà)

13. 大禍临〔臨〕头〔頭〕　　dàhuòlíntoú　　EX: "great calamity near head," disaster is at hand (6-198, 20-25)

14. 貫住　　　　　guànzhù　　　FV: concentrate (one's love, attention, etc.) on something (6-189)

page 423

15. 公子　　　　　gōngzǐ　　　　N: son (polite word)

16. 娘〔孃〕　　　niáng　　　　N: mother, mom (5-67 爹 diē 'father' and 娘 niáng are used, especially in North China, as equivalents of 父親 fùqin and 母親 mǔqin or 爸爸 bàba and 媽媽 māma; 2-57, 14-83)

17. 重量　　　　　zhòngliàng　　N: weight

18. 懺悔　　　　　chànhuǐ　　　FV: repent (of one's mistakes; 10-74)

19. 专(專)制　　zhuānzhì　　　SV/N: despotic, dictatorial/dictatorship, tyrannical government

20. 应(應)和　　yìnghé　　　　FV: mix, mingle

page 424

21. 亲(親)家太太　qìngjiā tàitai　N: lady who is the mother of a married woman (親家 refers to the parents of a husband or wife)

22. 月房　　　　　yuèfáng　　　N: lying-in room (room in which a woman gives birth)

23. 惨(慘)　　　cǎn　　　　　SV: terrible, tragic, miserable (4-1)

24. 根　　　　　gēn　　　　　M: (for long and narrow things like needles, blades of glass, hairs, strings, etc.; 7-67)

CHAPTER THIRTY-EIGHT

page 425

1. 支　　　　　zhī　　　　FV: prop up, support (14-70)

2. 下領　　　　xiàhàn　　　N: chin (9-37)

3. 鏡框　　　　jìngkuàng　　N: picture frame (3-45, 24-36)

4. 凝視　　　　níngshì　　　FV: "freeze" or fix one's eyes on, gaze at with great concentration (19-115, 22-51)

5. 爱(愛)国(國)布　aìguóbù　N: "love country cloth," type of cloth produced in China during the boycott of foreign goods

6. 边(邊)代袋　　biāndài　　N: pocket at the edge of a piece of clothing (12-124)

page 426

7. 开(開)奠　　　kaìdiàn　　VO: offer libations or sacrifice at a funeral

8. 安葬　　　　ānzàng　　　FV: bury in a grave (12-125, 15-58, 17-33)

page 427

9. 庙(廟)子　　　miaòzi　　N: temple (M: 座 zuò; 四川; 21-35)

10. 活轉来(来)　　huózhuǎnlaí　RC: come back to life

11. 丧(喪)服　　　sāngfú　　N: period of mourning

12. 續弦[絃]　　　xùxián　　VO: "add on a (new) lute string," remarry (of a man; 17-47)

13. 云(雲)兒　　　Yún'ér　　N: (人名)

14. 嘉定　　　　Jiādìng　　PW: (name of a city in Sìchuan province to the south of Chéngdū; also known as 樂山 Lèshān)

page 428

15. 管不管由你　　　guǎnbuguǎn yóu nǐ　PH: "whether you concern your-self (with me) or not is up to you" (cf. 信不信由你　xìnbuxìn yóu nǐ 'believe it or not'—the Chinese title of Robert Ripley's famous newspaper column)

16. 轉机（機）　　　zhuǎnjī　　　N: turning point

17. 謀事　　　moúshì　　　VO: look for a job

page 429

18. 求活　　　jiùhuó　　　RC: save (the life of), rescue

page 430

19. 相邻（鄰隣）　xiānglín　　　ADJ: adjacent

20. 丧（喪）事　　sāngshì　　　N: matters connected with someone's funeral (contrast with 33-58 喪失　sàngshī 'lose')

21. 三七　　　sān qī　　　PH: "three times seven (days)," three weeks (8-78, 29-119)

22. 不祥　　　bùxiáng　　　PH: inauspicious, unlucky (7-78)

23. 心如刀割　　xīnrúdāogē　　EX: "heart (feels) like knife cutting," a knife through the heart (29-53)

page 431

24. 扯　　　chě　　　FV: talk freely without a def-inite topic of conversation, chat (21-33)

25. 严（嚴）正　　yánzhèng　　SV: severe, stern

26. 礼（禮）制　　lǐzhì　　　N: rules for ceremonial conduct

27. 起旱　　　qǐhàn　　　VO: go by land route (as opposed to by water)

28. 繁华（華）　　fánhuá　　　SV/N: given to luxury, extravagant/ luxury, rich way of living (4-60)

page 432

29. 習气（氣）   xíqi   N: habit, custom, fad (often bad)

30. 公子哥兒   gōngzǐgeēr   N: dandy, playboy (37-15)

31. 漲水   zhǎngshuǐ   VO: rise, flood (of water)

32. 叛徒   pàntú   N: rebel (33-50)

33. 石印本   shíyìnběn   N: lithographic edition (of a publication)

34. 訃聞   fùwén   N: obituary notice

35. 行述   xíngshù   N: record of what someone did and said during his life, biography of a deceased person (often accompanies the obituary notice)

36. 讀書而后（後）明礼（禮），勤儉所以持家

Dú shū érhòu míng lǐ, qín jiǎn suǒ yǐ chí jiā

After studying the classics he understood the rules of propriety; he managed family affairs with diligence and frugality

37. 样（樣）本   yàngběn   N: sample of a printed text (33-12)

38. 撕烂（火闌）   sīlàn   RC: tear to shreds, rip to pieces (11-53, 20-10)

page 433

39. 筹（籌）   chóu   FV: raise (money; 7-35)

40. 推口   tuīkǒu   A: making excuses (31-33)

page 434

41. 难（難）住   nánzhù   RC: ask someone something so difficult or present someone with so complicated a problem that he is rendered completely at a loss; nonplus, stump

42. 戴孝   dàixiaò   VO: wear mourning dress

page 435

43. 难（難）题   nántí   N: difficult problem

44. 本科   běnkē   N: main course (of studies at a university, as distinct from preparatory courses)

45. 蓬勃   péngbó   SV: growing quickly, flourishing (20-70, 20-98)

page 436

46. 下联（聯、聫）   xiàlián   N: second line of a 1-135 對聫 duìlián or couplet

47. 家人同一哭
Jiārén tóngyī kū
The members of the family all weep

咏絮怜（憐）才
Yǒngxù lián caí
That the talent of the cultured one is gone is very sad

焚鬚增痛
Fén xū zēng tòng
My pain (at my sister's death) is as if my whiskers were burned

料得心縈幼兒
Liaòdé xīn yíng yoù'ér
I think your heart must be entwined around your babe

未获（獲）百般顾复（復）
Weì huò baǐbān gùfù
It has not received your tender care

待完职（職）任累高堂
Daì wán zhírèn leí Gaōtáng
Trouble the Gaō's to fulfill the responsibility you could not

48. 燕窩酥   yànwōsū   N: swallow's nest brittle (a delicacy, eaten as a snack)

49. 蒸   zhēng   FV: steam (food)

50. 頂綫 [線]   dǐngxiàn   N: cord at the top of something which enables one to hang it up

CHAPTER THIRTY-NINE

page 437

1. 不凡（幾）时（時） bùjǐshí   A: for a not long time, for a short time (here, = 不多久 bùduōjiǔ; 14-95, 19-132)

2. 帮（幫、幇）手 bāngshǒu   N: "helping hand," helper, assistant (14-113, 35-47)

3. 这（這）一向 zhè yíxiàng   A: recently

4. 出下去 chūxiaqu   RC: continue to be published (the RE 下去 xiàqù indicates continuation of the action of the verb, e.g., 做下去 zuòxiaqu 'keep on doing', 繼續下去 jìxuxiaqu 'continue', 活不下去 huóbuxiàqù 'cannot keep on living')

page 438

5. 鬼 guǐ   ADJ: cursed, damned

6. 立足 lìzú   VO: "establish (one's) feet," establish oneself (in society)

7. 充实（實） chōngshí   SV/FV: rich in content, complete and abundant/give real substance to, strengthen (2-62, 13-89)

8. 望 wàng   FV: look forward to, hope for

page 439

9. 露出破綻 lùchū pòzhan   PH: "expose a broken seam," (here) reveal a secret

10. 餞行 jiànxíng   FV: give a farewell party for someone

11. 当（當）   dàng   FV: pawn (22-55, 33-16)

12. 公   gōng   BF: everybody

13. 分摊（攤）   fēntān   FV: share (a financial burden; 9-130, 28-14)

page 440

14. 汪   Wāng   N: （人名; 2-76, 30-99)

15. 哪儿（個）騙你 不是人   Nǎge piàn ni búshi rén   PH: "Whoever deceives you isn't a person," "If I'm lying, I'm not a person," "On my honor hope to die" (1-101)

page 441

16. 多时（時）   duōshí   A: for a long time

17. 吹拂   chuīfú   FV: blow and brush against (as of the wind against cheeks; 10-65)

18. 斜纹布   xiéwénbù   N: twill (fabric made with diagonally woven threads; 5-32, 26-33)

19. 出自...手笔（筆）   chūzì...shǒubǐ   PH: "from the brush of," painted or written by (3-15)

20. 蓝空   lánkōng   N: "blue void," sky

21. 航行   hángxíng   FV: navigate, sail

22. 月明如水   yuèmíngrúshuǐ   EX: "moon bright like water," the moon is very bright

page 442

23. 包   bāo   FV: contract for or charter (a boat, plane, meal plan, etc.)

page 443

24. 罐头（頭）   guàntou   ADJ/N: canned/can (34-2)

25. 火腿   huǒtuǐ   N: ham

page 444

26. 机（機）械　　　　jīxiè　　　　SV/N: mechanical/mechanical tool
　　　　　　　　　　　　　　　　　　　　　　　(M: 件　jiàn)

27. 寒暖飽飢（饑）　hánnuǎnbǎojī　　EX: "cold-warmth, fullness-
　　　　　　　　　　　　　　　　　　　　　　　hunger," clothes and food

28. 关（關、鬮、関）切　guānqiè　　FV/N: be concerned about someone/
　　　　　　　　　　　　　　　　　　　　　　　concern for someone (2-49)

*29. 沿途　　　　　　yántú　　　　PW: along the way, on the road
　　　　　　　　　　　　　　　　　　　　　　　(P-22)

30. 接济（濟）　　　jiēji　　　　FV/N: provide, supply (someone
　　　　　　　　　　　　　　　　　　　　　　　with something urgently
　　　　　　　　　　　　　　　　　　　　　　　needed)/supplies

page 445

31. 平心而論　　　　píngxīn'érlùn　EX: "level-heartedly to discuss,"
　　　　　　　　　　　　　　　　　　　　　　　speak frankly and fairly

page 446

32. 谷欠訳又止　　　yùyányòuzhǐ　　EX: "wish to say, again stop,"
　　　　　　　　　　　　　　　　　　　　　　　want to speak but on second
　　　　　　　　　　　　　　　　　　　　　　　thought decide not to (=25-136
　　　　　　　　　　　　　　　　　　　　　　　欲語又止 yùyǔyòuzhǐ)

33. 直截了当（當）　zhíjiéliǎodàng　EX: "cut straightly, finish at
　　　　　　　　　　　　　　　　　　　　　　　the point of appropriateness,"
　　　　　　　　　　　　　　　　　　　　　　　simple and direct, straight-
　　　　　　　　　　　　　　　　　　　　　　　forward (also written 直捷
　　　　　　　　　　　　　　　　　　　　　　　了當 ; 18-15, 25-67)

34. 籠　　　　　　　lóng　　　　BF: cage (FF: 籠子 lóngzi; 10-7)

35. 金童玉女　　　　jīntóngyùnǚ　　EX: "gold boys, jade girls,"
　　　　　　　　　　　　　　　　　　　　　　　figures of young boys and
　　　　　　　　　　　　　　　　　　　　　　　girls attending upon Taoist
　　　　　　　　　　　　　　　　　　　　　　　immortals (12-47)

36. 矮板凳〔櫈〕　　ǎibǎndèng　　N: low stool or bench (without
　　　　　　　　　　　　　　　　　　　　　　　a back; 5-48)

37. 拆掉　　　　　　chāidiaò　　RC: disassemble, tear down
　　　　　　　　　　　　　　　　　　　　　　　(32-47, 33-21)

38. 前 清 誥 封 通 奉 大 夫 显（顯）考 高 公 諱 敦 斋（齋）

Qián Qīng gàofēng tōngfèngdàfū xiǎnkaǒ Gaō gōng huì Dùnzhaī

The funeral tablet of our late and honorable father Gaō Dùnzhaī,

府 君 之 灵（靈）位

fǔjūnzhī língweì

on whom was bestowed the title of <u>Tōngfèngdàfū</u> during the former
Qīng Dynasty

<u>page 447</u>

39. 躲〔躲〕懒〔懶〕   duǒlǎn   FV: try to avoid work, be lazy
                                          (4-73, 7-127)

CHAPTER FORTY

page 448

1. 左思右想　　zuǒsīyòuxiǎng　EX: "left think, right consider," think about all
sorts of different things

2. 籃子　　lánzi　N: basket (contrast with 藍
lán 'blue'; 19-9, 36-22)

3. 粪（糞）　　fèn　N: night soil, manure

4. 早点（點、点）心　zǎodiǎnxin　N: breakfast foods

5. 小販　　xiǎofàn　N: peddler, hawker

6. 晴朗無云（雲）　qínglǎngwúyún　EX: "clear and bright and
without clouds," clear
(19-90)

7. 麻雀　　máquè　N: sparrow (M: 隻 zhī; 28-96,
30-93)

8. 吱々喳々　　zhīzhīzhāzhā　ON: (sound of birds chirping;
15-14)

page 450

9. 碼头（頭）　　mǎtou　N: pier, dock

10. 陪笑　　péixiaò　FV: put on a smile (so as to
reassure someone)

11. 艙　　cāng　N: cabin (of a ship)

12. 餅干（乾）　　bǐnggān　N: cookie, cracker (M: 塊 kuài;
餅乾 are always hard and
dry as opposed to 點心
diǎnxin, which may be soft
and moist)

13. 行程　　xíngchéng　N: route, journey (6-22, 17-28)

page 451

14. 护（護）兵　　hùbīng　N: military guard (22-65)

15. 送行者   sòngxíngzhě   N: someone who sees someone
                                          else off on a trip

16. 依恋、(戀)地   yīliànde   A: reluctant to see someone
                                          leave, longing for someone
                                          (36-43)

page 452

17. 好生保重   haǒshēngbaǒzhòng   EX: take good care of oneself
                                          (21-87)

18. 清瑩   qīngyíng   SV: clear and bright (10-68)

19. 舟子   zhoūzǐ   N: boatman

20. 搖[摇]櫓[櫓]   yaólǔ   VO: work the sculls of a boat
                                          back and forth, row (19-63)

page 453

21. 悲惜   beīxī   FV: regret

22. 再見   zaìjiàn   IE: Good-bye

COMPARATIVE ROMANIZATION TABLE

Pīnyīn—Yale—Wade-Giles

PY	Yale	W-G	PY	Yale	W-G	PY	Yale	W-G
a	a	a	chong	chung	ch'ung	ei	ei	ei
ai	ai	ai	chou	chou	ch'ou	en	en	en
an	an	an	chu	chu	ch'u	eng	eng	eng
ang	ang	ang	chuai	chwai	ch'uai	er	er	erh
ao	au	ao	chuan	chwan	ch'uan			
			chuang	chwang	ch'uang	fa	fa	fa
ba	ba	pa	chui	chwei	ch'ui	fan	fan	fan
bai	bai	pai	chun	chwun	ch'un	fang	fang	fang
ban	ban	pan	chuo	chwo	ch'o	fei	fei	fei
bang	bang	pang	ci	tsz	tz'u	fen	fen	fen
bao	bau	pao	cong	tsung	ts'ung	feng	feng	feng
bei	bei	pei	cou	tsou	ts'ou	fo	fwo	fo
ben	ben	pen	cu	tsu	ts'u	fou	fou	fou
beng	beng	peng	cuan	tswan	ts'uan	fu	fu	fu
bi	bi	pi	cui	tswei	ts'ui			
bian	byan	pien	cun	tswun	ts'un	ga	ga	ka
biao	byau	piao	cuo	tswo	ts'o	gai	gai	kai
bie	bye	pieh				gan	gan	kan
bin	bin	pin	da	da	ta	gang	gang	kang
bing	bing	ping	dai	dai	tai	gao	gau	kao
bo	bwo	po	dan	dan	tan	ge	ge	ko
bou	bou	pou	dang	dang	tang	gei	gei	kei
bu	bu	pu	dao	dau	tao	gen	gen	ken
			de	de	te	geng	geng	keng
ca	tsa	ts'a	dei	dei	tei	gong	gung	kung
cai	tsai	ts'ai	deng	deng	teng	gou	gou	kou
can	tsan	ts'an	di	di	ti	gu	gu	ku
cang	tsang	ts'ang	dian	dyan	tien	gua	gwa	kua
cao	tsao	ts'ao	diao	dyau	tiao	guai	gwai	kuai
ce	tse	ts'e	die	dye	tieh	guan	gwan	kuan
cen	tsen	ts'en	ding	ding	ting	guang	gwang	kuang
ceng	tseng	ts'eng	diu	dyou	tiu	gui	gwei	kuei
cha	cha	ch'a	dong	dung	tung	gun	gwun	kun
chai	chai	ch'ai	dou	dou	tou	guo	gwo	kuo
chan	chan	ch'an	du	du	tu			
chang	chang	ch'ang	duan	dwan	tuan	ha	ha	ha
chao	chau	ch'ao	dui	dwei	tui	hai	hai	hai
che	che	ch'e	dun	dwun	tun	han	han	han
chen	chen	ch'en	duo	dwo	to	hang	hang	hang
cheng	cheng	ch'eng				hao	hau	hao
chi	chr	ch'ih	e	e	o	he	he	ho

PY	Yale	W-G	PY	Yale	W-G	PY	Yale	W-G
hei	hei	hei	lan	lan	lan	nen	nen	nen
hen	hen	hen	lang	lang	lang	neng	neng	neng
heng	heng	heng	lao	lau	lao	nong	nung	nung
hong	hung	hung	le	le	le	nou	nou	nou
hou	hou	hou	lei	lei	lei	ni	ni	ni
hu	hu	hu	leng	leng	leng	nian	nyan	nien
hua	hwa	hua	li	li	li	niang	nyang	niang
huai	hwai	huai	lia	lya	lia	niao	nyau	niao
huan	hwan	huan	lian	lyan	lien	nie	nye	nieh
huang	hwang	huang	liang	lyang	liang	nin	nin	nin
hui	hwei	hui	liao	lyau	liao	ning	ning	ning
hun	hwun	hun	lie	lye	lieh	niu	nyou	niu
huo	hwo	huo	lin	lin	lin	nu	nu	nu
			ling	ling	ling	nuan	nwan	nuan
ji	ji	chi	liu	lyou	liu	nuo	nwo	no
jia	jya	chia	long	lung	lung	nü	nyu	nü
jian	jyan	chien	lou	lou	lou	nüe	nywe	nüeh
jiang	jyang	chiang	lu	lu	lu			
jiao	jyau	chiao	luan	lwan	luan	pa	pa	p'a
jie	jye	chieh	lun	lwun	lun	pai	pai	p'ai
jin	jin	chin	luo	lwo	lo	pan	pan	p'an
jing	jing	ching	lü	lyu	lü	pang	pang	p'ang
jiong	jyung	chiung	lüe	lywe	lüeh	pao	pau	p'ao
jiu	jyou	chiu				pei	pei	p'ei
ju	jyu	chü	ma	ma	ma	pen	pen	p'en
juan	jywan	chüan	mai	mai	mai	peng	peng	p'eng
jue	jywe	chüeh	man	man	man	po	pwo	p'o
jun	jyun	chün	mang	mang	mang	pou	pou	p'ou
			mao	mau	mao	pi	pi	p'i
ka	ka	k'a	mei	mei	mei	pian	pyan	p'ien
kai	kai	k'ai	men	men	men	piao	pyau	p'iao
kan	kan	k'an	meng	meng	meng	pie	pye	p'ieh
kang	kang	k'ang	mi	mi	mi	pin	pin	p'in
kao	kau	k'ao	mian	myan	mien	ping	ping	p'ing
ke	ke	k'o	miao	myau	miao	pu	pu	p'u
ken	ken	k'en	mie	mye	mieh			
keng	keng	k'eng	min	min	min	qi	chi	ch'i
kong	kung	k'ung	ming	ming	ming	qia	chya	ch'ia
kou	kou	k'ou	miu	myou	miu	qian	chyan	ch'ien
ku	ku	k'u	mo	mwo	mo	qiang	chyang	ch'iang
kua	kwa	k'ua	mou	mou	mou	qiao	chyau	ch'iao
kuai	kwai	k'uai	mu	mu	mu	qie	chye	ch'ieh
kuan	kwan	k'uan				qin	chin	ch'in
kuang	kwang	k'uang	na	na	na	qing	ching	ch'ing
kui	kwei	k'uei	nai	nai	nai	qiong	chyung	ch'iung
kun	kwun	k'un	nan	nan	nan	qiu	chyou	ch'iu
kuo	kwo	k'uo	nang	nang	nang	qu	chyu	ch'ü
			nao	nau	nao	quan	chywan	ch'üan
la	la	la	ne	ne	ne	que	chywe	ch'üeh
lai	lai	lai	nei	nei	nei	qun	chyun	ch'ün

PY	Yale	W-G	PY	Yale	W-G	PY	Yale	W-G
ran	ran	jan	suo	swo	so	yao	yau	yao
rang	rang	jang	ta	ta	t'a	ye	ye	yeh
rao	rau	jao	tai	tai	t'ai	yi	yi	i
re	re	je	tan	tan	t'an	yin	yin	yin
ren	ren	jen	tang	tang	t'ang	ying	ying	ying
reng	reng	jeng	tao	tau	t'ao	yong	yung	yung
ri	r	jih	te	te	t'e	you	you	yu
rong	rung	jung	teng	teng	t'eng	yu	yu	yü
rou	rou	jou	ti	ti	t'i	yuan	ywan	yüan
ru	ru	ju	tian	tyan	t'ien	yue	ywe	yüeh
ruan	rwan	juan	tiao	tyau	t'iao	yun	yun	yün
rui	rwei	jui	tie	tye	t'ieh			
run	rwun	jun	ting	ting	t'ing	za	dza	tsa
ruo	rwo	jo	tong	tung	t'ung	zai	dzai	tsai
			tou	tou	t'ou	zan	dzan	tsan
sa	sa	sa	tu	tu	t'u	zang	dzang	tsang
sai	sai	sai	tuan	twan	t'uan	zao	dzau	tsao
san	san	san	tui	twei	t'ui	ze	dze	tse
sang	sang	sang	tun	twun	t'un	zei	dzei	tsei
sao	sau	sao	tuo	two	t'o	zen	dzen	tsen
se	se	se				zeng	dzeng	tseng
sen	sen	sen	wa	wa	wa	zha	ja	cha
seng	seng	seng	wai	wai	wai	zhai	jai	chai
sha	sha	sha	wan	wan	wan	zhan	jan	chan
shai	shai	shai	wang	wang	wang	zhang	jang	chang
shan	shan	shan	wei	wei	wei	zhao	jau	chao
shang	shang	shang	wen	wen	wen	zhe	je	che
shao	shau	shao	weng	weng	weng	zhei	jei	chei
she	she	she	wo	wo	wo	zhen	jen	chen
shei	shei	shei	wu	wu	wu	zheng	jeng	cheng
shen	shen	shen				zhi	jr	chih
sheng	sheng	sheng	xi	syi	hsi	zhong	jung	chung
shi	shr	shih	xia	sya	hsia	zhou	jou	chou
shou	shou	shou	xian	syan	hsien	zhu	ju	chu
shu	shu	shu	xiang	syang	hsiang	zhua	jwa	chua
shua	shwa	shua	xiao	syau	hsiao	zhuai	jwai	chuai
shuai	shwai	shuai	xie	sye	hsieh	zhuan	jwan	chuan
shuan	shwan	shuan	xin	syin	hsin	zhuang	jwang	chuang
shuang	shwang	shuang	xing	sying	hsing	zhui	jwei	chui
shui	shwei	shui	xiong	syung	hsiung	zhun	jwun	chun
shun	shwun	shun	xiu	syou	hsiu	zhuo	jwo	cho
shuo	shwo	shuo	xu	syu	hsü	zi	dz	tzu
si	sz	szu	xuan	sywan	hsüan	zong	dzung	tsung
song	sung	sung	xue	sywe	hsüeh	zou	dzou	tsou
sou	sou	sou	xun	syun	hsün	zu	dzu	tsu
su	su	su				zuan	dzwan	tsuan
suan	swan	suan	ya	ya	ya	zui	dzwei	tsui
sui	swei	sui	yan	yan	yen	zun	dzwun	tsun
sun	swun	sun	yang	yang	yang	zuo	dzwo	tso

SIMPLIFIED CHARACTER-TRADITIONAL CHARACTER CONVERSION TABLE

Below is given a list of all simplified characters in the Nánguó edition of <u>Jiā</u> together with their corresponding traditional forms. The simplified characters are arranged first in order of the number of their strokes and then, within each group of characters having the same number of strokes, according to the direction of their initial stroke: first those beginning with a <u>héng</u> 橫 (一), then those with a <u>shù</u> 豎 (丨), then those with a <u>piě</u> 撇 (丿), then those with a <u>diǎn</u> 點 (丶), and finally those with a <u>héngzhé</u> 橫折 (丁). To find the traditional forms of an unfamiliar simplified character in the text, the student need only count the number of strokes in it and determine what kind of stroke its initial stroke is.

The edition of <u>Jiā</u> on which these notes are based does not include characters from the last groups of characters to be simplified by the government of the People's Republic of China. For example, the words <u>jiǎng</u> 'speak' and <u>shū</u> 'book' are represented here in their traditional forms 講 and 書 rather than the new simplified forms 讲 and 书 . This edition is also not completely consistent in its use of simplified characters, so that <u>liǎn</u> 'face', for example, is given as 脸 on page 55, line 16, but as 臉 on page 58, line 17. Finally, a few "semi-simplified" characters are used, such as 証 <u>zhèng</u> (traditional form 證, official simplified form 证) and 觉 <u>jué/jiào</u> (traditional form 覺, official simplified form 觉).

2 strokes

厂(廠)　几(幾)　了(瞭)

3 strokes

干(乾)　干(幹)　于(於)　亏(虧)　万(萬)　与(與)　亿(億)　个(個)　么(麼)　广(廣)　义(義)　飞(飛)　乡(鄉)

4 strokes

[一]
丰(豐)　开(開)　专(專)　云(雲)　艺(藝)　厅(廳)　历(歷)　区(區)

车(車)

[丿]
气(氣)　长(長)　从(從)　仅(僅)

[丶]
为(為)　斗(鬥)　忆(憶)

[乛]
丑(醜)　队(隊)　办(辦)　邓(鄧)　劝(勸)　双(雙)　凶(兇)

5 strokes

[一]
击(擊)　扑(撲)　节(節)　术(術)　龙(龍)　厉(厲)　布(佈)　灭(滅)

东(東)

[丨]
旧(舊)　帅(帥)　归(歸)　叶(葉)　号(號)　电(電)　只(隻)　占(佔)

[丿]
仪(儀)　丛(叢)　尔(爾)　乐(樂)　处(處)　务(務)

[丶]
兰(蘭)　关(關)　汉(漢)　宁(寧)　写(寫)　礼(禮)

[乛]
边(邊)　出(齣)　对(對)

台(臺)

6 strokes

[一]
动(動)　执(執)　扩(擴)　扫(掃)　亚(亞)　朴(樸)　机(機)　权(權)　过(過)　协(協)　压(壓)　夸(誇)　夺(奪)　达(達)　夹(夾)　划(劃)　迈(邁)

[丨]
师(師)　当(當)　吁(籲)　吓(嚇)　虫(蟲)　团(團)　岁(歲)

网(網)

[丿]
朱(硃)　迁(遷)　优(優)　伤(傷)　价(價)　华(華)　伙(夥)　伪(偽)　后(後)　会(會)　杀(殺)　众(眾)　爷(爺)　伞(傘)　杂(雜)

[丶]
壮(壯)　冲(衝)　妆(妝)　庄(莊)　庆(慶)　刘(劉)　齐(齊)　产　关　灯(燈)

忏(懺)　兴(興)　农(農)

[乛]
寻(尋)　尽(盡)(儘)　导(導)　孙(孫)　阶(階)　妇(婦)　戏(戲)　欢(歡)　买(買)

7 strokes

[一]
寿(壽)　进(進)　远(遠)　运(運)　坏(壞)　扰(擾)　折(摺)　坟(墳)　护(護)　壳(殼)　声(聲)　报(報)

将（將）亲（親）养（養）类（類）总（總）烂（爛）洒（灑）涤 恼（惱）举（舉）窃（竊）袄（襖）
［フ］险（險）观（觀）

10 strokes

［一］艳（豔）蚕（蠶）赶（趕）执（執）热（熱）壶（壺）获（獲）（穫）恶（惡）莹（瑩）桥（橋）

标（標）栏（欄）树（樹）桦（樺）
［丨］战（戰）点（點）临（臨）尝（嘗）哑（啞）显（顯）虽（雖）响（響）
［丿］毡（氈）选（選）适（適）种（種）复（復）（複）覆 胆（膽）胜（勝）独（獨）
［丶］弯（彎）变（變）

备（備）
［丶］恋（戀）庙（廟）郑（鄭）卷（捲）单（單）泪（淚）怜（憐）学（學）宝（寶）廉（廉）实（實）
［フ］肃（肅）萧（蕭）隶（隸）参（參）艰（艱）

9 strokes

［一］帮（幫）赵（趙）垫（墊）挤（擠）荐（薦）带（帶）荣（榮）

变（變）庙（廟）郑（鄭）卷（捲）单（單）泪（淚）怜（憐）学（學）宝（寶）廉 实（實）

势（勢）拦（攔）苎 莹 柜（櫃）松（鬆）丧（喪）画（畫）卖（賣）郁（鬱）奋（奮）态（態）
［丨］齿（齒）虏（虜）国（國）罗（羅）图（圖）
［丿］制（製）刮 铲 征 舍 肿（腫）胁（脅）周

势（勢）范（範）松（鬆）丧（喪）画（畫）卖（賣）郁（鬱）奋（奮）态（態）

邻（鄰）犹（猶）条（條）系（係）（繫）
［丶］冻（凍）状（狀）应（應）弃（棄）这（這）灿（燦）灶（竈）怀（懷）穷（窮）补（補）
［フ］灵（靈）汇（匯）际（際）陆（陸）陈（陳）

8 strokes

［一］环（環）拣（揀）担（擔）拥（擁）

拟（擬）严（嚴）劳（勞）克（剋）苏（蘇）杆（桿）极（極）两（兩）丽（麗）医（醫）励（勵）还（還）来（來）
［丨］坚（堅）时（時）县（縣）里（裏）园（園）邮（郵）听（聽）
［丿］乱（亂）体（體）佣（傭）御（禦）余（餘）谷（穀）彻（徹）

[一]
墙(墻) 愿(願)
[丨]
踊(踴) 蜡(蠟) 蝇(蠅)
[丿]
稳(穩)

15 strokes

[一]
聪(聰)

19 strokes

[一]
庞(龐)
[丿]
赞(讚)

20 strokes

[乛]
缠(纏)

屡(屢)

13 strokes

[一]
摆(擺) 摊(攤) 献(獻) 楼(樓) 碍(礙)
[丿]
辞(辭) 筹(籌) 触(觸)
[丶]
数(數) 滩(灘) 誉(譽) 寝(寢)
[乛]
叠(疊)

14 strokes

隐(隱)

12 strokes

[一]
趋(趨) 挽(輓) 联(聯) 椭(橢) 确(確)
[丿]
筑(築) 征(徵) 御(禦)
[丶]
装(裝) 觉(覺) 蚕(蠶) 娄(婁) 湿(濕) 证(證) 焰(燄)
[乛]

梦(夢) 检(檢)
[丨]
悬(懸)
[丿]
盘(盤) 脸(臉) 猎(獵)
[丶]
盖(蓋) 断(斷) 兽(獸) 减(減) 渊(淵) 渗(滲) 惧(懼) 惊(驚) 惨(慘)
[乛]
隋 随(隨)

恋(戀) 桨(槳) 浆(漿) 斋(齋) 准
离(離) 烛(燭) 烬(燼) 涩(澀) 涌(湧) 宾(賓)
[乛]
恳(懇) 剧(劇) 难(難)

11 strokes

[一]
厢(廂) 据(據) 职(職) 营(營)

桩(樁) 样(樣) 础(礎) 致
[丨]
虑(慮) 监(監) 紧(緊) 党(黨) 晒(曬) 罢(罷)
[丿]
牺(犧) 敌(敵) 积(積) 称(稱) 笔(筆) 借(藉) 爱(愛) 脑(腦)
[丶]

INDEX

This index contains all words and expressions in the present notes which reoccur in chapters of Jiā after the one in which they were introduced. A student who comes across a word which was given earlier but whose pronunciation and or meaning he has forgotten, may locate in this index the chapter and entry number of the first occurrence and in this way find the information he is seeking.

The index is arranged according to the total number of strokes in each character of a word or expression exactly as it appears in Jiā. For example, 头 would be ordered as 5, 糊 as 15, 糊塗 as 15.13, and 糊里糊塗 as 15.7.15.13. If more than one item falls into a stroke group, the system of ordering by initial stroke that was discussed in the introduction to the Simplified Character-Traditional Character Conversion Table (i.e., 一 , 丨 , 丿 , 丶 , 乛 , cf. p.258) is employed. Although such an arrangement may seem somewhat cumbersome at first, it was felt that since both traditional and simplified characters occur in this edition, and since many entries contain more than a single character, this ordering would be the most practical. Furthermore, this system has the added pedagogical advantage of making the student write the word he wishes to find.

After each entry in the index is given a number reference to the place in the notes where the item was introduced. The number before the hyphen indicates chapter (P=Preface), while the number after it indicates entry number. Thus, P-3 would indicate the third item in the notes to the Preface, 7-19 the nineteenth item in the notes to chapter seven, and so on.

漿流笑紋		憎厭	32-42	頰撒	2-20	薄命	4-119
蕩	19-88						
輪	6-175	**15.15**		瞞踱踏	34-34	**16.9**	
嘲	3-17	撫摩	10-79			懊惱	17-4
皺紋	14-6	嘻之	36-37	**[丶]**	24-7	**16.10**	
15.11		摩撫	26-26		10-15	醒悟	1-81
鋪	6-44	**15.15.6**		謎窺燃	1-53	嘴唇	7-57
蓋慈惠堂	2-92	緩之地	17-96		9-87	頰唐	5-63
課	1-100	**15.16**			16-47	**16.10.10**	
熟習	14-118	髮髮髮	4-69	隱	1-21	靜悄之	9-90
熟腳	28-53	嚇嘴錢	19-101		10-29	**16.10.16**	
褲悴	1-36	賞駡	12-10	**16.4.9**		燒紙錢	29-117
憔問	7-92	嘲靜	26-48	辦公室	7-3	**16.11**	
慰	8-114	僻	1-24	**16.4**		靜寂夢	1-119
15.12		**15.19**		薪水	2-63	靈激情	15-117
賭博然	16-12	請願	8-53	嘴巴	23-82	濃密	25-26
毅濕	7-151	**15.20**		**16.6**		震	17-59
潤橋	9-149	髮辮	2-15	整齊激動	6-78	**16.12**	
躺	22-47	**15.22**			1-99	操場頸項	8-54
15.13		閱讀	6-187	**16.6.10.8**		嘴衛硬道	17-69
憂秘跡嘆諒	3-118	**15.24**		濃妝艷抹	9-81		2-33
踪嘆解	1-71	髮髮賓	3-133	**16.6.13**			2-84
糊塗	10-53			錫灯盞	5-76	**16.13**	
	31-21	**16**		**16.7**		橫溢	25-31
	14-76	**[一]**		擋住	8-80	**16.14**	
15.14		橫賴飄磚	14-102	**16.8**		橫豎	3-146
蕩漾遺漏懷慨	3-111		26-11			**16.6.6**	
	1-42		5-56			黑犬之地	1-116
	2-85		13-12				

CORNELL EAST ASIA SERIES

For ordering information, please contact the Cornell East Asia Series, East Asia Program, Cornell University, 140 Uris Hall, Ithaca, NY 14853-7601, USA; phone (607) 255-6222, fax (607) 255-1388.

5-94/.4M/BB